ENGLISH WORDS

from

LATIN *and* GREEK

ELEMENTS

CC 306: 4.95 14

ENGLISH WORDS

from

LATIN AND GREEK

ELEMENTS

Donald M. Ayers

THE UNIVERSITY OF ARIZONA PRESS
Tucson   Arizona

About the Author . . .

DONALD M. AYERS wrote this volume from the vantage point
of a professor with primary interest in Latin literature, as
well as a special concern for the classical background of
English vocabulary and the value of a knowledge of this in
vocabulary building for both general and technical studies.
He joined the faculty of the Classics Department of the
University of Arizona in 1951, having previously taught
Classics at Vanderbilt University.

Eleventh Printing 1982

THE UNIVERSITY OF ARIZONA PRESS

Copyright © 1965
The Arizona Board of Regents
All Rights Reserved
Manufactured in the U.S.A.

I.S.B.N.–0–8165–0403–2
L.C. No. 64–17264

PREFACE

IN THESE times when students in greater and greater numbers are seeking higher education, and when, as a consequence, classes are becoming so large that personal contact between student and professor has been reduced to the barest minimum, it is more necessary than ever for college students to master subject matter through their own efforts. Yet for many of our students, because of inadequacies in their vocabulary, the understanding of textbooks and lectures is slow and painful. It has been stated on the basis of a study of student academic mortality at one large university, for instance, that the lack of an adequate vocabulary is the most important single factor contributing to failure in college.* Other statistical studies have also shown the close correlation between extent of vocabulary and success in college. There has consequently been a general recognition of the need for word study even at the university level.

A number of different methods for increasing vocabulary have been tried with more or less success. The study of Greek and Latin word elements, the learning of lists of unfamiliar terms, practice in recognizing the meaning of words from context, the listing of new words encountered in reading, all have their own special merits. The present book, which is the result of several years' experience in teaching a vocabulary course at the University of Arizona, is devoted primarily to the study of Greek and Latin stems or bases and affixes. This approach to vocabulary building, since it can be largely systematized, lends itself especially to classroom procedure. Also, since this method of word study is more general in its application, it is better suited to the needs of students with varied backgrounds and interests.

It seems likely, however, that a combination of methods will yield the best results in vocabulary building. I have therefore tried to incorporate insofar as possible the benefits derived from the other approaches. The second of these methods mentioned above,

---

*G. Rexford Davis, *Vocabulary Building*, New York, 1951, p. 1.

the so-called direct method, that is, the learning of specially pre
pared word lists, is valuable because the student concentrates on
words which occur rarely enough to be unfamiliar but are found
sufficiently often in college reading to cause difficulty. If the words
to be studied are carefully chosen, the immediate gains from this
procedure are quite large, though there is of course little transfer
in the case of words not specifically considered. In order to include
the advantages derived from this type of training I have chosen for
the main exercises wherever feasible words with which the majority
of students are likely to be unfamiliar but which it would be desirable for them to know. In selecting such words I have been guided
by a list prepared by the Freshman English staff of the University
of Arizona, a list which all freshman students are required to learn,
and by a list which I have compiled on the basis of notebooks sub-
mitted by my students which contain new words that they have
encountered in reading for other courses.

The third of the methods for vocabulary building mentioned
above, the recognition of meaning from context clues, has the merit
of concentrating the student's attention on the use of a word in a
sentence, for the precise meaning of a term can only be understood
from its context. This method, however, tends to have the defect of
encouraging the student to guess at unfamiliar words without
checking his guesses in a dictionary. I have tried to introduce into
the main exercises some of the advantages from this type of approach by generally including the words to be studied there in a
sentence or phrase, taken where possible from the works of standard
authors or from current periodicals. Such words, however, are
always to be defined with the aid of a dictionary. As to the fourth
method, the instructor will probably expect the students to keep
notebooks of new words as part of the course requirements.

The basic emphasis of this book nevertheless remains on Greek
and Latin prefixes, stems or bases, and suffixes. The difficulty which
is most frequently encountered in this approach to word study arises
from the fact that often there is a considerable difference between
the etymological or root meaning of a word and its current meaning.
Thus, in determining the meaning of *urbane,* it is not of much help
to know that the Latin word *urbs* means "city." Some vocabulary
building textbooks have attempted to avoid this problem by omitting from consideration those words in which such a wide variation
between root meaning and current meaning occurs. The present

book, however, does not make an attempt to do so. There are several reasons for this. First, the problem can be overcome to some extent by instruction in the general patterns of semantic change, which are discussed in several of the lessons in this book. Second, examples of change in meaning furnish one of the most interesting and instructive aspects of word study. Not only does the student gain some insight into the patterns of human thought ᴠy studying words which have changed their meaning, but often such words reflect something of the history of ideas. As Bradley says in reference to the word *oxygen*, the etymology of which shows that the French chemists who named the element mistakenly thought it was the distinctive constituent of acids (Greek *oxys*, "sharp," "acid," and *gignesthai*, "to be produced), ". . . if we do happen to know the literal sense we may learn from it an interesting fact in the history of science."* After all, one of the best ways for a book such as this to achieve its goal is to make the student interested in words themselves and not merely to hold out to him as an incentive the practical rewards to be gained from having a large vocabulary. Finally, while semantic change is often a serious obstacle to the use of a knowledge of bases and affixes in attacking an unfamiliar word, recognizing the meaning of newly encountered terms is only one side of vocabulary building. Not the least of the reasons for learning Greek and Latin elements is their mnemonic value; a knowledge of these will serve as an excellent device for fixing words in the memory once their meaning has been determined, and this should be true even when semantic change has taken place.

Although most textbooks devoted to vocabulary building give some attention to Greek and Latin word elements, I have felt that there is need for such a book as this. Many texts, while they list all of the important prefixes and suffixes and a great many stems or bases, confine consideration of these to only a few lessons, and they do not give sufficient practice in recognizing these elements ever to make the knowledge of them an effective tool for increasing vocabulary. The exercises in this book are therefore designed to give systematic drill in these elements as well as to acquaint the student with words which it will be useful for him to know. In each lesson the basic exercise consists of words which contain the roots and affixes studied in that lesson and in previous ones. The student

---

*Henry Bradley, *The Making of English*, New York, 1904, p. 109.

is expected to be able to analyze these words fully and to define them. In addition, one or two other exercises of varying nature are usually included, which the instructor may assign at his own discretion. A number of these are suitable to be done in class.

Several excellent textbooks (which are among the books listed on pp. x-xi) do treat very adequately the classical element in English and give thorough practice in applying this knowledge. Their aim, however, is somewhat different from that of the present work; they attempt to impart some knowledge of the Latin and Greek languages, partly, perhaps, with the intention of attracting students to language courses. They consequently tend to be written more from the standpoint of Latin and Greek than of English and give considerable attention to Latin and Greek grammar, a matter which, I have found, the student who is primarily trying to improve his vocabulary regards as extraneous.

The material in this book has therefore been presented insofar as possible from the point of view of English. Stems or bases (e.g., DUC-, NOMIN-) have been given rather than actual Latin and Greek words (e.g., *ducere, nomen, nominis*), and the meanings attached to them are not necessarily those of the Latin but rather those which they have when used in English derivatives. Suffixes are treated not so much with regard to their origin as to their present form and meaning. Thus, for example, no distinction has been made between the English adjectival suffixes *-ary,* derived from Latin *-aris* (as in *military*), and *-ary,* derived from *-arius* (as in *arbitrary*). For the same reason the discussion of grammatical points has been kept to a minimum.

ACKNOWLEDGMENTS

I would like to express my appreciation to my colleagues at the University of Arizona who were kind enough to read sections of the manuscript of this book and who offered many valuable suggestions. My especial thanks are due Professor G. D. Percy of the Department of Classics; Professors Robert H. Hurlbutt (now of the University of Nebraska) and Charles F. Wallraff of the Department of Philosophy; Professors Marie P. Hamilton, William F. Irmscher (now of the University of Washington), and Jack W. Huggins of the Department of English; and Professor Loyal A. T. Gryting of the Department of Romance Languages.

I would also like to express my gratitude to the University of Arizona for most generously granting me a sabbatical leave in order to complete this work.

I likewise take this opportunity to thank the editors of *The Atlantic Monthly, Harper's Magazine,* and *Time* for their kind permission to quote sentences from these magazines to illustrate the use of the words studied in the exercises.

Donald M. Ayers

BOOKS ON THE STUDY OF WORDS

The following list is by no means exhaustive but contains a number of useful books dealing with various aspects of the material covered in the present work. It includes popular works as well as those which are technical and scholarly.

Owen Barfield, *History in English Words,* new ed. (London, 1954, Faber and Faber)

Charles B. Brown, *The Contribution of Greek to English* (Nashville, 1942, Vanderbilt University Press)

——*The Contribution of Latin to English* (Nashville, 1946, Vanderbilt University Press)

Eli E. Burriss and Lionel Casson, *Latin and Greek in Current Use,* 2nd ed. (New York, 1949, Prentice-Hall)

Charles E. Funk, *Thereby Hangs a Tale* (New York, 1950, Harper and Brothers)

——*A Hog on Ice (and Other Curious Expressions)* (New York, 1948, Harper and Brothers)

Wilfred Funk, *Word Origins and Their Romantic Stories* (New York, 1950, Wilfred Funk)

James B. Greenough and George L. Kittredge, *Words and Their Ways in English Speech* (New York, 1901, Macmillan; paperback edition, 1961)

Bernard Groom, *A Short History of English Words* (London, 1949, Macmillan)

W. C. Grummel, *English Word Building from Latin and Greek,* (Palo Alto, Calif., 1961, Pacific Books)

John N. Hough, *Scientific Terminology* (New York, 1953, Rinehart)

Charles Jennings, Nancy King, and Marjorie Stevenson, *Weigh the Word* (New York, 1957, Harper and Brothers)

Edwin L. Johnson, *Latin Words of Common English* (Boston, 1931, D. C. Heath)

Roland Kent, *Language and Philology* (New York, 1923, Longmans, Green)

C. S. Lewis, *Studies in Words* (Cambridge, 1960, Cambridge University Press)

George H. McKnight, *English Words and Their Background* (New York, 1923, Appleton)

Oscar E. Nybakken, *Greek and Latin in Scientific Terminology* (Ames, Iowa, 1959, Iowa State College Press)

Eric Partridge, *Name into Word* (New York, 1950, Macmillan)

——*Origins: a Short Etymological Dictionary of Modern English* (London, 1958, Routledge and Paul)

——*The World of Words,* 3rd ed. (London, 1948, Hamish Hamilton)

T. H. Savory, *The Language of Science* (London, 1953, Andre Deutsch)

Mary S. Serjeantson, *A History of Foreign Words in English* (New York, 1936, Dutton; New York, 1961, Barnes and Noble)

J. A. Sheard, *The Words We Use* (London, 1954, Andre Deutsch)

Walter W. Skeat, *An Etymological Dictionary of the English Language,* rev. ed. (4th) (Oxford, 1946, Clarendon)

Mignonette Spilman, *Medical Latin and Greek* (Salt Lake City, 1957, Edwards Bros., Ann Arbor`

George R. Stewart, *Names on the Land* (New York, 1945, Random House)

Edgar H. Sturtevant, *Linguistic Change* (Chicago, 1917, University of Chicago Press; paperback edition, 1961, Phoenix Press)

Isaac Taylor, *Words and Places,* abridged and ed. by Beatrice S. Snell (London, 1925, Thomas Nelson)

George H. Vallins, *The Making and Meaning of Words* (London, 1949, A. and C. Black)

Ernest Weekley, *Etymological Dictionary of Modern English* (London, 1921, John Murray)

——*More Words Ancient and Modern* (London, 1927, John Murray)

——*The Romance of Names* (London, 1914, John Murray)

——*The Romance of Words* (London, 1912, John Murray)

——*Surnames* (London, 1917, John Murray)

——*Words Ancient and Modern* (London, 1926, John Murray)

——*Words and Names* (New York, 1933, Dutton)

CONTENTS

PAGE

Introduction: The Indo-European Family of Languages 1
The Background of the English Vocabulary 7

PART I: WORD ELEMENTS FROM LATIN

Lesson I: The Dictionary 16
Lesson II: Definition; Latin Bases 23
Lesson III: Prefixes 28
Lesson IV: Prefixes 34
Lesson V: Prefixes 37
Lesson VI: Combinations of Bases; Numerals 41
Lesson VII: Hybrids 45
Lesson VIII: Adjective-Forming Suffixes 48
Lesson IX: Word Analysis; Adjective-Forming Suffixes 52
Lesson X: Adjective-Forming Suffixes 57
Lesson XI: Semantic Change; Metaphorical Usage;
                 Adjective-Forming Suffixes 61
Lesson XII: Specialization and Generalization of Meaning;
                 Adjective-Forming Suffixes 66
Lesson XIII: Functional Change; Adjective-Forming Suffixes .. 70
Lesson XIV: Degeneration and Elevation of Meaning;
                 Noun-Forming Suffixes 74
Lesson XV: Change from Abstract to Concrete;
                 Noun-Forming Suffixes 79
Lesson XVI: Weakening; Noun-Forming Suffixes 83
Lesson XVII: Change of Meaning Due to Changing Concepts;
                 Diminutive Suffixes 86
Lesson XVIII: Euphemism; Noun-Forming Suffixes 92
Lesson XIX: Folk Etymology; Noun-Forming Suffixes 96
Lesson XX: Clipped Words; Verb-Forming Suffixes 100
Lesson XXI: Blends; Verb-Forming Suffixes 104
Lesson XXII: Doublets 107
Lesson XXIII: Uncommon Usages of Words 112
Lesson XXIV: Uncommon Usages of Words 117
Lesson XXV: Latin Words in English 120
Lesson XXVI: Latin Phrases in English 123
List of Suffixes 127
List of Bases 128

PART II: WORD ELEMENTS FROM GREEK

PAGE

Introduction 136
Lesson I: Words from Greek Mythology 139
Lesson II: Words from Greek History and Philosophy 150
Lesson III: Greek Bases 159
Lesson IV: Combinations of Bases 165
Lesson V: Prefixes 169
Lesson VI: Prefixes 173
Lesson VII: Adjective-Forming Suffixes 176
Lesson VIII: Adjective-Forming Suffixes 180
Lesson IX: Place Names; Noun-Forming Suffixes 183
Lesson X: Expressions; Noun-Forming Suffixes 190
Lesson XI: Words and Religion; Noun-Forming Suffixes 195
Lesson XII: Words and Religion; Noun-Forming Suffixes
                (Combining Forms) 200
Lesson XIII: Sea Terms; Noun-Forming Suffixes
                (Combining Forms) 206
Lesson XIV: Words from Sports and Games; Noun-Forming
                Suffixes (Combining Forms) 210
Lesson XV: Military Terms; Verb-Forming Suffix 216
Lesson XVI: Words from the Arts; Numerals 220
Lesson XVII: Words from Law 225
Lesson XVIII: Literary Terms 229
Lesson XIX: Terms from Various Occupations 233
Lesson XX: Scientific Language; Suffixes Used in Medical Terms 237
Lesson XXI: Combining Forms Used in Medical Terms 243
Lesson XXII: Combining Forms Used in Medical Terms 246
Lesson XXIII: Combining Forms Used in Scientific Terminology . 251
Lesson XXIV: Suffixes Used in Scientific Terminology 255
Lesson XXV: Diminutive Suffixes 259
List of Suffixes and Combining Forms 265
List of Bases 266

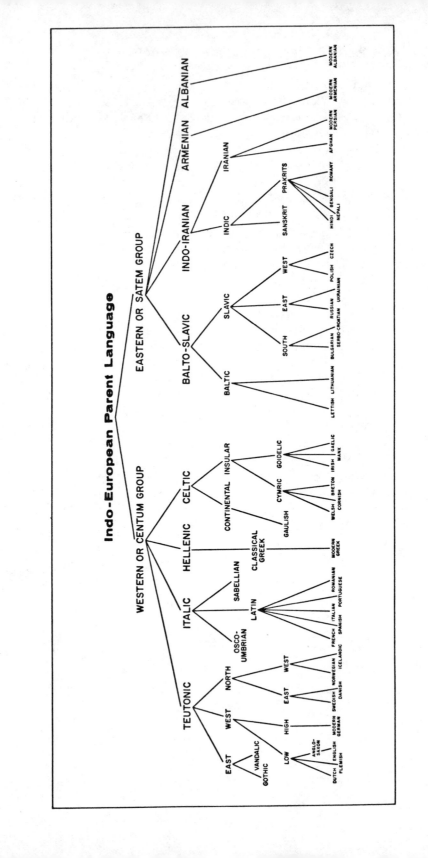

Indo-European Parent Language

INTRODUCTION

I   The Indo-European Family of Languages

OUR ENGLISH vocabulary is not something to be studied in isolation but is related in one way or another to many of the other languages of the world. The proper beginning for us, therefore, is to view the place of English in perspective, amid the many tongues of mankind.

Those students who have studied German undoubtedly have noticed a remarkable similarity between that language and their own. The German word *Milch* is very close in sound to the English *milk;* likewise, German *Wasser* and English *water, Brot* and *bread, Fleisch* and *flesh* closely resemble each other, not to mention a great many additional examples. This resemblance to English, moreover, is true not of German alone, but is also the case with other Northern European languages. Perhaps we can see this similarity best if we place side by side in systematic form the words for *mother, father,* and *brother* as they appear in various tongues.

ENGLISH	GERMAN	DUTCH	DANISH
mother	Mutter	moeder	moder
father	Vater	vader	fader
brother	Bruder	broeder	broder

While the spelling of these words makes their similarities obvious, we would be even more struck by their likeness if we heard them pronounced. For instance, a German "v" (as in *Vater*) sounds the same as an English "f"; also, a brief consideration of one's own speech will show that the sounds represented by "t," "th," and "d" are closely related.

1

Now at first glance we might conclude that the similarities among these languages are due to borrowing, that because these languages are spoken by people living relatively close to one another, such words were adopted from one of the languages by the others. This is not the case, however, as we shall see later. For one thing, there is usually no need for languages to borrow such simple, fundamental words.

If we extend this table to cover a wider area, we shall find the same similarity, though not to so great a degree.

SPANISH	FRENCH	LATIN	CLASSICAL GREEK
madre	mère	mater	meter
padre	père	pater	pater
*	frère	frater	*(phrater)

Finally, let us broaden our examination to include most of Europe and part of Asia.

IRISH	RUSSIAN	LITHUANIAN	POLISH	SANSKRIT	PERSIAN
māthair	mat'	motyna	matka	mātṛ	mādar
athair				pitṛ	pidar
brāthair	brat	brōlis	brat	bhrātṛ	birādar

Now we have already said that the similarity between these languages was not to be explained in terms of borrowing. The cause of their resemblance lies rather in the fact that they are descendants of a single parent language. Thus, all the important languages of Europe (except Finnish and Hungarian) and some of the languages of Asia belong to one family known as the Indo-European family of languages.

The original Indo-European parent language, which became extinct long before written records existed, was spoken by a prehistoric people whose homeland was somewhere in Eastern Europe. The exact location of their origin, however, remains an unsolved problem. Sometime between 3000 and 2000 B.C. this primitive people, still living in the Stone Age, began a series of migrations. During the centuries that followed, successive waves of Indo-Europeans moved westward into Europe and southward into Persia and

---

*There are some gaps and irregularities in this pattern; the Spanish for brother is *hermano*, related to English *germane*, while the Greek *phrater* means "member of a clan" (originally, "of a brotherhood").

India, and the language of these invaders for all practical purposes obliterated the languages of the earlier inhabitants in much the same way that, in the United States, English has superseded the languages of the American Indians. Possibly the only survivor of the pre-Indo-European tongues of Europe is Basque, spoken in a mountainous corner of Spain, where the original inhabitants were able to maintain their way of life against the invaders.

But language is constantly changing, and as the various groups of Indo-Europeans became isolated from one another in the vast tracts of Europe and Asia, the language of each group began to evolve in its own peculiar fashion. Eventually a number of distinct dialects arose, and in the course of centuries there was no longer one common tongue, but a series of completely different languages, each of which in turn produced still more numerous descendants, and so on, until the present multitude of languages in Europe and Southwest Asia emerged. In diagrammatic form the relationship of the Indo-European languages resembles a family tree, some branches having died out, others having given rise to many descendants. A somewhat simplified diagram of this will be found facing p. 1. The modern descendants of the common Indo-European parent may be divided into eight principal groups or branches.* Four of these belong to the Western or *Centum* subfamily, and the other four belong to the Eastern or *Satem* subfamily. (This classification is made on the basis of the word for "hundred" in the various languages, whether it more nearly approximates the Latin *centum* or the Zend *satem*.)

1. TEUTONIC

We should perhaps consider the Teutonic branch first, for to it belongs English. The primitive Teutonic, which antedates the earliest written records, eventually came to be divided geographically into three groups of languages, East, North, and West. The East Teutonic languages did not survive into modern times, but we know their principal representative, Gothic, from early translations of the New Testament into that language. The language of the Vandals, the barbarian raiders who sacked Rome in 455 A.D., also belonged to this group. The North Teutonic languages are

---

*In this classification there are frequently listed two other branches now extinct, Tocharian and a group of languages once spoken in the Balkans and Asia Minor, but since these have no present-day representatives, they are not considered here.

spoken today in the Scandinavian countries, Denmark, Norway, Sweden, and Iceland. West Teutonic is represented principally by Modern German, Dutch, Flemish, and English.

2. ITALIC

When Rome was only a small village of rude huts on the banks of the Tiber, there were several Italic languages having equal status with Latin, but, as Rome achieved a dominant position in the ancient world, these disappeared, and Latin alone remained. The modern descendants of Latin, usually called Romance languages, show by their geographical distribution something of the extent of the Roman Empire. In France and Spain the Roman Conquest resulted in the complete displacement of the earlier languages by Latin. So today French, Spanish, and Portuguese, as well as Italian, are classed as Romance languages. Far to the east, Romanian is likewise a descendant of the language of Roman colonists and soldiers.

3. HELLENIC

The Hellenic branch of the Indo-European family is today represented by Modern Greek, which is the descendant of the Classical Greek of Plato and Aristotle and the common Greek dialect of the Eastern Mediterranean area in which the New Testament was written.

4. CELTIC

Over two thousand years ago the Celtic languages were spoken throughout a wide area of Western Europe, generally comprising France (or Gaul), part of Spain, and Great Britain. But, as we have seen, after the Roman Conquest Latin replaced the Celtic languages on the Continent, and, as we shall see later, Teutonic Anglo-Saxon largely replaced the Celtic speech in Britain. In sections of the British Isles which were difficult for the invaders to reach, however, Celtic languages still exist, notably in Ireland and Wales.

5. BALTO-SLAVIC

A. The Slavic languages are spoken in Russia, on the Balkan Peninsula in Bulgaria and Yugoslavia, and in Poland and Czechoslovakia.

B. The Baltic group is today of far less importance. It comprises mainly Lithuanian and Latvian or Lettish, the languages of two of the Baltic States forcibly absorbed by the Soviet Union in 1940.

6. INDO-IRANIAN

A. The oldest literary works in any Indo-European language are written in an Indian language, Sanskrit. As early as 1500 B.C. a number of very beautiful sacred books were composed in this language. Because of its antiquity and therefore closer resemblance to its Indo-European parent, Sanskrit is of great interest to linguists; only when European scholars became familiar with it did they realize fully the common origin of the many languages which we have been discussing. Sanskrit, however, is no longer spoken, but like Latin, has become a learned language.

From early Indian dialects called Prakrits existing at the same time as Sanskrit ultimately came many of the languages of present-day India and Pakistan, such as Hindi (Hindu), Bengali, and Nepali. Romany, the language of the Gypsies, likewise belongs to this group for, although the Gypsies have wandered widely throughout Europe and even America, their homeland was long ago in the northwestern part of India.

B. Closely related to the Indic group is the Iranian. Here is to be found the language of Iran or, as it used to be called, Persia. Modern Persian contains a great many Arabic elements, but is nevertheless considered Indo-European. Between India and Iran is the small nation of Afghanistan, which likewise speaks an Iranian language.

7. ARMENIAN

Modern Armenian, the sole member of this group, is a language native to a small area east of the Black Sea, partly in Turkey and partly in Russia.

8. ALBANIAN

The only surviving representative of the Albanian branch is Modern Albanian, spoken in a small nation just north of Greece.

Because all of these languages have come from a common ancestor, they are called cognate languages, and the similarities between them, which are not confined merely to vocabulary but include elements of grammar as well, might be compared to the physical similarities which exist between brothers and sisters, or between cousins.

We must remember, however, that the Indo-European is only one of a number of language families throughout the world. The other families have not been studied so thoroughly as Indo-European and consequently no universal agreement has been reached as to the exact extent of many of them. The following is a list of some of the more important families together with representative languages.

SEMITIC Hebrew, Arabic, Syrian, Ethiopic, Phoenician (extinct)

HAMITIC the ancient Egyptian of the Pharaohs, Berber or Libyan

INDO-CHINESE Chinese, Burmese, Siamese, Tibetan

URAL-ALTAIC Mongolian, Finnish, Estonian, Turkish, Magyar (Hungarian)

DRAVIDIAN the languages of Southern India and Ceylon

MALAY-POLYNESIAN the languages of the Malay Peninsula, Indonesia, the Philippines, and many of the Pacific Islands including Hawaii

AFRICAN NEGRO

JAPANESE and KOREAN

AMERICAN INDIAN

Between the various families no definite natural relationship has been established. Thus, while English and Greek can be traced back to a common ancestor and are cognate languages, this is not true of English and, let us say, Hebrew, or Chinese and Turkish.

II The Background of the English Vocabulary

Descent from a common ancestor is not the only type of relationship between languages. A relationship which is more obvious and which has greatly influenced the vocabulary of our language is that which has come about through borrowing; and to see the effect of this we should know something of the history of the English language.

During the Stone and early Bronze Ages the British Isles were inhabited by a non-Indo-European race about which next to nothing is known. Around 1000 B.C., however, the Celts, Indo-Europeans as we have seen, began to arrive in Britain and to conquer the prehistoric inhabitants, eventually completely wiping out their language. Thus, for some centuries the languages of the British Isles were of the Celtic group, and a few of their descendants, Welsh and Irish, for instance, are spoken today.

In the first century A.D. the Romans began the conquest of Britain and for the next several hundred years were in control of most of it. Romanization was proceeding on the island in much the same fashion as on the Continent, when the Roman occupation was cut short by the withdrawal of the legions, which were sent to buttress the tottering Empire against the onslaughts of the Eastern barbarians. The language of the British Celts, therefore, was never replaced by Latin as in France.

But something did happen to the Celtic languages of Britain, for it has already been pointed out in the preceding section that English is a Teutonic language. In the fifth century, after the Roman troops had been withdrawn, the Celts, having been exposed for some time to the softening effects of civilization, found themselves unable to resist the incursions of the fierce northern tribes which had never been subdued by the Romans. The Celtic leaders sought the aid of certain Germanic peoples living on the Continent to help them in their struggle. The Germans, however, found the island so much to their liking that they decided to remain and in fact conquered most of what is now England for themselves. These

7

Teutonic tribes were known as the Angles, Saxons, and Jutes; their language is called Anglo-Saxon and it became the basis of Modern English. As a matter of fact, our language took its name ("Anglish") from that of one of the tribes.

From the very first, however, Anglo-Saxon or Old English was subjected to outside influences. Even before the Angles and Saxons came to Britain, while they were still living on the mainland of Europe, they had come in contact with Roman civilization. For a time large parts of Germany were under Roman domination, and from the Roman soldiers and the inevitable traders who traveled in their wake, the languages of the Teutonic tribes received a number of Latin words. These words generally indicate the new products and concepts which were acquired from contact with a higher civilization. Thus, when they arrived in England, the Anglo-Saxons already had such borrowed words in their vocabulary as *straet* (from Latin *via strata,* "paved road"), which became in Modern English *street;* also, *ciese* (cheese), *win* (wine), *cuppe* (cup), and *pund* (pound).

Old English Period (450–1150)

Once the Anglo-Saxons were in Britain, contact with the earlier inhabitants brought some Celtic words, mostly place names like *Kent* and *London,* into Old English. Then, too, some words from Latin and Greek, such as *altar, candle,* and *priest,* were introduced during this period by Christian missionaries sent from Rome.

Beginning in the eighth century, England was subjected to repeated invasions by Danish marauders, many of whom settled in the areas of Britain which they had conquered. Despite the valiant efforts of English leaders like King Alfred the Great, the invaders could not be dislodged, but continued to live side by side with the Anglo-Saxons. The Danes were eventually assimilated, and their language has likewise left its mark upon English.

Middle English Period (1150–1500)

The greatest event in the shaping of the English language, however, was the Norman Conquest. In 1066 William of Normandy defeated King Harold at the Battle of Hastings and became ruler of England. The Anglo-Saxon nobles were replaced by a French-speaking aristocracy who regarded themselves primarily as Frenchmen and who looked upon England as occupied territory. Norman-French became the official language of the country, the language of the law courts, the schools, and the army.

In such a situation, the speech of the conquerors was bound to exert an influence upon English. Yet English remained as the language of the masses and kept its basically Teutonic structure. For a time Norman-French, spoken by the nobles, and English, spoken by the lower classes, existed side by side in the conquered land without affecting each other as much as is often supposed.

Around 1200, the Norman rulers of England lost many of their holdings on the Continent, including Normandy, and henceforth began to regard themselves as Englishmen rather than as Frenchmen, and by 1500, English had reasserted itself; but it was an English far different from the language of the Angles and Saxons. In the preceding three centuries many French-speaking aristocrats, as they learned English, had automatically introduced French words into their speech when they could not remember the new language or when the English synonym had been forgotten through disuse. Many who spoke English as a native tongue had learned French, not at this time the Norman-French of the conquerors but Parisian French, which had become the cultural and commercial language of Europe. Since it was more polished than their own language which had declined somewhat in the centuries when it was used in the main only by the uneducated classes, they naturally borrowed French words to make up deficiencies in their native tongue. Often both the French word and its English equivalent were kept, sometimes with varying shades of meaning, and this has tended to make our vocabulary more rich and varied. Thus we have both *begin,* which is native English, and *commence,* of French origin, *sin* and *crime, wretched* and *miserable, shun* and *avoid.* During the centuries when the distinction between Frenchman and Englishman was disappearing, the English vocabulary was enriched by the addition of thousands of French words. The language of this period is called Middle English and reached its fullest development in the writings of Chaucer.

Modern English Period (1500–)

By 1500, a new force had begun to exert itself on the English language, this time the result of an intellectual movement rather than of a military conquest. This was the Renaissance or Revival of

Learning, which was marked by the rapid advance of the sciences, a renewal of interest in the Greek and Roman classics, the rise of nationalism, and by such events as the Protestant Reformation, the invention of the printing press, and the discovery of the New World. The growth of national consciousness brought with it a desire on the part of Englishmen and Frenchmen and Italians and others to write books in their native tongues rather than in Latin, which had been the universal language of learned men throughout the Middle Ages. Many English writers, however, felt that their own language was still not sufficiently developed to meet the demands of the new learning; therefore, to remedy what they considered deficiencies in vocabulary they borrowed wholesale from Latin, which most of them knew almost as well as English. Further, the revival of interest in the ancient classics brought with it a flood of new ideas, especially from Greece; and when a new concept is imported from another culture, there is a strong tendency to import the word that denotes the concept as well.

The additions to English from Greek and Latin in this period are so many that it would be useless to try to give examples; most of the words which will be studied in this book entered our language during or after the Renaissance. Not only were words borrowed in great numbers directly from the pages of Greek and Roman authors but countless new words were coined by combining elements from the classical languages. In fact, the practice of using Greek and Latin as the basis of new scientific terms is one that still continues. In this way, for example, when the telephone was invented, instead of forming the name for the device from native elements, English combined Greek *tele,* "far" and *phone,* "sound."

Thus we have seen in outline the major forces which have shaped our vocabulary. But, of course, any contact with foreign nations, even a relatively minor contact, brings with it new additions, and English, perhaps because of its conglomerate background, has shown a greater tendency to borrow than most languages. The sources of its words therefore are world-wide, often reflecting the great extent of British commerce and colonization.

The modern European languages, especially those of France, with its leadership in cooking and fashion, and Italy, with its preeminence in the arts, have continued to supply us with a store of words. From the Near East, Persian, for instance, has given to English such common terms as *check, divan, pajamas,* and *tiger.*

Arabic has supplied *cotton, admiral, sirup, assassin,* etc. In the Middle Ages, Arabian science was considerably in advance of European; a number of our early scientific terms consequently came to us from the East. Many of these, *algebra, alcohol,* and *alkali,* for example, can be recognized from the fact that they begin with *al-,* the Arabic definite article. From the languages of India, long ruled by the British, have come, among others, *punch* (the beverage), *bungalow, loot, thug,* and *dungaree.* The Far East has provided fewer loan words, yet Chinese has given *tea, typhoon,* and *catsup,* while Japan has supplied *tycoon* and *kimono.* From Malayan have come *bamboo, bantam,* and perhaps *launch* (a boat). The islands of the Pacific have given us *tattoo, taboo,* and *hula.*

The borrowings by English in the New World remind us of the different cultures with which the colonists and pioneers came in contact. First of all, our language absorbed words from the Indians such as *caucus, raccoon, hickory,* and *skunk.* Some words came from the French in America. *Prairie* and *butte,* for instance, testify to the extensive early French explorations. *Levee, picayune,* and *bayou* came into our language from the French settlements in Louisiana. The Dutch colonists in New York State added to our vocabulary *boss, cookie, stoop* (porch), and *scow.* Later, from the Spanish-speaking culture of the Southwest we acquired words like *ranch, canyon, stampede,* and *mustang.* In the nineteenth century, immigrants from various countries added some of their native stock of words to our vocabulary; *smithereens* and *blarney,* for instance, were contributed by the Irish, and *pretzel, hamburger,* and *delicatessen* by the Germans.

Thus we have seen something of the composite nature of English and the many sources of its words. No other important language possesses such a complexity and variety of vocabulary, and this richness, while it has increased the difficulty of English, has made it an extremely flexible instrument. It would be interesting, therefore, to trace to their ultimate origins words from all of the tongues which have made up such a wealth of vocabulary; but this book, since its aim is to increase word knowledge systematically, will concentrate on only two of these languages, Latin and Greek. There are several reasons for doing this.

First, many of the languages previously mentioned have provided only a handful of loan words; the bulk of our borrowing has been from Latin and Greek. We have already seen how long such borrowing has been going on, starting in the period when the Angles and Saxons were still dwelling on the mainland of Europe, and continuing down to the present. (Remember that French is a direct descendant of Latin, so that most words borrowed from this source, as a result of the Norman Conquest or at other times, must be considered of Latin origin. In fact, it is impossible to tell in some instances whether a word entered English directly from Latin or by way of French.) This borrowing has been so extensive that words of classical origin make up the greater part of the English vocabulary. Such a statement naturally needs some qualification; it does not mean that the majority of words in this paragraph, for example, are from Latin and Greek. But of all the different words listed in an unabridged dictionary it has been estimated that more than three-fourths are of classical origin.* Furthermore, this percentage is increasing, for most of the words being added to English at the present time have to do with science, and, as was already mentioned, it is customary in coining new scientific terms to use Greek and Latin elements. It is true that many of the terms in a large dictionary are rarely used, but even among the 10,000 words which occur most frequently in English slightly more than half are ultimately derived from classical sources.†

Second, the longer, more difficult words, the ones which give the most trouble to college students, are generally those from Latin and Greek. Those of native Teutonic origin tend to be the short, basic, everyday words like *man, mother, run,* and *house,* which everyone knows, the learned and technical native words having fallen into disuse in the Middle Ages when English was used chiefly by unlettered speakers. In a list of 426 difficult but useful words compiled by the Freshman English staff at the University of Arizona for special vocabulary study—words like *ameliorate, cogent, epitome,* and *heterogeneous* — 404 are derived from the classical languages.

Third, the study of the more difficult words borrowed from Greek and Latin can to a great extent be systematized. That is, such words are usually composed of individual recognizable elements which have been used over and over again in the formation

---

*W. A. Oldfather, "The Future of the English Vocabulary," *Classical Outlook,* 19(1942), pp. 33-34.

†Edward Y. Lindsay, *"An Etymological Study of the Ten Thousand Words in Thorndike's Teacher's Word Book,"* Indiana University Studies, XII, No. 65, Bloomington, 1925.

of many different words. For example, one of the most widely used of these basic elements from Latin is the base DUC-, DUCT-, which has the general meaning of "to lead." In combination with various elements called prefixes and suffixes this basic form is to be found in a surprisingly large number of English words. The following list comprises the individual entries in a standard desk dictionary. (The negatives of these words have not been included.)

duct, ductile
abduce, abducent, abduct, abduction
adduce, adducent, adduct, adduction, adductor
aqueduct
conduce, conducive, conduct, conductance, conduction, conductive, conductivity, conductor
deduce, deduct, deduction
educe, educt, eductive
induce, inducement, induct, inductance, inductee, inductible, induction, inductive, inductivity, inductor
introduce, introduction, introductory
produce, producer, producible, product, production, productive, productivity
reduce, reduction
reproduce, reproduction, reproductive
seduce, seduction, seductive
subduct
traduce
transducer, transduction
viaduct

The idea of "lead" can usually be found somewhere in the meaning of those words which are familiar.

A further note is necessary, however. As has been mentioned, most of the words to be studied in this book entered English during the Renaissance or later, directly from Latin and Greek, and, since they were generally borrowed or coined by scholars and scientists, they lend themselves to systematic treatment. But many of the words which entered indirectly, by way of French or some other language, do not show as much regularity of form. Thus, also derived from the same Latin word as those in the preceding list are *duke*, *duchess, ducat, doge, dock, subdue, endue,* and *conduit.*

ASSIGNMENT

I. Which of the following languages are cognate with English?

1. Hindi
2. Hungarian
3. Korean
4. Russian
5. Arabic
6. Portuguese

II. To which branch of the Indo-European family does each of the following languages belong?

1. Bulgarian
2. Romanian
3. Sanskrit
4. Spanish
5. Greek
6. Welsh
7. Swedish

III. With the aid of a dictionary find the language from which each of the following is ultimately derived.

1. almanac
2. bizarre
3. boomerang
4. chair
5. cherub
6. chocolate
7. crag
8. dollar
9. galore
10. geyser
11. gingham
12. hominy
13. horde
14. hurricane
15. julep
16. khaki
17. magazine
18. mammoth
19. paradise
20. robot
21. sapphire
22. sherbet
23. swastika
24. tungsten

IV. With the aid of a dictionary trace the linguistic route of each of the following words into Modern English.

1. apricot
2. bishop
3. butter
4. car
5. chemist
6. orange

PART ONE
WORD ELEMENTS FROM LATIN

LESSON I   The Dictionary

A student will find that the most valuable tool in improving his vocabulary is a good dictionary. Many people, however, do not realize just how much information a dictionary contains. In looking up a word they note only its definition and spelling.

The individual entries in a good abridged or desk dictionary, such as *Webster's New Collegiate Dictionary* (abbreviated here WNCD), *The American College Dictionary* (ACD), or *Webster's New World Dictionary* (WNWD),* give the following information (though not necessarily in the order listed here):

I. Form of the Word

This includes not only the most commonly accepted spelling but also the more usual variant forms (e.g., *theater,* but also *theatre*). Also, the division of a word into syllables is shown; this indicates how a word should be divided when it is necessary to break it at the end of a line. Likewise, in the case of certain words, capitalization (compare, for example, the meanings of *Democratic* and *democratic*), the use of italics (for foreign words and phrases), hyphens (as in *white-headed*), and apostrophes (as in *fool's gold*) are indicated.

II. Pronunciation

The phonetic values of the individual letters in a word are indicated by a set of symbols (e.g., *ā, ä, ò,* etc.) in parentheses after each entry. Many people unfortunately do not take the trouble to determine what sounds are represented by these symbols, which vary somewhat from dictionary to dictionary. This is not a difficult task, however, for at the bottom of the page, or on the inside of the covers, or in the introductory material there is a key which shows, by giving familiar words as examples, the pronunciation indicated by each of the symbols (e.g., *ā* is pronounced as in *day; ä,* as in *bother; ò,* as in *saw,* etc.). The syllable on which the accent or stress falls is marked, and in some instances a secondary accent is also indicated. Remember that your dictionary is not attempting to set the pronunciation of a word but is only describing

---

Webster's Seventh New Collegiate Dictionary, G. and C. Merriam Company, Springfield, Mass., 1963

The American College Dictionary, Random House, New York, 1962

Webster's New World Dictionary, College Edition, The World Publishing Company, Cleveland and New York, 1962

how educated users generally pronounce it; in many cases, therefore, several different accepted pronunciations will be given.

III. Grammatical Information

A dictionary will list the part of speech of the entry, whether noun, verb, etc. Of course, a word may serve as more than one part of speech, as, for instance, *travel,* which can be either a verb or a noun; in such a case the meanings are given for both uses. There will also be listed, *if irregular,* the past tense and participles of verbs (e.g., under the word *drive* are given *drove, driven,* and *driving*), the plural forms of nouns (e.g., *children* and *mice*), and the comparative and superlative forms of adjectives (e.g., under the word *much* are listed *more* and *most*).

IV. Etymology

We have already seen in connection with the introductory exercise that a dictionary indicates the various languages from which a word has come into modern English. A dictionary will also give the meaning of the word in these languages (if different from the meaning in English) and will explain its origin insofar as it is known.

V. Definition

Besides modern meanings of words dictionaries also give older meanings, including those which have passed out of use. Note that dictionaries differ in the manner in which they present the different meanings of a word. Some, WNCD for instance, list the definitions in historical order, that is, in the chronological order in which they have developed in English. ACD gives meanings in the order of frequency with which they now occur. WNWD arranges definitions according to a "semantic order," which allows the reader to follow the logical development of the various meanings of a word. It is therefore an unwise practice to assume that the first definition is automatically the most usual one.

VI. Special Information

It is often necessary to give the person consulting a dictionary some guidance as to the use of a word, for words do not all have equal status, and their meanings may vary with the particular area of subject matter in which they occur. A dictionary consequently will use special labels. These are of three types:

1. usage or status labels — *slang, colloquial,* etc.
2. subject labels — *medicine, geology, nautical,* etc.
3. geographical labels — *British, Southern U. S.,* etc.

The following usage labels in particular are often misunderstood:

Colloquial means "used in conversation," "informal." A word or definition so labeled is not unacceptable but is more appropriate in ordinary conversation and in letters to friends than in formal speech or writing. This label is not to be confused with *slang*. *Pesky,* meaning "annoying," is an example of a colloquial usage.

Dialect refers to a term or definition like *auld* (the Scottish form of "old") peculiar to a given geographical area and indicates that the word differs from standard usage.

Obsolete means that a word or a particular definition of a word has entirely disappeared from current usage as, for example, the meaning of *explode,* "to drive an actor off the stage by noisy disapproval."

Archaic means that a word or definition is generally obsolete but is still kept for certain special uses, as, for instance, *hath,* which is confined mainly to church ritual.

VII. Synonyms

One of the most useful services performed by a dictionary is the listing of synonyms (and, to some extent, antonyms). Of course, there are special dictionaries devoted entirely to this, but a good abridged dictionary can give much useful information to a person trying to avoid repetitious use of the same word. Often, also, a paragraph is included explaining the varying shades in the meanings of synonyms. For example, if one is looking for the synonyms of *filthy,* he will be referred by the dictionary to the entry *dirty,* where he will find listed *dirty, filthy, foul, nasty,* and *squalid.* Then the slight differences between these synonyms in meaning or usage will be described, such as that *filthy* suggests something both dirty and offensive, while *foul* implies something which is revoltingly offensive and is putrid or stinking.

VIII. Idiomatic Uses

When a word is used in an idiomatic expression, it often acquires a very special meaning which needs to be defined in the same way as a separate entry. For example, listed under the word *take* are *take after, take amiss, take to, take on,* etc.

IX. Miscellaneous

A student will also find it useful to know that dictionaries list the names of prominent persons and important places, together with brief identifying information about each. WNCD gives this material in a special section at the back, while ACD and WNWD list proper names alphabetically in the body of the work. In addition, abbreviations and their meanings are included, as well as a considerable amount of other miscellaneous information.

It is necessary to indicate in very brief form much of the information contained in a dictionary. Because many people are unfamiliar with the concise manner in which their dictionary is written, they fail to get the full benefit from looking up a word and, in fact, sometimes misinterpret the information that they do find. The exercises in this lesson are therefore designed to familiarize the student with his dictionary and to give him practice in using it.

ASSIGNMENT

I. A. Give the variant spellings of the following which are listed in your dictionary:

1. abridgment
2. adviser
3. archaeology
4. catchup
5. fulfill
6. judgment
7. movable
8. naïve
9. sirup
10. taboo.

B. Indicate whether the following pairs of words remain separate, are hyphenated, or are written as one word:

1. anti Semitic
2. anti slavery
3. black list
4. black market
5. folk dance
6. folk lore
7. good humor
8. good humored
9. non alcoholic
10. pre medical
11. red handed
12. hot headed

II. A. Indicate the pronunciation of the following:

1. The **ch** of *chiropodist* is pronounced like (1) the **c** in *certain* (2) the **c** in *can* (3) the **sh** in *shell* (4) the **ch** in *chair*.

2. The **a** of *forbade* is pronounced like the **a** in (1) *land* (2) *gate* (3) *father* (4) *about*.

3. the **ei** of *heinous* is pronounced like (1) the **i** in *bite* (2) the **e** in *equal* (3) the **e** in *tent* (4) the **a** in *gate*.
4. The **ei** of *Freiburg* (a city) is pronounced like (1) the **a** in *gate* (2) the **e** in *equal* (3) the **i** in *bite*.
5. The **a** of *naïve* is pronounced like the **a** in (1) *land* (2) *gate* (3) *father* (4) *about*.
6. The **g** of *orgy* is pronounced like the **g** in (1) *gem* (2) *get* (3) *tongue*.
7. The **a** of *pathos* is pronounced like the **a** in (1) *land* (2) *gate* (3) *father* (4) *about*.
8. The **o** of *pathos* is pronounced like the **o** in (1) *pot* (2) *tone* (3) *wisdom*.
9. The **ae** of *alumnae* is pronounced like (1) the **a** in *gate* (2) the **i** in *bite* (3) the **a** in *about* (4) the **e** in *equal*.
10. The **au** of *chauvinism* is pronounced like (1) the **o** in *tone* (2) the **aw** in *awful* (3) the **ow** in *cow* (4) the **oo** in *too*.
11. The **a** of *Xenophanes* (a Greek philosopher) is pronounced like the **a** in (1) *land* (2) *gate* (3) *father* (4) *about*.
12. The first **e** of *egress* is pronounced like the **e** in (1) *agent* (2) *equal* (3) *tent*.

B. Circle the syllable on which the primary accent falls in each of the following:

1. adamant
2. adamantine
3. advertisement
4. anathematize
5. Aristides (a Greek statesman)
6. clandestine
7. formidable
8. impotent
9. incomparable
10. maniacal
11. misanthrope
12. Seattle

III. A. Give the plural or plurals of the following:

1. analysis
2. antenna
3. château
4. grotto
5. loaf
6. mongoose
7. moose
8. phenomenon
9. spoonful
10. stimulus
11. stratum
12. summons

B. Give all the past tenses and participles of the following verbs:

1. abide		7. drag	
2. awake		8. dwell	
3. awaken		9. plead	
4. bid		10. spit (to eject saliva)	
5. cleave (to split)		11. stride	
6. dive		12. wring	

IV. Describe the origin of each of the following:

1. amethyst	6. grog
2. ammonia, ammoniac	7. guy (a person)
3. blurb	8. namby-pamby
4. chortle	9. O.K.
5. gerrymander	10. paraphernalia

V. For each of the following, give a meaning labeled *obsolete* or *archaic:*

1. careful	7. naughty
2. comply	8. quaint
3. curious	9. quick
4. discover	10. remark (verb)
5. exult	11. shrewd
6. lewd	12. silly

VI. A. Give the usage or status label (if any) of each of the following:

1. ain't	7. irregardless
2. calaboose	8. larrup
3. fake (counterfeit)	9. lave (to wash)
4. galluses	10. lief (dear)
5. galoot	11. phony
6. gat (gun)	12. poke (sack)

B. Give the geographical label (if any) of each of the following

1. agley	7. pantechnicon
2. billabong	8. petrol
3. brae	9. pone (bread)
4. burn (brook)	10. pub
5. cayuse	11. pucka
6. dogie	12. van (baggage car)

VII. A. Give all the synonyms listed in your dictionary for the following:

1. abhor	6. monetary
2. calamity	7. paramount
3. claim	8. solid
4. gentle	9. sparkle
5. inert	10. speak

B. Distinguish between the following pairs of synonyms:

1. begin — commence	7. riddle — enigma
2. copious — ample	8. specific — special
3. curious — inquisitive	9. sudden — abrupt
4. fair — impartial	10. timely — opportune
5. faithful — loyal	11. value — prize
6. meaning — significance	12. vulgar — common

VIII. Give the meaning of each of the following idiomatic expressions:

1. beg the question	7. full tilt
2. do for	8. hang fire
3. dog in the manger	9. make away with
4. down at the heel	10. pop the question
5. fall foul of	11. put about
6. fight shy of	12. stand down

IX. A. Identify each of the following persons:

1. Jane Addams	7. Jozef Pilsudski
2. Sir Alexander Fleming	8. William Sidney Porter
3. Théophile Gautier	9. Henry Purcell
4. Richard Hakluyt	10. Saladin
5. Lao-tse	11. Thucydides
6. Paracelsus	12. Vasari

B. Locate each of the following places:

1. Bab el Mandeb	7. Monterrey
2. Bahrein Islands	8. Namur
3. Dodecanese Islands	9. Port Arthur
4. Funchal	10. Penang
5. Jakarta	11. Peshawar
6. Malabar	12. Sandwich Islands

C. Give the meanings of the following abbreviations:

1. cf.	7. F.R.S.
2. ca.	8. K.C.B.
3. D.D.S.	9. NEA
4. D.O.	10. N.E.D.
5. d.t.	11. Skt.
6. ESP	12. v.t.

LESSON II   Definition

In most of the lessons in this book, students will be asked to define words, for the ability to define is one of the surest tests of a knowledge of word meanings. The easiest way to arrive at a definition is to look it up in a dictionary; but, if a person merely copies the dictionary wording in an unthinking fashion, he is not likely to retain any lasting memory of it. Rather, with the aid of a dictionary, one should try to define an unfamiliar term in his own words. To do this, however, it is necessary to know something of the requirements for an adequate definition.

I. *A definition should be equivalent to the term to be defined.*

In the first place, a definition should be neither too broad nor too narrow. To define *saw* as "a tool" would be to define it too broadly, for there are many other kinds of tools besides saws. On the other hand, a definition such as "an instrument with teeth used for cutting wood" is too narrow, since some saws are used to cut metal. In the same way, the definition of *pen* as "a writing instrument" is too broad because it would include pencils, typewriters, and so on. But "a writing instrument with its own supply of ink" is too narrow a definition for it excludes every type of pen but a fountain pen.

In the second place, for a definition to be equivalent, a noun should be defined as a noun, a verb as a verb, and so on. In defining the noun *penury,* for example, do not say "poor" or "to be poor"; rather, use a noun or noun phrase, such as "want" or "lack of resources." When one defines a verb like *alleviate,* he should express its meaning not as an adjective, "less severe," but as a verb, "to make less severe." In the case of an adjective, one should use another adjective or adjective phrase. Thus *gregarious* does not mean "a herd," but "tending to gather in a herd."

II. *A definition should give the essential characteristics of the term to be defined and not merely make a statement about the term.*

Essential characteristics are rather elusive and relative, and they will vary with the purpose of the definition. But if, for instance, one defines *democracy* as "a type of government which has the interests of its citizens at heart," while this statement is no doubt true, he has provided no real explanation of the word. A more serviceable definition would be "government by the people." Likewise, to define a *traitor* as "a man whom everybody hates" does not tell much about the meaning of the word. Samuel Johnson, who compiled the first great English dictionary, occasionally yielded to his prejudices or to a spirit of playfulness in giving definitions, with the result that he has provided some famous examples of this type of shortcoming. Dr. Johnson, who cared little for the Scotch, defined *oats* as "a grain, which in England is generally given to horses, but in Scotland supports the people."

III. *A definition should be simple and clear, and expressed if possible in terms more familiar than the one to be defined.*

Again, the classic example of failure to observe this rule is Dr. Johnson's definition of *network,* "anything reticulated or decussated, at equal distances, with interstices between the intersections."

Above all, a definition should not contain the term to be defined nor any derivative of it. Do not define *imperturbable,* for example, as "incapable of being perturbed."

IV. *A definition should not be expressed in negative terms where affirmative can be used.*

It is not very helpful to be told that a *sofa* is "neither a bed nor a chair," or that a *Protestant* is "a Christian who is not a Catholic." On the other hand, some terms like *imperturbable* and *improvident* have to be defined negatively.

Latin Bases

As was indicated in the introduction, many of the longer and more difficult words of the English vocabulary are compounds formed from several individual elements. These elements are of three kinds, known as bases (sometimes called roots or stems),* prefixes, and suffixes, and a relatively small number of them have been used again and again in various combinations to form different words. In this lesson you will be introduced to Latin bases, that is, Latin words as they appear in English derivatives without the various characteristic Latin endings, *-us, -a, -um, -are,* etc. Throughout the book these bases will be printed in capital letters followed by a dash; e.g., FIRM-, GRAV-, MOD-. In later lessons we shall see how, by the addition of various prefixes and suffixes, many English words have been formed from a single base. For example:

con-FIRM-at-ion
in-FIRM-ity
in-FIRM-ary
FIRM-ament
re-af-FIRM-at-ion
af-FIRM-at-ive

Frequently, of course, Latin bases appear in English without the addition of any prefix or suffix.

I. Sometimes a base by itself forms an English word.

Latin Base	Meaning	English Derivative
FIRM-	firm, strong	firm
VERB-	word, verb	verb
FORT-	strong	fort

II. In other cases a final silent *e* is added in English. (This *e* is not a suffix and has no meaning.)

Latin Base	Meaning	English Derivative
GRAV-	heavy	grave
FIN-	end, limit	fine

Dictionaries, in describing the origin of an English word derived from Latin, will give the actual Latin word rather than the base; e.g., the

---

*Technically, *root, stem,* and *base* are not synonymous, *root* being a much broader term than the other two. This book, since it is primarily concerned with these elements as they are to be found in English words and not as they appear in Latin or Greek, makes varying use of all three types in the exercises, whichever type seems in a particular instance more useful for the student. Since, however, in the great majority of cases it is the base that has been listed, I have used this term throughout. (See Oscar E. Nybakken, *Greek and Latin in Scientific Terminology,* Ames, Iowa, 1959, pp. 3–5.)

word *verb* is listed as coming from the Latin *verbum.* In some cases, also, a dictionary will give two forms of a Latin word; e.g., our word *origin* is derived from the Latin *origo, originis* (the nominative and genitive cases). If one keeps in mind the English words, however, the roots, VERB- and ORIGIN-, will be readily apparent; in this book, bases as they appear in English will be our primary concern.

ASSIGNMENT

I. Learn the following bases and their meanings. Study each base so that you can recognize it when it occurs in a long compound word.

ALIEN-	of another	GRAV-	heavy
ART-	art, skill	LINE-	line
FIN-	end, limit	NUL(L)-	nothing
FIRM-	firm, strong	PART-	part
FORT-	strong	VERB-	word, verb
GRAND-	great	VEST-	garment

II. The bases listed above all appear as English words by themselves or with the addition of a final *e*; however, without using a dictionary, list as many other words formed from each of them as you can. For example, from the base ALIEN-, in addition to *alien,* have come *alienate, alienist,* and *inalienable.* Then check these words in a dictionary to make sure that they actually contain the particular Latin base. For instance, *investigate* has nothing to do with VEST-, "garment," but is formed from another base VESTIG-, "trace." It will be found that the meanings given for the bases do not always exactly fit the definitions of the words containing them, for over the years various changes of meaning have occurred, some of which will be studied in later lessons. Nevertheless, in most cases, a connection between the meaning of the base and the modern definition can be seen.

III. List the base and its meaning in each of the following italicized words and define the word as it is used in the sentence or phrase.

Example: the *gravity* of his illness; base, GRAV-, "heavy"; definition, "seriousness"

1. For an *infinitesimal* fraction of a second his fingers closed again on the small object. — Joseph Conrad

2. . . . the policy of shutting down plants entirely in bad times greatly *aggravates* economic crises, particularly in small one-factory towns. *—Harper's Magazine*

3. He took great pride in the ancient *lineage* of his family.

4. Just as an aggressive war is an admission of moral bankruptcy, the *nullification* of civil liberties is an admission of defeat. — *Atlantic Monthly*

5. . . . they are endowed by their Creator with certain *unalienable* Rights. —Thomas Jefferson

6. His fluency betrayed him into *verbiage,* and his descriptions are more diffuse than vigorous. — John Addington Symonds

7. Before the *investiture* . . . he apprized him of the difficulty and importance of his great office. — Edward Gibbon

8. The *definitive* book on this subject was written last year.

9. Preaching, not teaching, was his *forte.* —William Allen White

10. An ambitious man might make his own *aggrandizement,* by the aid of a foreign power, the price of his treachery to his constituents. — *The Federalist*

11. The governments and society of Europe, for a year at least, regarded the Washington Government as dead, and its ministers as *nullities.* —Henry Adams

12. . . . one *gravid* mouse developed a . . . tumor that disappeared after she littered . . .*—Time*

13. . . . I suggest that you get a report of a hearing that interests you and read the *verbatim* record of the statements made . . . — *Harper's Magazine*

14. . . . travelled for hours in those long thoroughfares that seemed to stretch away into *infinitude.* —W. H. Hudson

15. In the speech he gave a clear *affirmation* of his former pledge.

16. While he thus disgusted his subjects by his haughty deportment, he *alienated* their affections by the imposition of grievous taxes. — William Hickling Prescott

17. But he looked again, and the face and person seemed gradually to grow less strange, to change . . . into *lineaments* that were familiar. — Dickens

18. Religion by force, especially of the state, is a moral *travesty* and a contradiction of terms for modern man. — *Harper's Magazine*

IV. Describe what is wrong with each of the following definitions:

1. diffident: a person who lacks self-confidence
2. raceme: a simple inflorescence of the centripetal or indeterminate type, in which the several or many flowers are borne on somewhat equal axillary pedicels along a relatively lengthened axis or rachis
3. supine: not standing upright
4. perjury: dishonesty
5. impervious: not pervious
6. dog: man's best friend
7. redundancy: quality of being redundant
8. mutton: a kind of meat
9. carnivorous: eating human flesh
10. benign: not harmful
11. chemist: a scientist
12. vigilance: to watch carefully
13. poultry: a collective term for chickens
14. magnanimous: greatness of mind
15. uncle: the brother of one's father
16. introvert: a quiet person
17. calumny: an accusation
18. drunkenness: habitual inebriety
19. patriotism: the last refuge of a scoundrel
20. improvident: when a person lacks foresight or thrift

LESSON III   Prefixes

More often than not the Latin bases which will be studied appear in English with the addition of prefixes, that is, elements placed in front of the bases to modify their meanings. Most of these elements were originally Latin prepositions or adverbs. Thus:

ab-	from	+	DUCT-	to lead	abduct
con-	with	+	DUCT-		conduct
de-	off	+	DUCT-		deduct

This, of course, is not something confined to words of Latin derivation. There are a number of native English prefixes, seen in words like *by• stander, off•spring, fore•arm,* and *with•stand.*

An English word may contain more than one prefix, as in *dis•af• fected, non•con•ductor,* and *re•pro•duction.*

There are two special points which must be kept in mind in learning to recognize prefixes.

I. Often, when a prefix is used before certain consonants, its basic form undergoes phonetic change. Such changes have arisen in the unconscious process of pronouncing words. For example, the basic form of the Latin prefix meaning "not" is *in-,* as in *inglorious.* If words were only written and not spoken, we could accordingly expect *in•possible;* but, if we try to pronounce the word in this fashion, we find that as soon as we stop thinking about the usual form of the prefix, we automatically start saying "impossible."

The most usual type of change is that in which the last consonant of a prefix becomes the same as the first consonant of a base. This process is called *assimilation.* For example:

ad-	to	+	GRAV-	heavy	+	*-ate*	aggravate
ad-		+	SIMIL-	like	+	*-ation*	assimilation
con-	together	+	LECT-	to gather			collect
dis-	apart	+	FER-	to bring			differ
ex-	from	+	FECT-	to make			effect
in-	not	+	LEG-	law	+	*-al*	illegal
ob-	toward	+	FER-	to bring			offer
sub-	under	+	CUMB-	to lie			succumb

A student will find that a knowledge of prefixes and an awareness of the process of assimilation will help him to spell more correctly, for double consonants are one of the sources of spelling difficulty in English. When one realizes that assimilation has taken place in the case of words like *ag•gression, as•sist, col•lide, oc•cur, etc.,* he will be less likely to fall into the error of writing one consonant when he should write two.

II. Another element of difficulty in connection with prefixes arises from the fact that occasionally the base itself exhibits slight changes in form when a prefix is added. For example:

Latin Base		English Derivatives
SACR-	holy	sacred, sacrament, but also conSECRate, deSECRate
APT-	to fit	apt, aptitude, but also inEPT
FACT-	to make	factory, manufacture, but also afFECT, deFECT
SED-	to sit	sedentary, but also preSIDe

Since such changes are relatively infrequent and are difficult to classify, in the case of bases subject to this process, the variant form will be given in parentheses thus:

SACR-	(SECR-)	holy
FACT-	(FECT-)	to make
SED-	(SID-)	to sit

Learn the following prefixes and their meanings. (The first form given for each prefix is the basic or most usual one.)

Prefix	Meanings	Examples
ab-, a-, abs-	away, from	abduct, abnormal
(This prefix is never assimilated, so do not confuse it with *a* followed by a double consonant, which is from *ad-*.)		avert abstract
ad-, ac-, etc.	to, toward	adopt, admire
(Occasionally this prefix appears simply as *a-*, usually before *-sc-*, *-sp-*, and *-st-*; e.g., *aspire, ascribe.* When in doubt, however, assume that the prefix *a-* is a form of *ab-*, "away.")		access, aggression attract, allocate

| *ambi-* | both, around | ambidextrous |
| *ante-* | before, in front of | anteroom, antecedent |

(Do not confuse this with *anti-,* a Greek prefix meaning "against.")

circum-	around	circumference, circumscribe
con-, com-, co-, etc.	with, together, very	connect, conduct compose, compress collect, correspond co-operate
contra-, contro- (through French, *counter-*)	against	contradict controversy counteract
de-	down, off, thoroughly	descend, dejected
dis-, di-, dif-	apart, in different directions, not	dispute, disable divert, divorce differ

These prefixes can be found listed in a good abridged dictionary, where they are generally more fully discussed.

ASSIGNMENT

I. Learn the following bases and their meanings:

Latin Base	Meanings	English Derivatives
CED-, CESS-	to go, to yield	concede, precede excess, process
DUC-, DUCT-	to lead	induce, reduce conduct, reduction
JUR-	to swear	perjure, jury
LEV-	light (in weight)	levity, elevate
LOQU-, LOCUT-	to speak	colloquial, eloquent elocution, interlocutor
LUD-, LUS-	to play, to mock	interlude, delude illusion

PREC-	prayer	precarious
TRUD-, TRUS-	to push, to thrust	protrude
		intrusion, inobtrusive
VEN-, VENT-	to come	intervene
		invent, prevent

II. List the prefix and base, together with their meanings, in each of the following italicized words. Define each word as it is used in the sentence or phrase. In this and similar exercises the bases contained in the italicized words are ones assigned in the lesson or in previous lessons. If you cannot remember the meaning of a particular base, however, refer to the section at the end of Part I, where are listed all bases which students are expected to learn.

Example: *adjuration, ad-,* "to"; JUR-, "to swear"
     definition: a solemn entreaty

1. How could he *abjure* the faith that was intertwined with the dearest affections of his heart? —William Hickling Prescott

2. Russia, historically desirous of dominating the Balkans, will use Soviet policy to stimulate rather than *alleviate* Greek troubles. —*Harper's Magazine*

3. Into this jungle of *abstruse* learning Pico plunged with all the ardor of his powerful intellect. —John Addington Symonds

4. He began with a hesitating *circumlocution,* in order to prepare her mind for bad news. —George Meredith

5. . . . the noise and nerve-numbing will continue — and get worse with the *advent* of supersonic commercial traffic. —*Time*

6. I shall now proceed to *delineate* dangers of a different and, perhaps, still more alarming kind. —*The Federalist*

7. . . . whenever a particular statute *contravenes* the Constitution, it will be the duty of the judicial tribunals to adhere to the latter and disregard the former. —*The Federalist*

8. Friendship takes place between those who have an *affinity* for one another. —Thoreau

9. Congress *convened* in August for a special session.

10. Since his *accession* to the Crown, Charles the Fifth had been chiefly engrossed in the politics of Europe. —Prescott

11. Here, in the twinkling of an eye, he *divested* himself of his coat. —Dickens

12. . . . evidence, mainly negative in kind, has been *adduced* to prove the story of it a fabrication. —Francis Parkman

13. The right inherent in society, to ward off crimes against itself by *antecedent* precautions . . . —Mill

14. There is no need to dwell here on the evils of *collusion* . . . to fix prices and to restrict production. —*Harper's Magazine*

15. Shall we acquire the means of effectual resistance by lying supinely on our backs and hugging the *delusive* phantom of hope, until our enemy shall have bound us hand and foot? —Patrick Henry

16. By a powerfully welded chain of *deductive* evidence, the guilt of the robbery and apparent murder had been fixed on Clifford. —Hawthorne

17. How, it was asked on the other side, can the fundamental laws of a monarchy be *annulled* by any authority but that of the supreme legislature? —Macauley

18. But the life I lead . . . is not *conducive* to health. —Dickens

19. Thus, for a third time, Beatrix's ambitious hopes were *circumvented*. —Thackeray

20. . . . I should *deprecate* strongly the overemphasizing of party differences now, and recommend that we all bind ourselves with unflagging energy and unbroken union to the national task. —Sir Winston Churchill

III. Form words by combining the following elements, changing the spelling of the prefix where necessary.

Example: *con* + lusion   collusion

1. *ad-*	+ lusion		6. *ob-*	+ clusion
2. *sub-*	+ fuse		7. *in-*	+ ruption
3. *ad-*	+ rogate		8. *ad-*	+ monition
4. *dis-*	+ tract		9. *ob-*	+ trusive
5. *ex-*	+ fusive		10. *con-*	+ rosive

LESSON IV Prefixes

Learn the following prefixes and their meanings:

Prefix	Meanings	Examples
ex-, e-, ef-	out, from, completely	expel, exasperate eloquent, evade efficient

(In English, when *ex-* precedes a base beginning with *s,* the *s* is dropped.)

ex- + SPECT- to look		*expect*
ex- + SECUT- to follow		*execute*

Prefix	Meanings	Examples
extra-, extro-	outside, beyond	extraordinary extrovert
in-, im-, etc. (through French, *en-, em-*)	in, into, against	inject impose, impel illuminate, irrigate endure, embrace
in-, im-, etc.	not	ineffective, inequality immoral, impartial illegal, irresponsible

(This prefix and the preceding one are the same in form, but it is well to treat them as two separate prefixes so that one will be less likely to confuse their meanings. The word *inflammable,* sometimes written on gasoline cans, is a good illustration of the necessity for keeping these two prefixes distinct; the word does not mean that the liquid will *"not* burn," but that it will burst *"into* flame.")

Prefix	Meanings	Examples
infra-	below, beneath	infrared
inter-	between, among	interrupt, intercept
intra-, intro-	within	intramural, intravenous introduce
non-	not	nonresident

(This prefix is less emphatic than *in-* or the native English *un-;* compare *nonreligious* and *irreligious, non-American* and *un-American.*)

| *ob-,* etc. | toward, against, completely | obstruct, obstacle occur, offer, oppress |

(In many words it is difficult to see the force of the foregoing prefix.)

| *per-* | through, wrongly, completely | permeate, persecute perfect |

ASSIGNMENT

I. Learn the following bases and their meanings:

Latin Base	Meanings	English Derivatives
CRUC-	a cross	crucify
GREG-	flock, herd	congregate, segregate
PED-	foot	pedal, pedestrian
PUNG-, PUNCT-	to prick, point	puncture, punctual
SACR-, (SECR-)	sacred	sacrament consecrate
SENT-, SENS-	to feel, to think	sentiment, consent sensation
TURB-	to disturb	disturb
VERT-, VERS-	to turn	revert aversion
VI-	way, road	via, previous

II. List the prefixes and bases, together with their meanings, in the following italicized words. Define each word as it is used in the sentence or phrase.

1. He is so condescending to the son he so *egregiously* deludes, that you might suppose him the most virtuous of parents. —Dickens

2. I should not *obtrude* my affairs so much on the notice of my readers if very particular inquiries had not been made by my townsmen concerning my mode of life. —Thoreau

3. . . . . and if the assertion were proved to be false or the pledge to have been broken, he should be liable to the penalties of *perjury*. —John Stuart Mill

4. He saw that his crime was likely to produce nothing but hatred and *obloquy.* —Macaulay

5. . . . a *perverse* will that indulged children invariably acquire. —Emily Brontë

6. . . . a mysterious force called psi . . . which carries powers of *extrasensory* perception . . . —*Time*

7. . . . a small, frosty lady *imperturbable* even in the face of a severe automobile accident sustained last summer at the age of ninety-four . . . —*Harper's Magazine*

8. The *illusory* study of astrology, so captivating to the unenlightened mind, engaged no share of his attention. —William Hickling Prescott

9. . . . patients who undergo amputations continue to have "sensations" ranging from pleasant tingling to *excruciating* pain. —*Time*

10. . . . came so close to dismissal that only the indignant *intercession* of his mother saved him. —*Time*

11. In the second edition of his treatise he *expunged* or modified the passages which had given the manager offence. —Washington Irving

12. They cursed their fate, condemned their life, and wasted their breath in deadly *imprecations* upon one another. —Joseph Conrad

13. As might be expected of one who had spent a solitary childhood, he was something of an *introvert.*

14. The two functionaries advised their friend to *expedite* matters as much as possible, and lose no time in getting his fleet ready for sea. —Prescott

15. . . . one-third of our citizens, although literate by census standards and able to read and write well enough to get along, are *impervious* to book learning. —*Harper's Magazine*

16. The most *execrable* crimes are sometimes committed without apparent temptation. —Samuel Johnson

17. A woman who has *inadvertently* parked her car in a loading zone may have to wait in court nearly all day . . . —*Harper's Magazine*

18. He had been at the pains to transcribe the whole book, with blottings, *interlineations,* and corrections. —James Boswell

19. The stick with which the deed had been done, although it was of some rare and very tough and heavy wood, was broken in the middle under the stress of this *insensate* cruelty. —A. Conan Doyle

20. . . . bore in their faces the signs of extreme *perturbation;* they were plainly people who had passed a sleepless night. —Henry James

III. By adding one of the following prefixes, *counter-, de-, dis-, in-, non-,* and also the native English *un-,* make negatives of the following words or reverse their meaning. Consult your dictionary to make sure that the word which you form actually exists. Example: resident — nonresident

1. persuasive	6. combustible
2. militarize	7. inclination
3. enfranchise	8. clockwise
4. resistance	9. sensitize
5. resistible	10. audible

LESSON V Prefixes

Learn the following prefixes and their meanings:

Prefix	Meanings	Examples
post-	after, behind	postpone, postscript
pre-	before, in front of	prevent, predict
pro-	forward, in front of, for	promote, produce
re-, red- (before vowels)	back, again	renew, recede, recall redemption
retro-	backward, behind	retroactive
se-, sed- (before vowels)	aside, away	secede, segregate sedition

sub-, sus-, suc-, etc.	under, up from under, secretly	submerge, submarine suspend, sustain succumb, suffer support
super-	◦ above, over	superhuman, superfluous
trans-, tran-, tra-	across, through	transfer, transparent transcend, transcribe traverse, travesty
ultra-	beyond, exceedingly	ultraviolet, ultra-modern

There are several other Latin prefixes which occur so rarely that it is not worthwhile to learn them. These are: *juxta-,* "beside," "near to," seen mainly in the word *juxtaposition; preter-,* "beyond," in *preternatural;* and *subter-,* "below," "secretly," in *subterfuge.*

ASSIGNMENT

I. Learn the following bases and their meanings:

Latin Base	Meanings	English Derivatives
CLUD-, CLUS- (through French, CLOS-)	to shut	exclude, include conclusion disclose, enclosure
CUR(R)-, CURS- (through French, COURS-)	to run, to go	recur, current excursion concourse
GRAD-, GRESS-	to step, to go	gradual (literally, by steps) progress, aggression
PEND-, PENS-	to hang, to weigh, to pay	dependent, suspend dispense, expense

(The last meaning of the foregoing base arose from the fact that, before coins came into use, payment was made by weighing out gold and silver.)

PLE-, PLET-	to fill	implement complete, deplete
SPEC- (SPIC-), SPECT-	to look	specimen, conspicuous inspect, respect

UND- (through French, -OUND)	wave	abundant, undulate abound, redound
VID-, VIS-	to see	evident, provide visual, provision
VOC- (VOK-)	voice, to call	vocal, invocation provoke, revoke

II. List the prefixes and bases, together with their meanings, in the following italicized words. Define each word as it is used in the sentence or phrase.

1. . . . a brevity which excludes everything that is *redundant* and nothing that is significant . . .—Lytton Strachey

2. . . . the gorilla infant will, in the course of time, develop an enormously powerful and *protrusive* muzzle. —*Harper's Magazine*

3. This tendency represents a *regression* to a more primitive stage of religion.

4. Though not of a *retrospective* turn, he made the best effort he could to send his mind back into the past. — Hawthorne

5. Cards were easily made out of old parchment drumheads, and in a few days most of the prize-money, obtained with so much trouble and suffering, had changed hands, and many of the *improvident* soldiers closed the campaign as poor as they had commenced it. — William Hickling Prescott

6. He had come home to lay an empire at the feet of his sovereign, and to demand in return the redress of his wrongs and the *recompense* of his great services. —Prescott

7. The sierra was so precipitous that it seemed to *preclude* all further progress. — Prescott

8. It was now evident that instant retreat was necessary; and the command being issued to that effect, the men . . . slowly began their *retrograde* movement. —Francis Parkman

9. All concerned . . . should be asked to report on the measures which they are taking to *implement* these instructions . . . — Sir Winston Churchill

10. I have not the sense of perfect *seclusion* which has always been essential to my power of producing anything. — Hawthorne

11. . . . the United Nations, with the United States *concurring,* passed a resolution promising to discuss the future of Formosa . . . —*Harper's Magazine*

12. . . . the *propensity* of mankind to exalt the past, and to depreciate the present. — Edward Gibbon

13. There goes in the world a notion that the scholar should be a *recluse* . . . —as unfit for any handiwork or public labor as a penknife for an axe. — Emerson

14. . . . their country was vanquished simply because its *transgressions* against civilized behavior aroused the organized anger of most of humanity. — *Harper's Magazine.*

15. Once more he bent his footsteps towards the scene of his living martyrdom, saddened with a deep *presentiment* that he was advancing to his death. — Francis Parkman

16. Thanks to its long and distinguished history as the only effective weapon against the *recurrent* fevers of malaria, quinine is still highly regarded . . . —*Time*

17. The dusty old trunk contained many objects *evocative* of the past.

18. . . . cunning, ambitious, and unprincipled men will be enabled to *subvert* the power of the people, and to usurp for themselves the reigns of government. — Washington

19. He was obliged to pause and decide whether he would surrender and obey, or whether he would give the refusal that must carry *irrevocable* consequences. —George Eliot

20. It may be added that without this *supplemental* provision, the great and essential power of regulating foreign commerce would have been incomplete and ineffectual. — *The Federalist*

III. By changing the prefix, form the antonym of each of the following words.

Example: exhale — inhale

1. assent	7. converge
2. supersonic	8. persuade
3. prelude	9. discord
4. depreciate	10. inflate
5. associate	11. retrogress
6. ante-bellum	12. accelerate

LESSON VI   Combinations of Bases

Many words have been formed by combining two Latin bases. Sometimes a connecting vowel, usually *i,* has been inserted between the bases in order to make pronunciation easier. For example:

SACR- sacred + (i) + FIC- to make   sacrifice
EQU- equal + (i) + VAL- to be worth + *-ent* equivalent

In particular the bases which denote numbers are frequently found in combination with other bases. Learn the following numerical bases and their meanings:

SEMI-	half, partly	semiannual
UN-	one	uniform, unanimous
PRIM-	first	primary, primitive
DU-	two	duet, dual
BI-, BIN- (before vowels)	two, twice	bicycle, binoculars
TRI-	three	tricycle, triangle
QUADR(U)-	four	quadrangle, quadruple
QUART-	fourth	quarter
QUINT-	fifth	quintuplet, quintet
SEXT-	sixth, six	sextet
SEPT-, SEPTEM-	seven	septet, September*
OCT-	eight	octet
OCTAV-	eighth	octave
DECI-, DECIM-	tenth	deciliter, decimal
CENT-	hundred	century, centennial
MILL-	thousand	millimeter, mill

---

*Originally the Romans began their new year on March 1; thus, September was the seventh month, October, the eighth, and so on. When the beginning of the year was put back to January 1, the names of the months were left unchanged.

This list does not contain all the bases for the sequence from one to ten. Some have been omitted since they appear in few English words or only in very technical terms. These are: SESQUI-, "one and a half times," SECOND-, 'second," TERTI-, "third," QUINQUE-, "five," SEX-, "six," SEPTIM-, "seventh," NOVEM-, "nine," NON-, "ninth," and DECEM-, "ten."

Roman Numerals

While we are studying the Latin bases for numbers, we might also consider Roman numerals, which are used to indicate volume numbers of periodicals, dates such as those on buildings and motion pictures, the introductory pages and chapter numbers of books, and for various other purposes. Most students have probably studied Roman numerals before, so this part of the lesson will be largely a review, but a worthwhile review nonetheless, for these symbols occur just often enough to be troublesome but not often enough to make one accustomed to their use.

The symbols which are chiefly used are:

I = 1	X = 10	D = 500
V = 5	L = 50	M = 1000
	C = 100	

If a smaller numeral follows a larger one, the two are added (e.g., XI = 10 plus 1 = 11); if a larger numeral follows a smaller one, the smaller is subtracted from the larger (e.g., IX = 10 minus 1 = 9). If a numeral stands between two larger numerals, it is subtracted from the second, and the remainder is added to the first (e.g., XIX = 10 plus 9 = 19).

Examples:

III 3	VIII 8	MDCCCLXIII 1863
IV 4	IX 9	MCMLIX 1959
VII 7	XII 12	
	XXVII 27	
	XLIV 44	
	LXXVI 76	

ASSIGNMENT

I. List the prefixes (if any) and bases, together with their meanings, in the following italicized words. Define each word as it is used in the sentence or phrase.

1. In regard to intellectual ability he is in the second *quartile* of the applicants who took the examination.

2. He *appended* a qualifying footnote to the statement.

3. During the last three months an element of baffling *dualism* has complicated every problem of policy and administration. We had to plan for peace and war at the same time. — Sir Winston Churchill

4. . . . because of the city's [Berlin's] *quadripartite* occupational status . . . —*Time*

5. A temporary *recession* of business activity is expected this year.

6. . . . another voice shouted occasional replies; and this *interlocutor* seemed to be on the other side of the hedge. —Thomas Hardy

7. The president of the university addressed the *convocation*.

8. The long narrow plain was interrupted in several places by *transverse* canals.

9. I am *averse* to listening to the complaints of the customers.

10. This is an extremity to which no government will of choice *accede*. —*The Federalist*

11. Any system of compulsory wage arbitration would have to be *tripartite,* with representatives of the workers, employers, and the public making up the tribunal. — *Harper's Magazine*

12. . . . the wall which had been constructed by the ancient kings of Assyria to secure their dominions from the *incursions* of the Medes. — Edward Gibbon

13. A *centigrade* thermometer . . .

14. All they had hitherto suffered, the *desecration* of their temples, the imprisonment of their sovereign . . . —William Hickling Prescott

15. He devoted Sunday afternoons to his *avocation* of landscape painting.

16. This outpost settlement had had its membership *decimated* during the Arab riots. — *Harper's Magazine*

17. Victory is traditionally *elusive*. Accidents happen. Mistakes are made. — Churchill

18. I heard her sigh low. She was *pensive* a few minutes, then rousing herself, she said cheerfully . . . —Charlotte Brontë

19. . . . let it be named from the fishes that swim in it, the wild fowl or *quadrupeds* which frequent it . . . —Thoreau

20. (a) The colonies . . . of the gibbons and perhaps of other *primates* not far away from the line of human descent . . . — *Harper's Magazine*
    (b) . . . the election of a new Archbishop of Athens (who is also *primate* of the country) is a matter of high national interest. — *Time*

II. With the aid of a dictionary explain the connection between the numerical bases which were presented in this lesson and the following words.

   Example: *primate,* (1) one who occupies the "first" rank (2) one of the highest or "first" order of mammals, including man and the apes.

   1. unicorn
   2. primer
   3. primeval
   4. biscuit
   5. trivial
   6. trillion
   7. Septuagint
   8. octogenarian
   9. centurion
   10. mile

III. Write the following in Arabic numerals:

   1. XVIII
   2. XLIX
   3. CVII
   4. DCLX
   5. DCCCXLIV
   6. MDCCXXXIX
   7. XXXII
   8. LVII
   9. CCXIV
   10. MCCXIX

IV. Write the following in Roman numerals:

1. 1776
2. 89
3. 244
4. 1332
5. 669

LESSON VII   Hybrids

In the previous lesson, words formed by combining two bases were considered. Usually such combinations are made up of elements which have been taken from the same language, but sometimes words are found composed of bases or prefixes and suffixes drawn from two or more different languages. Such combinations are called hybrids. Many hybrids are so common that we are scarcely aware of their composite background; *gentleman* (*gentle*, ultimately of Latin origin; *man*, from Anglo-Saxon) and *petrify* (*petra*, Greek; *-fy*, Latin) are examples. Some philologists frown on the formation of hybrids; nevertheless, many such words are to be found in English, and no amount of disapproval will remove them from the language. In Part III of the assignment are a number of these words made up of diverse elements.

ASSIGNMENT

I. Learn the following bases and their meanings:

ANIM-	mind, feeling, life	animal, animated
ANN(U)- (ENNI-)	year	annals, annual perennial
BENE-	well, good	benefactor, benefit
BENIGN-	kind	benign
EQU-	equal, even	equal, equidistant
MAGN-	great	magnitude, magnify
MAL(E)- MALIGN-	bad	maladjusted, malicious malignant
MULT-	many	multitude, multiply

PLIC-, PLICIT-,	to fold, to	complicate, implicate
-PLEX (through	interweave, to	implicit,
French -PLY)	tangle	complex,
		imply, multiply
VOL-	to wish	voluntary

II. List the prefixes and bases, together with their meanings, in the following italicized words. Define each word as it is used in the sentence or phrase.

1. Not long afterwards he made a *magnanimous* public gesture of reconciliation towards German men of learning and letters. — *Atlantic Monthly*

2. It was plain that the Queen was sinking under smallpox of the most *malignant* type. —Macaulay

3. . . . another of the many proofs of the tenderness and *benignity* of his heart. —James Boswell

4. Miss Miller was . . . hurried in gait and action, like one who had always a *multiplicity* of tasks on hand. —Charlotte Brontë

5. . . . a bill then depending for making parliaments *triennial*. — Samuel Johnson

6. The *inanimate* objects were not changed, but the living things had altered past recognition. — Charlotte Brontë

7. (a) . . . it is most remarkable to find no record of its existence prior to the second *millennium* B.C. —*Harper's Magazine*

   (b) It seemed, in fact, as if the *millennium* were dawning upon the land; for the sword was beaten into a ploughshare, and the spear into a pruning-hook. — Washington Irving

8. The dentist treated him for a *malocclusion*.

9. Hitherto it had been simply a sentimental dalliance, and gossips had *maligned* the lady. —George Meredith

10. The answer was evasive — I should have liked something clearer; but Mrs. Fairfax either could not, or would not, give me more *explicit* information. —Charlotte Brontë

11. . . . the smile of broad *benevolence* wherewith he made it a point to gladden the whole world. — Hawthorne

12. Almagro's indignation, as well as that of his companions, was heightened by the *duplicity* of their enemy, who could practice such insidious arts, while ostensibly engaged in fair and open negotiation — William Hickling Prescott

13. She marshalled all her *volition,* all her self-control and strength, to shout . . . —Arnold Bennett

14. Hammarskjöld has cautiously moved behind a cloud of *equivocal* words to win an Arab-Israeli truce that has lasted four years. — *Time*

15. The inexorable political calendar provides for *biennial* congressional elections and *quadrennial* presidential elections at stated dates, regardless of when wars end. — *Harper's Magazine*

16. It was a bearded, hairy face, with wild, cruel eyes and an expression of concentrated *malevolence.* —A. Conan Doyle

17. In those days he spoke *grandiloquently* of "manufacturing wheat" and he was hailed . . . as "the Henry Ford of Agriculture." — *Harper's Magazine*

18. The fact that he did not approve of the present administration was *implicit* in his refusal to accept the appointment.

19. Nothing seems to make an impression on their minds; nothing short of being knocked down by a porter, or run over by a cab, will disturb their *equanimity.* —Dickens

20. He carried into the bookselling craft somewhat of the grandiose manner of the stage, and was prone to be mouthy and *magniloquent.* —Washington Irving.

III. With the aid of a dictionary, determine the languages from which the elements in each of the following hybrids have been drawn.

1. television
2. anteroom
3. megaton
4. ill-tempered
5. automobile
6. speedometer
7. denazify
8. antibody
9. aqualung
10. monaural

LESSON VIII   Suffixes

Along with bases and prefixes, suffixes have often been used in word formation. Suffixes are word elements attached to the end of a base, and, as with prefixes, most of us are familiar with them in the case of native English words. For example:

kind	+	*-ness* quality of	kindness
care	+	*-less* without	careless
boy	+	*-ish* like	boyish

In the same way, many English words of Latin origin have been formed by the addition of suffixes. For example:

FIN-	end	+ *-al*	pertaining to	final
NUMER-	number	+ *-ous*	full of	numerous
POPUL-	people	+ *-ar*	pertaining to	popular

Suffixes differ from prefixes in that they not only modify the meaning of a base, but also determine the part of speech of the word thus formed. In the case of the previous examples, adjectival suffixes were attached to noun bases to form adjectives. We shall be dealing with three types of suffixes, adjective-forming, noun-forming, and verb-forming. In some instances, however, a suffix normally classed as adjective-forming will actually be found to form a noun. This is because of a tendency, present in most languages, for adjectives to be used as nouns. Thus, in English *good* is generally an adjective, but in the sentence, "The good die young," it is used to mean "good people." Similarly, the words *numeral* (NUMER-, "number" + *-al,* "pertaining to") and *pedal* (PED-, "foot" + *-al*) usually occur as nouns despite the fact that *-al* is classed as an adjective-forming suffix.

More than one suffix is sometimes found in a single word. For example:

CLASS- class, rank	+ *-ic* belonging to	+ *-al* pertaining to	classical
EQU- equal	+ *-al* pertaining to	+ *-ity* state of	equality
POPUL- people	+ *-ar* pertaining to	+ *-ity*	popularity

When a suffix which ends in *e* is followed by an additional suffix, the *e* is generally dropped. For example:

VERB- word	+ *-ose* full of	+ *-ity* quality of	verbosity
URB- city	+ *-ane* pertaining to	+ *-ity*	urbanity

Learn the following adjective-forming suffixes and their meanings:

I. *-al* (*-ial, -eal*), "pertaining to," "like," "belonging to," "having the character of"

VOC-	voice	+ -al	vocal
VERB-	word	+ -al	verbal
EQU-	equal	+ -al	equal

II. *-ane, -an* (*-ian*), same meanings as the preceding.

VETER-	old	+ -an	veteran
URB-	city	+ -an	urban
MUND-	world	+ -ane	mundane

A. The suffix *-an* (*-ian*) frequently forms words which are used as nouns and so comes to mean "one connected with."

| LIBR- | book | + -ary place for | + -an | librarian |
| BARBAR- | foreign | + -ian | | barbarian |

III. *-ar*, "pertaining to," "like," "belonging to," "having the character of."

POPUL-	people	+ -ar	popular
REGUL-	rule	+ -ar	regular
FAMILI-	family, household	+ -ar	familiar

IV. *-ose* (*-iose*), "full of"

| VERB- | word | + -ose | verbose |
| COMAT- | lethargy | + -ose | comatose |

V. *-ous*, (*-ious, -eous*), "full of," "having the character of," "like."

FAM-	fame, report	+ -ous	famous
POPUL-	people	+ -ous	populous
VARI-	varied	+ -ous	various

The various suffixes can be found listed in a good dictionary, where they are generally discussed more fully than in this book.

ASSIGNMENT

I. Learn the following bases and their meanings:

| AQU(A)- | water | aquatic, aqueduct |
| CARN- | flesh | carnage, incarnation |

CORPOR-, CORP- (CORPUS-)	body	incorporate corpuscle
JUDIC-	judgment	judicial, prejudice
OMN-	all	omnipotent, omnipresent
RECT-	right, straight	rectangle, rectify
SIMIL-, SIMUL-	like	similar, simulate
TEMPOR-	time	temporary, contemporary
TENU-	thin	extenuate
VOR-	to devour	voracious

II. List the prefixes, bases, and suffixes, together with their meanings, in the following italicized words. Define each word as it is used in the sentence or phrase.

Example: *interlinear; inter-,* "between," LINE, "line," *-ar,* "pertaining to"; definition: "between lines"

1. But they greeted first with disbelief and then with dismay the disclosures of the *devious* bypaths into which resentment . . . had led their senior Senator . . . *—Harper's Magazine*

2. . . . a speech that was plain, straight, and pungent, enriched by a meaty, homely, and *colloquial* metaphor, a concrete descriptive power that made use of the good straight words of common speech . . . —Thomas Wolfe

3. In the dark and on all fours he resembled some *carnivorous* animal prowling amongst corpses. — Joseph Conrad

4. He was disgusted by the hideous wilderness, and declared that he greatly preferred . . . trim flower beds and *rectilinear* avenues. — Macaulay

5. . . . the separation between spiritual and *temporal* authority (which placed the direction of men's consciences in other hands than those which controlled their worldly affairs). — John Stuart Mill

6. . . . Malaya is run by a coalition Alliance Party, which has established a *tenuous* racial harmony among Malaya's 6,500,000 polyglot population. — *Time*

7. . . . to throw as much sanctity as possible into his face, and in particular, to abstain from all appearances of mirth and

pleasantry, which were looked upon as the marks of a *carnal* mind. — Joseph Addison

8. But his type of *verbose* and overornamental oratory was becoming outmoded. —Samuel Hopkins Adams

9. Rosie had not attempted to inflict *corporal* punishment beyond an occasional punch or slap . . . —W. H. Hudson

10. He had *aqueous* gray eyes, and a sallow bumpy skin. — Thomas Wolfe

11. An English ruin is more beautiful often in its decay than even it was in its *primal* strength. —Hawthorne

12. Governments of *dissimilar* principles and forms have been found less adapted to a federal coalition of any sort. —*The Federalist*

13. . . . the *crucial* need for economic stability.

14. The artillery, also, was so *injudiciously* placed as to be entirely useless. — Washington Irving

15. One of New England's *perennial* chores, as perennial as winding the clock and putting out the cat, is adjusting to the mutable American economy. — *Harper's Magazine*

16. Above all, Ben Franklin was a man of the 18th century Enlightenment, with its indiscriminate, *omnivorous,* ravenous appetite for all facts about all nature. — *Time*

17. As he grew older, Trujillo embarked on *grandiose* projects of no merit, lost $35 million on an international fair that flopped in 1956 . . . —*Time*

18. . . . the affected, wordy style that a schoolboy might use to a fancied, *incorporeal* sweetheart. —Emily Brontë

III. Distinguish in meaning the following pairs of words. These pairs have the same bases but different suffixes.

1. official–officious
2. aquatic–aqueous
3. equal–equable
4. continuous–continual
5. urban–urbane
6. judicial–judicious
7. imperial–imperious
8. funeral–funereal
9. human–humane
10. military–militant

LESSON IX Word Analysis

Now that you have been introduced to the three elements used in word formation, bases, prefixes, and suffixes, you will be able to separate the words in the exercises into their component parts. Henceforth, when asked to analyze a word, list its elements and their meanings, as in Part II of the previous exercise. By developing this technique of word analysis you will acquire a valuable method for attacking unfamiliar words of Latin or Greek origin. When you first encounter a new word, if you break it down into base, prefix, and suffix, it will seem less strange and puzzling, and in many cases its meaning can be guessed with the help of the context, that is, the rest of the sentence or phrase in which it is used. Even if one can recognize only some of the elements that a word contains, this technique will be useful. Furthermore, after analyzing unfamiliar words, a student will find them much easier to remember, for the various bases, prefixes, and suffixes which will be studied are excellent mnemonic devices; it will be of considerable aid to the memory if one can link the unfamiliar with the familiar, if, for example, one is aware that *perturbation* contains the same base as *disturb*.

Word analysis, however, is not an infallible method of determining the meanings of words. It must be used with care and intelligence. A good dictionary will still be indispensable, for the student should verify his guesses made on the basis of analysis and context. There are in particular two areas of difficulty in analyzing words. In the first place, confusion can sometimes arise because two or more Latin bases are spelled the same way. To cite an extreme instance of this, *transparent, parent,* and *preparation* contain three different bases, each spelled alike but with separate meanings, PAR-, "to appear," PAR-, "to give birth," and PAR-, "to make ready." Sometimes, also, a word may seem to contain a familiar Latin base and yet not come from Latin at all. *Artichoke* has nothing to do with ART-, "skill," but is apparently of Arabic origin.

In the second place, the combined meaning of base, prefix, and suffix, which is called the *etymological meaning,* is frequently not the same as the current meaning. For instance, the etymological meaning of *precarious,* "pertaining to prayer," (PREC-, "prayer") seems at first glance rather remote from its usual meaning of "hazardous, insecure." It is not likely that one could deduce the current meaning simply by using a knowledge of word elements. Only by comparing the etymological meaning with the current meaning does one come to realize that a "precarious" situation was originally one completely out of human control, dependent only upon prayer and entreaty. Again, on the basis of the meanings of its elements, *transgressor* is "one who steps across" (*trans-*, "across" + GRED-, GRESS-, "to step," "to go," + *-or*, "one who"). The connection with its current meaning "sinner" is not readily apparent until one sees that originally the sense of the word was "one who steps across the bounds of righteousness." The verb *decimate*, as we saw from its root, would seem to have something to do with "tenth," yet it normally refers to the destruction of a large part of a group, as in the sentence, "The enemy troops were *decimated* by machine gunfire." Not until we learn that at one time the word referred to the practice of punishing mutinous soldiers by executing every tenth man and that it came to be used loosely, can we connect the two senses. Thus, in many cases, a student must be careful to distinguish the current meaning from the etymological meaning.

Such differences between current meanings and etymological meanings offer many problems in connection with word analysis. But there is a positive side to this. As was mentioned in the preface, one of the most effective ways of improving vocabulary is to become "word-concious," to develop an interest in words for their own sake. The words which the student will find most interesting are not those which can be analyzed in a more or less cut and dried fashion, but those which have changed their meanings in the course of centuries, and so present a problem which challenges the imagination. When one finds a word which is capable of analysis but which means something quite different from the sum of its parts, if he has any intellectual curiosity at all, he will try to determine how its present sense developed.

Usually a dictionary will be of help in this, and often one will find an interesting explanation for such a development, an explanation which may reflect some custom or belief or event of the past, or some characteristically human way of looking at things. For instance, *lunatic* contains the base meaning "moon" (also found in *lunar*), reminding us that once insanity was thought to be caused by the influence of the moon. The etymological meaning of *candidate* is "clad in white," a word arising from the practice of Roman politicians who, when campaigning for office, wore artificially whitened togas as a symbol of personal purity.

Note that the analysis of words into prefixes, bases, and suffixes frequently does not correspond to their division into syllables. Thus, *bellicose* is made up of the elements *bell-*, "war," *-ic*, "pertaining to," and *-ose*, "full of," but is divided into syllables *bel-li-cose*.

ADJECTIVE-FORMING SUFFIXES

Learn the following suffixes and their meanings:

I. *-(u)lent, -(o)lent,* "full of," "disposed to"

FRAUD-	deceit	+ *-(u)lent*	fraudulent
VI-	force	+ *-(o)lent*	violent

II. *-ic, -tic,* "pertaining to," "like"

CIV-	citizen	+ *-ic*	civic
CLASS-	class, rank	+ *-ic*	classic
RUS-	country	+ *-tic*	rustic

III. *-ary,* "pertaining to," "connected with," "having the character of"

LITER-	letter, literature	+ *-ary*	literary
MILIT-	soldier	+ *-ary*	military
TEMPOR-	time	+ *-ary*	temporary

A. If this suffix is followed by an additional element, the final *y* appears as *i.*

PREC-	prayer	+ *-ary*	+ *-ous*	precarious
ANTIQU-	old	+ *-ary*	+ *-an*	antiquarian

B. The suffix *-ary* frequently forms words which are used as nouns and so comes to mean "one connected with."

ANTIQU-	old	+ *-ary*	antiquary
DIGNIT-	worth	+ *-ary*	dignitary

IV. *-ile, -il,* "pertaining to," "like," "belonging to," "having the character of"

JUVEN-	youth	+ *-ile*	juvenile
HOST-	enemy	+ *-ile*	hostile
CIV-	citizen	+ *-il*	civil

ASSIGNMENT

I. Learn the following bases and their meanings:

BELL-	war	belligerent, rebellion
GENER-, GEN-	race, kind	general, generate, degenerate
LATER-	side	lateral, multilateral

LUMIN-	light	illuminate
PECUNI-	money	pecuniary
SANGUIN-	blood	sanguine
SEN-	old	senate, senior
SERV-	to serve, to save	servant, service conservation, preserve

II. Analyze the following italicized words and define them as they are used in the sentence or phrase.

Examples: an *egregious* error; *e-,* "from"; GREG-, "flock"; *-ious,* "having the character of"; "distinguished for bad quality" *perennially* complaining; *per-,* "through"; ENNI-, "year"; *-al,* "pertaining to"; *-ly,* English adverbial suffix; "constantly"

1. The principal doctor was lost in the imbecilities of a *senile* optimism. —Lytton Strachey

2. A *bellicose* dictatorship in Germany, Japan, or even Italy could develop into a danger to the whole world. —*Harper's Magazine*

3. An *equilateral* triangle . . .

4. An intimacy with Dr. Johnson, the great literary *luminary* of the day, was the crowning object of his aspiring and somewhat ludicrous ambition. —Washington Irving

5. The *turbulent* multitude continued roaming and shouting and howling about the city during the day and a part of the night. —Irving

6. . . . *consanguineous* marriages.

7. He was generally clad in a long, patched livery coat . . . which bagged loosely about him, having evidently belonged to some *corpulent* predecessor. —Dickens

8. Our political experiment in representative government always was *precarious* to the very verge of disaster but it remains safer than anything else. —*Harper's Magazine*

9. . . . estimating the *pecuniary* value of every man's labour at one dollar a day. —Thoreau

10. . . . might unduly alarm U. S. allies fearful of *bilateral* U. S.-Soviet negotiations. —*Time*

11. Though this *gregarious* man is an inveterate joiner and belongs to "every fraternal order in Muncie . . ." —*Harper's Magazine*

12. Further away . . . meandered a small stream so filled with *aquatic* grasses and plants that the water was quite concealed. —W. H. Hudson

13. . . . . gradual coronary-artery shutdown, which developed so slowly that smaller, *collateral* artery branches grew and took over the work of the closing artery. —*Time*

14. Religions differ so much in their accidents that in discussing the religious question we must make it very *generic* and broad. —William James

15. If you make the criminal code *sanguinary*, juries will not convict. —Emerson

16. . . . . the flickering brightness from the inside shining up the chimney and making a *luminous* mist of the emerging smoke. —Thomas Hardy

17. They had not learned the noble dialects of Greece and Rome . . . and they prized instead a cheap *contemporary* literature. —Thoreau

18. The will of the monarch produced a false and *servile* unanimity, and no more than two patriots had courage to speak their own sentiments, and those of their country. —Edward Gibbon

19. Some of the most expensive schools . . . have such generous scholarships and loan funds that they attract more *impecunious* students . . . —*Time*

20. All idea of a trade embargo upon Japan, whether *unilateral* or by joint international action, was now given up. —*Harper's Magazine*

III. With the aid of a dictionary, separate the following into syllables:

1. luminary	4. redundant
2. malevolent	5. sanguinary
3. precarious	6. senile

LESSON X Adjective-Forming Suffixes

Learn the following suffixes and their meanings:

I. *-ine,* "pertaining to," "like," "of"

FEMIN- woman + *-ine* feminine

CAN- dog + *-ine* canine

(There are a number of adjectives formed by means of this suffix from the names of various living creatures; for example, FEL-, "cat," *feline;* ASIN-, "ass," *asinine;* BOV-, "cow," *bovine;* AQUIL-, "eagle," *aquiline,* etc.)

II. *-ate* (occasionally *-ite*), "possessing," "being," "characterized by" (often equivalent to the English past participial ending *-ed*)

ad- + CUR- care + *-ate* accurate

ad- + EQU- equal + *-ate* adequate (literally, made equal to)

FAVOR- favor + *-ite* favorite

ORN- to adorn + *-ate* ornate (literally, adorned)

III. *-ant, -ent (-ient),* equivalent to the English present participial ending *-ing*

URG- to press + *-ent* urgent (literally, pressing)

ad- + PAR- to appear + *-ent* apparent (literally, appearing)

VIGIL- to watch + *-ant* vigilant (literally, watching)

A. This suffix frequently forms words which are used as nouns, and so it comes to mean "person who," "that which."

AG- to do + *-ent* agent (literally, person doing)

in- + HABIT- to live + *-ant* inhabitant (literally, person living in)

ad-	+ HER-	to stick	+ *-ent*	adherent (literally, person sticking to)
	SERV-	to serve	+ *-ant*	servant (literally, person serving)

ASSIGNMENT

I. Learn the following bases and their meanings:

CUMB-, CUB-	to lie down	succumb incubator

FID-
  (FIDEL-)
	faith,
	  (faithful)
		confident
		  fidelity, infidel

HER-, HES-	to stick	adhere adhesive, cohesion
ORDIN-	order	ordinary, subordinate
PLAC-	to please, to appease	placid
POT-	to have power	potent, potential

SAL- (SIL-)
  SALT- (SULT-)
	to leap	salient
		  resilient
		  insult, result

SED- (SID-), SESS-	to sit, to settle	sediment, sedative preside, session

II. Analyze the following italicized words and define them as they are used in the sentence or phrase.

1. He was too *diffident* to do justice to himself; but when his natural shyness was overcome, his behaviour gave every indication of an open affectionate heart. —Jane Austen

2. This intention of abandoning Astoria was, however, kept secret from the men, lest they should at once give up all labor, and become restless and *insubordinate*. —Washington Irving

3. When the calm, *complacent,* self-satisfied tranquilities of the Victorian era had exploded into the world convulsions and wars of the terrible twentieth century . . . —Sir Winston Churchill

4. La Casa yielded to no impulses of rage. He remained sober, cold, *sedate* . . . —John Addington Symonds

5. Superficial observers will speak of the paganism of the Renaissance, its unblushing license, its worldliness . . . as though these qualities were not *inherent* in human nature, ready at any moment to emerge. —Symonds

6. What will be singled out as the *salient* event of our time by future historians, centuries hence . . . ? —*Harper's Magazine*

7. In times of public danger, the dull claims of age and of rank are sometimes *superseded*. —Edward Gibbon

8. Elsewhere metropolitan America has adopted a diet proper to the *sedentary* life, but the Western city dweller eats a cowhand's meal. —*Harper's Magazine*

9. Human shapes, interferences, troubles, and joys were all as if they were not, and there seemed to be on the shaded hemisphere of the globe no *sentient* being save himself. —Thomas Hardy

10. . . . the ideally best form of government is that in which the sovereignty . . . is vested in the entire *aggregate* of the community. —John Stuart Mill

11. In this country the Army is *subservient* to civilians; it depends for its money and its policies on civilian superiors. —*Harper's Magazine*

12. The *pungent,* acrid smell of rotting leaves, of flowers, of blossoms and plants dying in the poisonous and cruel gloom. —Joseph Conrad

13. According to their notions of *corporate* guilt, the plague which destroyed thousands of their countrymen was regarded as punishment for the crimes of a few.

14. How complex, sensitive, *resilient,* is the society we have evolved over centuries, and how capable of withstanding the most unexpected strain! —Churchill

15. The ten Iroquois . . . glided like shadows into the midst of the camp, where, by the dull glow of the smoldering fires,

they could distinguish the *recumbent* figures of their victims.
—Francis Parkman

16. A failure by Great Britain to produce a strong, *coherent,* resolute Government . . . would alter the entire balance . . . —Churchill

17. He was actuated by an *inordinate,* an unscrupulous, a remorseless zeal for what seemed to him to be the interest of the state. —Macaulay

18. No one who has sworn to support the Constitution can conscientiously vote for what he understands to be an unconstitutional measure, however *expedient* he may think it. —Abraham Lincoln

19. He made the common mistake of attributing to the government, which in such matters is powerless, the doings of parliament, which in such matters is *omnipotent.* —Trollope

20. (a) . . . the necessity that is *incumbent* on every writer to form some plan or design before he enter on any discourse or narration. —David Hume.
(b) The *incumbent* Vice-President was unacceptable to the South and to large portions of the middle classes. —*Harper's Magazine*

III. The following words contain bases which have been studied previously. With the aid of a dictionary, by consulting the etymology and the various meanings given for the word, explain the connection between the meaning of the base and the current meaning of the word.

1. annals	9. jury
2. carnation	10. magnate
3. confinement	11. obvious
4. impediment	12. prejudice
5. impend	13. punctuate
6. incorporate	14. segregate
7. incubate	15. senate
8. invent	16. travesty

LESSON XI Semantic Change

In analyzing words we have seen that in some cases there is a considerable difference between the etymological and the current meaning; for one reason or another, in the course of centuries, many meanings have tended to alter. Thus, to select two examples from the previous exercise, *expedient,* which once meant "freeing one caught by the foot," has come to mean "advantageous;" *salient* no longer means "jumping" but "obvious." This process whereby words vary their meaning is called semantic change, as distinct from phonetic change, the alteration in the form or sound of words. While it is impossible to classify precisely all the manifold examples of semantic change, we can discover certain general patterns which apply in many instances, and it will be helpful to know these not only in connection with word analysis and the enlargment of vocabulary but also in reading the older English authors like Shakespeare and Milton. Thus, when the line occurs in Shakespeare's *King John,* "Leave them as naked as the vulgar air," the word *vulgar* is only comprehensible if one is aware that in Shakespeare's time it meant "common," and that since then it has generally come to have the meaning "low and coarse." Similarly, Shakespeare speaks of "mice, and rats and such small deer," for in his day *deer* could refer to any animal.

In this and later lessons various types of semantic change will be discussed.

METAPHORICAL USAGE

One type of semantic change is brought about by the use of words in a metaphorical sense. Metaphor is a figure of speech most frequently encountered in poetry, but it is also found in other types of writing as well. It consists in the transfer of a word from an object or idea which it literally denotes to an object or idea only suggested by the literal sense. Thus, we speak of the "eye" of a needle or the "arm" of a chair, although *eye* and *arm* are strictly speaking organs of the body. We say that a ship "plows" the ocean, even though plowing is literally an activity which takes place on land. We describe someone as "fired" with ambition, or "burning" with zeal, or "blazing" with wrath, although we do not mean that there is an actual fire within him. In order to suggest a resemblance we have simply transferred these terms from the sphere of activity where they literally belong to an area where they are figuratively applicable.

Frequently, when a word has taken on a metaphorical meaning, its original sense has been forgotten and thus its meaning changes. Although we are not usually conscious of their presence, our language is full of such faded metaphors, many of which arose from the activities connected with farming, once so great a part of everyone's basic experience. Thus, *rehearse* meant originally "to harrow over again." (A *hearse,* now a vehicle for carrying the dead, was once the framework surrounding a coffin on which candles were placed and which was so called because it resembled a harrow.) *Tribulation* comes from the Latin word *tribulum,* a threshing sledge, that is, a wooden platform studded with iron teeth which was drawn over the grain to remove its outer husk. *Delirium* is a combination of Latin *de-,* "off," and *lira,* "furrow," and at first meant "getting out of the furrow in plowing." The metaphorical extension of its meaning developed in the same way as the English slang phrase for *insane* "off his rocker." *Inoculate* first meant "to graft." The Latin *oculus* means literally "eye" as in *oculist* or *binocular,* but here refers to a bud (cf. the "eye" of a potato); so *inoculate* once meant to take a bud from one plant and insert it in another. Then the term was transferred to the sphere of medicine with the extended meaning, "to take material from one body and put it into another."

In addition to farming, we have metaphors from almost every other activity and experience embedded in our language, seafaring, trade, sport, war, etc. Because so many of our words acquired their current meaning as metaphors, which are the essence of poetry, and because in the passage of time the images which they originally represented have faded from men's consciousness, language was described as "fossil poetry" by Emerson, who wrote:*

> For though the origin of most of our words is forgotten, each word was at first a stroke of genius, and obtained currency because for the moment it symbolized the world to the first speaker and to the hearer. The etymologist finds the deadest word to have been once a brilliant picture. Language is fossil poetry. As the limestone of the continent consists of infinite masses of the shells of animalcules, so language is made up of images or tropes, which now, in their secondary use, have long ceased to remind us of their origin.

The following are some examples of semantic change arising from metaphorical usage which you have encountered in previous exercises.

> *Egregious* (*e-,* "out" + GREG-, "flock"), "outstandingly bad," originally implied the way in which one animal might stand out from the rest of the herd.

---

*Essays: Second Series, "The Poet."

Pensive (PEND-, PENS-, "to weigh"), "thinking deeply," takes its meaning from the figure of weighing one idea against another.

Luminary (LUMIN-, "light"), in its metaphorical sense of "famous intellectual" refers to someone who enlightens mankind.

ADJECTIVE-FORMING SUFFIXES

Learn the following suffixes and their meanings:

I. *-able, -ible,* "able to be," "able to," "tending to"

		PORT-	to carry	+	*-able*	portable
ad-	+	APT-	fit	+	*-able*	adaptable
		FLEX-	to bend	+	*-ible*	flexible

A. If this suffix is followed by an additional element, it becomes *-abil-, -ibil-*.

ad-	+	APT-	fit	+	*-able*	+	*-ity*	adaptability
		FLEX-	to bend	+	*-ible*	+	*-ity*	flexibility

II. *-ile,* "able to be," "able to," "tending to"

AG-	to do	+	*-ile*	agile
VOLAT-	to fly	+	*-ile*	volatile
REPT-	to creep	+	*-ile*	reptile

This suffix is distinguished from *-ile, -il,* "pertaining to," etc. (see Lesson IX) by the fact that it is normally attached to verbal bases.

III. *-acious,* "tending to," "inclined to"

AUD-	to dare	+	*-acious*	audacious
TEN-	to hold	+	*-acious*	tenacious

ASSIGNMENT

I. Learn the following bases and their meanings:

CRED-, CREDIT-	to believe, to trust	credential creditor, discredit
CULP-	blame, fault	culprit, exculpate
DOC-, DOCT-	to teach	document doctor, doctrine

FA-, FAT-	to speak	affable, infant preface
FALL-, FALS-	to deceive	infallible false
MUT-	to change	commute, mutation
TANG- (TING-), TACT-	to touch	tangent contingent contact, intact
TEN- (TIN-), TENT- (through French, TAIN-)	to hold	tenant, lieutenant continent detention, retention detain, retain
TRACT-	to drag, to draw	tractor, contract extract

II. Analyze the following italicized words and define them as they are used in the sentence or phrase.

1. The soldier who fell in battle was transported at once to the region of *ineffable* bliss in the bright mansions of the Sun. — William Hickling Prescott

2. The more *perspicacious* members could easily see the hidden purpose behind this seemingly honest proposal.

3. Yet he hated them with a hatred as fierce and *implacable* as if they had laid waste his fields, burned his mansion, murdered his child in the cradle. — Macaulay

4. In speeches and on TV, Castro rambled *loquaciously* on. —*Time*

5. . . . for while everyone well knows himself to be *fallible,* few think it necessary to take any precautions against their own fallibility. — John Stuart Mill

6. The fact narrated must correspond to something in me to be *credible* or intelligible. —Emerson

7. . . . a stronghold of privateers, the home of a race whose *intractable* and defiant independence neither time nor change has subdued. — Francis Parkman

8. The least slip or false movement would have thrown us at once within reach of these *voracious* fish, who frequently thrust themselves directly upon us. — Edgar Allan Poe

9. . . . while the *pertinacious* humming of unnumbered mosquitoes will banish sleep from his eyelids. — Parkman

10. The true harvest of my daily life is somewhat *intangible* and indescribable as the tints of morning or evening. It is a little star-dust caught, a segment of a rainbow which I have clutched. — Thoreau

11. This did not appear the worst nor by any means a *despicable* alternative. — Thoreau

12. In the United States are more than two million, the least *assimilable* of immigrants. —*Harper's Magazine*

13. The republicans hold, as a fixed *incontrovertible* principle, that sovereignty resides in the great mass of the people. — Thomas Paine

14. Gold is an extremely *ductile* metal.

15. Nothing in the whole adventure, not even the upset, had disturbed the calm and *equable* current of Mr. Pickwick's temper. — Dickens

16. . . . notions based on such patently *fallacious* ideas that even the economists had abandoned them before Mr. Berenson began to write. — *Harper's Magazine*

17. . . . the planets follow the *immutable* Law of Gravitation. — *Harper's Magazine*

18. He bore a much fairer character than most of his accomplices; but in one respect he was more *culpable* than any of them. — Macaulay

19. Some of them are unmannered, rough, intractable, as well as ignorant; but others are *docile,* have a wish to learn, and evince a disposition that pleases me — Charlotte Brontë

20. . . . the related argument that increased consumer purchasing power is an infallible remedy for unemployment is hardly *tenable.* —*Harper's Magazine*

III. With the aid of a dictionary give the original or etymological meaning of the following words which have undergone semantic change due to metaphorical usage.

1. cancer	7. insult
2. eradicate	8. muscle
3. flourish	9. pastor
4. focus	10. remorse
5. gladiolus	11. scruple
6. gland	12. seminary

LESSON XII   Specialization and Generalization of Meaning

Another type of semantic change is specialization, a process whereby the meaning of a word shifts from the general to the specific. Thus, *undertaker* originally meant "one who undertakes to do anything," but now has come to mean "one who undertakes the special task of preparing bodies for burial." *Disease,* as can be seen by analyzing the word, once referred to any "discomfort," but now has the narrower meaning of "illness," that is, a particular type of discomfort. *Liquor* once referred to any liquid, as its form suggests. (Some may perhaps be familiar with a survival of this in the old-fashioned term *pot liquor,* the liquid left in the pot after cooking meat.) Now, of course, liquor means a special kind of liquid, that containing distilled alcohol; the French loan word *liqueur* is even more specialized. To cite an example mentioned in the previous lesson, *deer* in Shakespeare's time meant any animal but now is applicable to only one specific type.

The following are some examples of specialization of meaning which have already been encountered in earlier lessons:

The base VERB- originally meant "word" and still does in *verbose* and *verbatim,* but in the case of *verb,* a particular type of word denoting action, it has narrowed its meaning.

Diffident once meant "not trusting," and Milton speaks of "diffidence of God;" but now it has acquired the more specific meaning of not trusting oneself, lacking self-confidence.

The base VEST- as a Latin word referred to any garment; now, however, *vest* is applied to a special type of clothing.

Sometimes just the opposite process takes place and the meaning of a word becomes broader. This type of semantic change is known as generalization. Thus, *decimate* (DECIM-, "tenth") originally referred to the destruction of one tenth of a military unit; now it refers to the destruction of any large part. The word *vaccine* comes from the Latin *vacca*, "cow," since the first such immunizing substance was obtained from that source. Though the name *vaccine* is still used, it is no longer applied only to material from cows, however, but to other substances as well, such as Salk vaccine (used against poliomyelitis), which is produced from monkey kidneys.

In its evolution a word may show both specialization and generalization. *Assassin* is a word which entered the languages of Europe during the Crusades, when the members of a certain Mohammedan sect, having vowed the killing of Christian leaders, made use of the narcotic hashish to work themselves into a state of frenzy sufficient for the dangerous task. *Assassin* (Arabic, *hashshashin*) consequently first meant "eater of hashish," then specifically "one who murders by surprise or treachery after eating hashish" and finally the term came to be applied generally to any treacherous murderer whether under the influence of drugs or not.

Some of the words in the previous exercises show generalization of meaning. For instance:

Expedite (*ex-* "from" + PED-, "foot"), as we have seen, originally meant "to free one caught by the foot," but now refers to the removal of any sort of difficulty.

From the sentence, "He was divested of his authority," it is obvious that *divest* (*di-,* "apart" + VEST-, "garment") is used to signify not just the taking off of clothing but the removal of other things as well.

Excruciate (CRUC-, "cross") once referred to the torture of crucifixion, but is now used in reference to any kind of pain.

As can be seen from the previous examples, when metaphorical usage occurs, a certain amount of generalization is involved as well.

ADJECTIVE-FORMING SUFFIXES

Learn the following suffixes and their meanings:

I. *-itious,* "tending to," "characterized by"

FICT-	to invent	+	*-itious*	fictitious
ex- + PED-	foot	+	*-itious*	expeditious

II. *-id,* "tending to," "inclined to"

FRIG-	to be cold	+	*-id*	frigid
RAP-	to seize	+	*-id*	rapid
HUM-	to be wet	+	*-id*	humid

III. *-ulous,* "tending to," "inclined to"

GARR-	to chatter	+	*-ulous*	garrulous
TREM-	to tremble	+	*-ulous*	tremulous

ASSIGNMENT

I. Learn the following bases and their meanings:

AC(U)-, ACR-	sharp	acid, acute
CAD- (CID-), CAS-	to fall, to befall	cadence accident, incident casual, occasion
CAP- (CIP-), CAPT- (CEPT-) (through French, CEIV-)	to take, to seize	recipient captive, capture except, reception receive
FAC- (FIC-), FACT- (FECT-)	to do, to make	faculty factory efficient effective, perfect
FERV-	to boil, to bubble	fervent, effervesce
FLOR-	flower	florist, floral
FLU-, FLUX-	to flow	fluid, influence flux, influx
PATI-, PASS-	to endure, to suffer	patient passive, passion
REG- (RIG-), RECT-	to straighten, to rule	regent dirigible direct, erect

II. Analyze the following italicized words and define them as they are used in the sentence or phrase.

1. The use of economic coercion to force changes in public policies is *incompatible* with democratic institutions. —*Atlantic Monthly*

2. The drama was condemned to trivialities which only too faithfully reflected the political stagnation and the literary trifling of a *decadent* civilization. —John Addington Symonds

3. The *fervid* eloquence of preachers who declaimed against the horrors of French persecution . . . had wrought up the people to such a temper . . . —Macaulay

4. The Chinese have sometimes found it difficult to comprehend *Occidental* modes of thought.

5. It is even more graceful than the weeping willow or any *pendulous* trees which dip their branches in the stream instead of being buoyed up by it. — Thoreau

6. In his general deportment he was pompous and important, affecting a species of *florid* elocution, which often became ridiculous. — Sir Walter Scott

7. This feudal reverence for the dignity of wealth amounted to belief in the existence of a wise overlordship of the *affluent*. —William Allen White

8. I was a youth of gay and happy temperament, with an *incorrigible* levity of spirit. —Hawthorne

9. Whether the smile began as a *factitious* one, to test her capacity in that art — nobody knows; it ended certainly in a real smile. — Thomas Hardy

10. I had sat for about twenty minutes turning the thing over in my mind and trying to find some possible explanation. The more I thought the more extraordinary and *inexplicable* did it appear. — A. Conan Doyle

11. The river here is almost as *turbid* as the Tiber itself; but, I remember, in the upper part of its course the waters are beautifully transparent. — Hawthorne

12. The severe censure passed by the Commons on the administration was next considered and was approved without one *dissentient* voice. —Macaulay

13. It was now impossible to establish in Ireland a just and *beneficent* government. —Macaulay

14. . . . audaciously pledged himself to bring proofs which would satisfy the most *incredulous.* —Macaulay

15. The psychological analyses, casuistical questions, rhetorical digressions, and pathetic situations . . . were exactly suited to the intellectual tastes and temper of *incipient* decadence. — Symonds

16. When sometimes a frying-pan caught fire . . . and the old man was seen backing out of the doorway, swearing and coughing violently in the *acrid* cloud of smoke . . . —Joseph Conrad

17. . . . our increasing ability to distinguish a genuinely superior man from one who appears to be superior by means of some *adventitious* factor, such as money, or nepotism, or the favor of influential friends. —*Harper's Magazine*

18. . . . had an intellect *capacious* enough to appreciate and sympathize with whatever of truth and ultimate value to mankind there might be in all theories. — John Stuart Mill

19. But in an age of *facile* painters who were more interested in mannered effects than content, he restored discipline and purity to art. — *Time*

20. The change was so gradual as to be almost *imperceptible,* but was not the less real. — Macaulay

LESSON XIII   Functional Change

One type of semantic change, a variety of which has already been mentioned in passing (see Lesson VIII), is functional change, the process whereby a word, without change of form, that is, without the addition of suffixes, comes to be used as a different part of speech. Thus, words which were originally adjectives appear as nouns, nouns become verbs, verbs become nouns, and so on. This is so common an occurrence that usually we are not aware of it, but this type of shift is frequently encountered in the case of words brought from Latin into English, and it explains why, for instance, suffixes which are normally used to form adjectives are often found in words now used as nouns; e.g., *reptile, agent, inhabitant.*

It would be pointless to run through all the various changes of this type, but we might mention a few of the more interesting ones. The colors, which are generally adjectives, are often used as nouns as, for example, a *red,* referring to a communist, or a *pink,* referring to a communist sympathizer, the *whites* of a person's eyes, the *blues,* the *greens* of a golf course. Another frequently encountered variety of such change occurs when nouns are used as verbs; so we say, "to *book* a criminal," "to *knife* a person," "to *iron* a shirt," and recently sports announcers have begun to describe a referee as "positioning" the football instead of "placing" it on a particular yard line.

ADJECTIVE-FORMING SUFFIXES

Learn the following suffixes and their meanings:

I. *-ive,* "tending to," "inclined to"

		ACT-	to do	+	*-ive*	active
ad-	+	TRACT-	to draw	+	*-ive*	attractive
ex-	+	FECT-	to do	+	*-ive*	effective

II. *-uous,* "tending to," "inclined to"

con-	+	TIN-	to hold	+	*-uous*	continuous
con-	+	SPIC-	to look	+	*-uous*	conspicuous

III. *-ory,* "tending to," "serving for"

intro-	+	DUCT-	to lead	+	*-ory*	introductory
con-	+	PULS-	to drive	+	*-ory*	compulsory
contra-	+	DICT-	to speak	+	*-ory*	contradictory

ASSIGNMENT

I. Learn the following bases and their meanings:

CERN-, CRET-	to separate, to distinguish	discernment secret, excrete
FUND-, FUS- (through French, FOUND-)	to pour, to melt	refund fusion, confusion foundry

GEN-, GENIT-	to produce, to give birth to	congenial, ingenious genital
PEL(L)-, PULS-	to drive, to push	propel, compelling impulsive, repulsive
PON-, POSIT- (through French, POUND-)	to place, to put	component deposit, position
(-POSE, though historically derived from a different verb, was confused in meaning with PON- so long ago that we will find it useful to consider it here.)		compound, pro-pound compose, oppose
SCI-	to know	science, conscience
STRING-, STRICT- (through French, STRAIN-)	to draw tight	stringent strict, restrict restrain
TORQU-, TORT-	to twist	torque torture, distort

II. Analyze the following italicized words and define them as they are used in the sentence or phrase.

1. Yet he read a great deal in a *desultory* manner, without any scheme of study, as chance threw books in his way and inclination directed him through them. —James Boswell

2. Night, that strange personality which within walls brings ominous *introspectiveness* and self-distrust, but under the open sky banishes such subjective anxieties . . . —Thomas Hardy

3. The *prefatory* chapters, which in most cases introduce the special subject of each history, contain a series of retrospective surveys over the whole history of Florence. —John Addington Symonds

4. The conversation was varied and *discursive,* the king shifting from subject to subject according to his wont. —Macaulay

5. All art has a *sensuous* element, colour, form, sound . . . —Symonds

6. The *constrictive* material of the diving suit scarcely allowed him to breathe.

7. ... the shiny and stagnant water in its *tortuous* windings amongst the everlasting and invincible shadows. —Joseph Conrad

8. Haunting Hess's mind was a *compulsive* fear and hatred of Communist Russia. —*Time*

9. Once inside the expression of his face was no more *discernible* by reason of the increasing dusk of the evening. —Thomas Hardy

10. The same *assiduous* cultivation was bestowed . . . to improve the minds of the sons and nephews of Constantine. —Edward Gibbon

11. Died . . . [of] a *congenital* heart condition . . . —*Time*

12. What people therefore saw of her in a *cursory* view was very little. —Thomas Hardy

13. His manner was not *effusive*. It seldom was; but he was glad, I think, to see me. —A. Conan Doyle

14. ... recommendation: that the colleges give each prospective law student an examination in *expository* writing at the end of his junior year to see if he needs extra work. —*Time*

15. ... for what can escape the eye
Of God all-seeing, or deceive his heart
Omniscient? —Milton

16. ... a *retentive* memory.

17. We love characters in proportion as they are *impulsive* and spontaneous. —Emerson

18. The effect of Locke's forcible and *perspicuous* reasoning is greatly heightened by his evident anxiety to get at the truth. —Macaulay

19. While the river margin was richly fringed with trees of *deciduous* foliage, the rough uplands were crowned by majestic pines and firs of gigantic size. —Washington Irving

20. There were few *cohesive* factors to weld these dissimilar provinces into a unified whole.

III. Originally, what part of speech were the following italicized words and what part of speech are they as used in the sentence or phrase?

1. to *stone* to death
2. the *front* part of the house
3. first *down* and ten to go
4. He *steeled* himself against misfortune.
5. The third *out* was made by the pitcher.
6. He *blacked* the other boy's eye.
7. He reported his *find* to the authorities.
8. The crowd uttered *oh's* of delight at the sight of the fireworks.
9. The deal is *off*.
10. The coach *mothered* the younger members of the team.

IV. Give some examples of your own of this type of change.

LESSON XIV   Degeneration and Elevation of Meaning

A number of words in English have undergone degeneration of meaning, a type of semantic change whereby a word which originally had a good, or at least a neutral, meaning has come to indicate or suggest something objectionable, low, or unpleasant. *Villain,* for instance, at one time signified merely "farm laborer," that is, one attached to a villa or country estate. Gradually, however, the word came to refer to one who had all the bad qualities which in an aristocratic age the gentry attributed to the lower classes. As you saw in Lesson XI, the same snobbish attitude is reflected by the evolution of the word *vulgar,* the etymological meaning of which (as distinct from the current meaning) is "pertaining to the common people" (cf. *divulge,* literally, "to spread among the common people"). *Hussy,* a term for a woman of low moral character, is a contraction of *housewife,* its original meaning. *Amateur* once was a complimentary term; it means literally "one who loves" and referred to a person who engaged in an activity for its own sake, not out of an ungentlemanly desire for pay. In our more commercial age, however, the word *amateur* is frequently applied to an inept person, a dabbler, one who cannot keep up with the well-trained professional.

This degeneration is well illustrated by the story of a college football coach who, disgusted by a particularly poor performance on the part of his players, remarked in a moment of forgetfulness that his team had played "like a bunch of amateurs."

Some instances of degeneration of meaning in words occurring in the previous exercises are the following:

Senile (SEN-, "old") has come to take into account only the worst characteristics of old age, especially feeble-mindedness. *Senate,* on the other hand, though formed from the same root, is associated with the best characteristics, wisdom and mature judgement.

Verbose, literally "full of words," now indicates a tiresome excess of language.

As with specialization, an opposite process sometimes occurs whereby a word comes to mean something more pleasing or dignified than it did originally. This is called elevation of meaning; it takes place less often than degeneration, however, for, as in most instances, it is easier to tear down than to rebuild.

A good example of elevation is *fame,* which originally signified any report, good or bad. Now, of course, it refers only to good report. Many titles of rank and office show elevation. *Lord* is a contraction of two Anglo-Saxon words meaning "loaf" and "guard," in other words, "bread keeper," a rather humble beginning for so exalted a title. *Constable* began as "chief groom of the stable" and rose to the point where, in the Middle Ages, it became the title of the highest military officer of France. Since then it has descended from its high station and now usually designates a minor official of the law. *Chancellor* once referred to an usher in a law court, the person stationed at the *cancelli,* the latticework separating the public from the judges.

An example of elevation with which you are already familiar is *urbane,* which was once a synonym for *urban,* "pertaining to a city." Sometime during its history the former rose in standing and acquired the meaning of "polite and polished," denoting the qualities which city dwellers like to think they possess; *urban,* however, kept its original meaning.

NOUN-FORMING SUFFIXES

The next six suffixes are equivalent to the native English suffixes used to form abstract nouns, *-ness (heaviness, newness)*, *-hood (child-*

hood, manhood), and *-dom* (*boredom, freedom*). Learn the following suffixes and their meanings:

I. *-ity* (*-ety, -ty*), "quality of," "state of"

GRAV-	heavy	+	*-ity*			gravity
SAN-	healthy	+	*-ity*			sanity
SOCI-	associate	+	*-ety*			society
NOV-	new	+	*-el*	+	*-ty*	novelty

A. If this is followed by an additional suffix, the final *y* disappears.

GRAV-	heavy	+	*-ity*	+	*-ate*	gravitate
SAN-	healthy	+	*-ity*	+	*-ary*	sanitary
DIGN-	worthy	+	*-ity*	+	*-ary*	dignitary

II. (*i*)*tude*, "quality of," "state of"

LONG-	long	+	*-(i)tude*	longitude
MULT-	many	+	*-(i)tude*	multitude
MAGN-	large	+	*-(i)tude*	magnitude

A. If this is followed by an additional suffix, it becomes *-(i)tudin-*.

LONG-	long	+	*-(i)tude*	+	*-al*	longitudinal
MULT-	many	+	*-(i)tude*	+	*-ous*	multitudinous

III. *-acy*, "quality or state of being or having"

ac-		+ CUR-	care	+	*-acy*	accuracy
in- + *ad-*	+ EQU-	equal	+	*-acy*	inadequacy
con-		+ FEDER-	league	+	*-acy*	confederacy

This is generally the noun form of the adjectival suffix *-ate*, "possessing," "being" (see Lesson X).

ASSIGNMENT

I. Learn the following bases and their meanings:

AM-	to love	amorous, amiable, amicable
CELER-	swift	accelerate, decelerate
DE-, DIV-	a god	deify, deism divine
LITER-	letter, literature	illiterate, literal

LUC-	light, to shine	lucid, elucidate
PROB- (through French, PROV-)	good, to test	probation approve, reprove
VER-	true	veritable, aver

II. Analyze the following italicized words and define them as they are used in the sentence or phrase:

1. . . . the rapture of a worshiper on his knees before his *deity* . . . —*Time*

2. Nor was his *rectitude* altogether proof against the temptations to which it was exposed in that splendid and polite, but deeply corrupted society. —Macaulay

3. Among these men there was a *stringent* code of honour, any infringement of which was punished by death. —A. Conan Doyle

4. He had a sudden moment of *lucidity* — of that cruel lucidity that comes once in life to the most benighted. He seemed to see what went on within him, and was horrified at the strange sight. —Joseph Conrad

5. The fog had by this time become more *translucent,* and the position of the sun could be seen through it. —Thomas Hardy

6. . . . the *inequity* of the struggle smothers the tragic sense, which demands a more equal conflict . . . —*Time*

7. Merely corroborative detail, intended to give artistic *verisimilitude* to a bald and unconvincing narrative. —W. S. Gilbert

8. The bull sprang again and again at his assailant, but the horse kept dodging with wonderful *celerity.* —Francis Parkman

9. The beautiful fables of the Greeks, being proper creations of the imagination and not of the fancy, are universal *verities.* —Emerson

10. Bear with unflinching *fortitude* whatever evils and blows we may receive. —Sir Winston Churchill

11. The historic interests of France in Syria, and the *primacy* of those interests over the interests of other European nations, are preserved. —Churchill

12. He was in high repute not only for piety but for *probity* and honor. —Francis Parkman

13. No method and no brilliance of teaching can improve these youths enough to make any appreciable difference in their *literacy*. —*Harper's Magazine*

14. . . . a test of visual *acuity*.

15. To the *efficacy* and permanency of your union a government for the whole is indispensable. —Washington

16. He would sometimes pass me haughtily and coldly, just acknowledging my presence by a distant nod or a cool glance, and sometimes bow low and smile with gentlemanlike *affability*. —Charlotte Brontë

17. He showed, at the some time, his implacable *animosity* towards the Christians, by commanding that everyone taken within his dominions should be . . . sacrificed with all the barbarous ceremonies. —William Hickling Prescott

18. His *percipient* mind easily picked out the fallacies in the proposal.

19. She would have cried for assistance, but age and *infirmity* had long ago deprived her of the power of screaming. —Dickens

20. . . . the obligation . . . to maintain inviolate the relations of peace and *amity* towards other nations. —Washington

III. By comparing the various meanings listed in your dictionary, including the etymological meaning, show how each of the following words has undergone degeneration of meaning.

Example: *blackguard;* once "servants in charge of pots and pans." now "villain"

1. artificial	6. grandiose
2. boor	7. knave
3. churl	8. sensual
4. egregious	9. slave
5. gossip	

IV. In the same way, show how each of the following words has undergone elevation of meaning:

1. frank
2. marshal
3. minister

4. nice
5. shrewd
6. sturdy

LESSON XV   Change from Abstract to Concrete

A further type of semantic change is that whereby a meaning shifts from the abstract to the concrete. In this and the previous lessons, suffixes have been considered which form abstract nouns, but one can see at once that sometimes these are found in words which do not refer to qualities but to things. Most of us find it difficult to think for very long at a time in abstract terms; we prefer concrete, down-to-earth realities. As a consequence, a word which originally referred to a state or quality may come to signify an object or act exhibiting that quality.

Thus, when we speak about "the *multitude* who attended a concert," we are referring to actual people, not to "the state of being many." In the sentence, "His room was full of curiosities from all parts of the world," *curiosity* here indicates a concrete object, not a quality. An unruly child is often spoken of as a *terror,* and a beautiful woman is called a *beauty.*

Occasionally a word shifts from a concrete to an abstract meaning. *Tragedy* first signified a play; then, in the sentence, "His life was full of tragedy," it has come to mean the quality exhibited by the play. *Tongue* refers not only to an actual organ of the body, but also to language, as in the phrase, "the gift of tongues." The word *brains* is often used for "intelligence," and *heart* for "courage."

NOUN-FORMING SUFFIXES

Learn the following suffixes and their meanings:

I. -(*i*)*mony,* "quality of," "state of"

| TEST- | witness | + | -(*i*)*mony* | testimony |
| MATR- | mother | + | -(*i*)*mony* | matrimony |

A. If this is followed by an additional suffix, the final *y* appears as *i.*

| TEST- | witness | + | -(*i*)*mony* | + | -*al* | testimonial |
| MATR- | mother | + | -(*i*)*mony* | + | -*al* | matrimonial |

II. *-acity*, "quality of being inclined to"

AUD-	to dare	+	*-acity*	audacity
CAP-	to take	+	*-acity*	capacity
RAP-	to seize	+	*-acity*	rapacity

This is the usual noun form of the adjective *-acious*, "tending to," "inclined to" (see Lesson XI).

III. *-y*, "quality of," "state of," "act of," "result of"

CUSTOD-			guard	+	*-y*	custody
per-	+	JUR-	to swear	+	*-y*	perjury
contro-	+	VERS-	to turn	+	*-y*	controversy

A. If this is followed by an additional suffix, it appears as *i*.

CUSTOD-	guard				+	*-y*	+	*-al*	custodial
contro-	+	VERS-	to turn	+	*-y*	+	*-al*	controversial

IV. *-ate*, "office of," "holder(s) of the office of"

	SEN-	old			+	*-ate*	senate
	MAGISTR-	officer, master			+	*-ate*	magistrate
e- +	LECT-	to choose	+	*-or*	+	*-ate*	electorate

ASSIGNMENT

I. Learn the following bases and their meanings:

CID-, CIS-	to kill, to cut	insecticide, fratricide incision, precise
MATR-, MATERN-	mother	matron maternity
PATR-, PATERN-	father	patron paternity
PATRI-	fatherland, country	repatriate
PLEN-	full	replenish, plenty
SANCT-	holy	sanctify, sanctuary
SEQU-, SECUT-	to follow	sequence, consequence prosecute, consecutive
SOL-	alone	solitude, desolation
VIV-	to live	vivid, revive

II. Analyze the following italicized words and define them as they are used in the sentence or phrase.

1. He betrayed the leader whom he most affected to serve. His whole career was treachery to his own government. His life was one long *perfidy*. —William Hickling Prescott

2. Such is the *tenacity* of my imagination that the image formed in it continued in all its power and freshness. —Washington Irving

3. He looked up, however, and when aware of her presence a deep flush of shame *suffused* his handsome countenance. —Sir Walter Scott

4. It is curious to observe the tendency which the dialogue of Lord Byron always has to lose its character of a dialogue, and to become a *soliloquy*. —Macaulay

5. The gigantic productiveness of the American economy ready to erupt into such a *plenitude* of goods as the world has never seen . . . —*Harper's Magazine*

6. (a) He had been taught by bitter experience how much baseness, perfidy, and ingratitude may lie hid under the *obsequious* demeanour of courtiers. —Macaulay

   (b) When an Inca died . . . his *obsequies* were celebrated with great pomp and solemnity. —Prescott

7. While at anchor at this place, much ceremonious visiting and long conferences took place between the *potentate* of the island and the partners of the company. —Washington Irving

8. His language is *diffuse* and lumbering. —John Addington Symonds

9. The gay sights, the air, the music, and the excitement . . . had quickened her blood and made her eyes sparkle with *vivacity*. —Thomas Hardy

10. Since then, Freeman has earned a national reputation as the caustic and *incisive* interviewer of the known and the renowned . . . —*Time*

11. . . . a gutter campaign featuring a phony *composite* photograph showing Tydings in apparently friendly conversation with Communist Earl Browder . . . —*Time*

12. But, if they determine to try the chance of war, they will, if they are wise, entrust to their chief that *plenary* authority without which war cannot be well conducted. —Macaulay

13. He was an ardent *proponent* of compulsory military service.

14. Mr. Gladstone viewed Victoria through a haze of awe which was almost religious — as a *sacrosanct* embodiment of venerable traditions. —Lytton Strachey

15. In his official letters he expressed with great *acrimony* his contempt for the King's character and understanding. —Macaulay

16. In 1872 occurred the first execution in Cleveland's term, the climax of a sensational case of *matricide*. —Allan Nevins

17. By courtesy of his creditors, there still remained in his possession a small remnant of his *patrimony*. —Edgar Allan Poe

18. . . . Bulgarian *plenipotentiaries* had actually opened armistice negotiations with Anglo-American representatives in Cairo. —*Harper's Magazine*

19. But the *veracity* of the narrative has never been questioned. —*Atlantic Monthly*

20. He points out how Ferdinand . . . used the pretext of religious zeal in order to achieve the conquest of Granada . . . and how his perfidies in Italy, his perjuries in France, were colored with a *sanctimonious* decency. —Symonds

III. Use each of the following words in two sentences of your own making, the first expressing an abstract meaning for the word, the second a concrete meaning.

Example: *delicacy* (1) She handled the situation with great delicacy.
(2) The table was loaded with delicacies.

1. authority
2. scholarship
3. impurity
4. novelty
5. justice
6. favor
7. divinity
8. likeness
9. brotherhood
10. inheritance

LESSON XVI   Weakening

A type of semantic change closely related to generalization and to degeneration occurs when the meaning of a word becomes less forceful and vivid. This process is called weakening and is to be found in the case of many of the overused words in our language. *Awful* once meant "inspiring awe," but it is hard to find much of this meaning left in a sentence like, "You've been gone an awfully long time." *Wonderful* (literally, "exciting wonder") and *nice* (strictly, "exhibiting careful discrimination"), as they are ordinarily used, are also examples of weakening. *Presently* once meant "immediately," that is, "at the present moment," but when a person says, "I'll be with you presently," some time will probably pass before he appears. *Mister* was formerly *master* and implied a great deal more respect than it does now. In the sentence, "Doubtless he will come," *doubtless* no longer means "certainly," but "probably."

Examples of weakening are to be found in words derived from some of the bases that have been studied. When we say, "He is a man of infinite wisdom," *infinite* (*in-*, "not" + FIN-, "end," "limit"; literally "endless") is probably an exaggeration. The original meaning of the base CUR(R)-, CURS-, is "to run," but in most of its derivatives its sense has been weakened simply to "go," as in *excursion, concur,* and *recur.*

NOUN-FORMING SUFFIXES

Learn the following suffixes and their meanings:

I. *-ion,* "act of," "state of," "result of"

com-	+	PLET-	to fill	+	*-ion*	completion
pre-	+	VENT-	to come	+	*-ion*	prevention
pro-	+	DUCT-	to lead	+	*-ion*	production

II. *-ment,* "result of," "means of," "act of," "state of"
(Various connective vowels usually precede this suffix.)

ex-	+	CIT-	to arouse	+	*-(e)ment*	excitement
		LIG-	to bind	+	*-(a)ment*	ligament
		MON-	to warn, to advise	+	*-(u)ment*	monument
		REG-	to rule	+	*-(i)ment*	regiment

III. *-men,* "result of," "means of," "act of," "state of"
(Various connective vowels usually precede this suffix.)

SPEC- to look + -(*i*)*men*   specimen

ASSIGNMENT

I. Learn the following bases and their meanings:

CRE-, CRESC-, CRET-	to grow	crescent, excrescence concrete
I-, IT-	to go	transient, ambient initial, transition
JUNCT- (through French, JOIN-, JOINT-)	to join	junction, conjunction adjoin, disjoin
LEG- (LIG-), LECT-	to choose, to pick out, to read	legible, legend eligible elect, select
MON-, MONIT-	to warn, to advise	admonish, monument monitor, premonition
RUPT-	to break	rupture, erupt, interrupt
SOLV-, SOLUT-	to loosen, to free	solve, absolve solution, absolute
TRIT-	to rub, to wear	trite, detriment

II. Analyze the following italicized words and define them as they are used in the sentence or phrase.

    1. ... the Aga Kahn was a fabulous figure who managed to combine the affluence and honors of an Oriental potentate with the *predilections* of a European playboy. —*Time*

    2. . . . sometimes read my unspoken thoughts with an *acumen* to me incomprehensible. —Charlotte Brontë

    3. Meanwhile the utter confusion subsequent upon the downfall of the Roman Empire and the *irruption* of the Germanic races . . . —John Addington Symonds

4. Nor have I scrupled, in so flagrant a case, to allow myself a severity of *animadversion* little congenial with the general spirit of these papers. —*The Federalist*

5. A healthy individual does not spend most of his life examining treatments and *regimens*. —*Harper's Magazine*

6. The mass would be likely to remain nearly the same, assimilating constantly to itself its gradual *accretions*. —*The Federalist*

7. Hunger is always the cause of tumults and *sedition*. —Lord Chesterfield

8. If at any time a shade of sadness stole across his brow, it was but *transient*, like a summer cloud, which soon goes by. —Washington Irving

9. Emma was very *compassionate*; and the distresses of the poor were as sure of relief from her personal attention and kindness, her counsel and her patience, as from her purse. —Jane Austen

10. For *absolution*, penitents must talk directly to a priest . . . —*Time*

11. As this *admonition* was accompanied with a threatening gesture and uttered with a savage aspect, the little boy rubbed his face harder, as if to keep the tears back. —Dickens

12. The crime which is asserted is tried not before a *dispassionate* neutral bench, but before the very persons alleged to be victims. —*Atlantic Monthly*

13. She was wrapped in a white robe of some kind, whilst down her shoulders fell a twining *profusion* of marvellously rich hair. —Thomas Hardy

14. . . . to pour into the pockets of the investing classes, especially in the East, a heavy unearned *increment*. —Allan Nevins

15. The surgeon performed an *excision* of the tumor.

16. . . . the Socratic philosophy rose like the sun in heaven, and spread its illumination over the whole intellectual *firmament*. —John Stuart Mill

17. At the same time it must not be supposed that the Renaissance burst suddenly upon the world in the fifteenth century without *premonitory* symptoms. —Symonds

18. An inveterate lighter and chewer of cigars, which he uses as *adjuncts* to conversation . . . —*Time*

19. The Japanese are showing signs of grave weakness. The *attrition* of their shipping, especially their oil tankers . . . has become not merely evident but obvious. —Sir Winston Churchill

20. He had not yet got his *complement* of men, nor of vessels; and was very inadequately provided with supplies of any kind. —William Hickling Prescott

III. Distinguish in meaning between the following pairs of words which are often confused.

1. adverse–averse	7. ingenious–ingenuous
2. compulsive–compulsory	8. lurid–livid
3. congenital–congenial	9. presumptuous–presumptive
4. discrete–discreet	10. sensuous–sensual
5. illicit–elicit	11. tortuous–torturous
6. imminent–immanent	12. turbid–turgid

LESSON XVII Change of Meaning Due to Changing Concepts

Some of the most interesting differences between etymological and current meanings have resulted from the influence on our language of discarded scientific ideas. The word *quintessence* is an example of this. The ancient Greeks believed that there were four basic substances which composed the universe: earth, air, fire, and water. In addition to these, Aristotle postulated a fifth element, which was so much lighter and subtler than the others that it was difficult to classify and so was termed simply "fifth being." This name entered our language as *quintessence* (QUINT-, "fifth," and *essence*). In the Middle Ages the fifth element came to be regarded by the alchemists as the most essential part of any substance. With the advance of scientific knowledge the idea of five elements was discarded, but the word *quintessence* remained, having lost its older significance of "fifth element" and keeping only the meaning of "the concentrated essence of anything" or, by extension, "the most perfect manifestation of some quality," as in the expression, "He is the quintessence of conceit."

One outmoded concept which has given rise to a whole series of such changes is known as the humoral theory of physiology. For over two thousand years the prevailing medical view was that soundness of mind and body depended on the proper mixture of four liquids or humors, as they were called, for the original meaning of humor is "liquid" (related to *humid*). These four "humors" were blood, phlegm, yellow bile, often simply termed bile, and black bile. Individual psychological differences were thought to be determined by the predominance of one or another of these fluids, and a person who had a proper mixture of them was supposedly pleasant and cheerful, in other words, good-humored. A person who behaved in an absurd or fantastic fashion was supposed to be suffering from an excess of some one of these fluids and so was termed "humorous." Eccentricity is, of course, likely to arouse laughter, and so *humor* acquired its modern meaning of "quality which excites amusement."

If we examine their derivations, we find that some other very common words reflect this concept that a mixture of humors causes a particular state of mind or body. A person's *temperament* (Latin, *temperare*, "to mix in due proportion") was the special combination of these fluids which resulted in his own individual personality. *Temper* was originally a synonym of *temperament*, but it has generally acquired the more specialized meaning of proneness to anger. In connection with metal the suggestion of a mixture formerly carried by this word comes out more clearly; the temper of steel refers to the blending of carbon, iron, etc. *Distemper*, which means literally "a disturbance of the proper mixture," likewise became specialized, describing a physical illness in animals rather than a psychological state. *Complexion* (Latin, "combination," from *con-* and *plectere*, "to weave") was also once synonymous with *temperament;* its current meaning arose from the belief that the special blend of the different humors was shown in the color of the face.

The different kinds of temperament were designated by the name of the particular humor which predominated. An excess of blood (SAN-

GUIN-, see Lesson IX) made a person *sanguine,* and thus of a cheerful hopeful disposition, which is the current meaning of the word. A preponderance of phlegm made one stolid and unemotional, and so the term *phlegmatic* came to have this meaning. The Greek term for bile is *chole;* since this humor was thought to bring about an angry nature, a quick-tempered person is now sometimes termed *choleric.* The cause of melancholy (Greek, *melas,* "black," and *chole,* "bile") was held to be the presence of too much black bile.

Another equally outmoded notion which influenced the meanings of a number of words was astrology, with its basic assumption that the stars and other heavenly bodies control earthly affairs. *Disaster* means literally "ill-starred" (from Latin, *dis-,* and Greek, *aster,* "star," found in such words as *astronomy* and *astrology*). According to astrological teachings the stars influenced not only events but human nature as well. An individual born under the planet Jupiter, or Jove, was supposedly *jovial.* Saturn, it was felt, caused men to be serious and gloomy, a temperamament called *saturnine;* while the planet Mercury produced a *mercurial,* that is, volatile, personality. The heavenly bodies were thought also to affect the health of human beings; consequently, *lunatic* means literally "moonstruck" (from Latin, *luna,* "moon"), while *influenza* is simply Italian for "influence," reflecting the notion that some influence emanating from evil stars caused this disease.

DIMINUTIVE SUFFIXES

The following are diminutive suffixes, that is, suffixes which denote something small or young. They have the same function as the native English suffixes *-kin,* in *lambkin* and *manikin; -let,* in *booklet* and *leaflet;* and *-ling,* in *duckling* and *darling;* or the French suffix *-et, -ette,* in *islet, cigarette,* and *statuette.*

Learn the following suffixes and their meanings:

I. *-cule* (often *-cle,* since the *-u-* is sometimes suppressed), "little"

MOLE-	mass	+	*-cule*	molecule
MUS-	mouse	+	*-cle*	muscle (but musc*u*lar)
PART-	part	+	*-(i)cle*	particle (but partic*u*lar)

II. *-el,* "little"

NOV-	new	+	*-el*	novel
MORS-	bite	+	*-el*	morsel
PAN(N)-	cloth	+	*-el*	panel

III. *-il,* "little"

PUP-	boy, girl	+	*-il*	pupil
CODIC-	book, document	+	*-il*	codicil

IV. *-ole, -ule* (often *-le,* since the *-u-* is sometimes suppressed), "little"

VACU-	empty	+	*-ole*	vacuole
AURE-	golden	+	*-ole*	aureole
CAPS-	box	+	*-ule*	capsule
GLOB-	ball	+	*-ule*	globule
SCRUP-	sharp stone	+	*-le*	scruple (but scrup*u*lous)
CIRC-	ring	+	*-le*	circle (but circ*u*lar)

Diminutive suffixes in their original Latin form appear in many common English words.

FORM-	form	+	*-ula*	formula
CUP-	tub	+	*-ola*	cupola
CALC-	limestone, pebble	+	*-ulus*	calculus
GLADI-	sword	+	*-olus*	gladiolus
CEREB(R)-	brain	+	*-ellum*	cerebellum

ASSIGNMENT

I. Learn the following bases and their meanings:

CALC-	limestone, pebble	calculate, calcium
FRANG- (FRING-), FRACT-	to break	frangible fraction
GRAN-	grain	granary, granite
JOC-	joke	jocular

MINOR-, MINUS-, MINUT-	small, smaller	minority minute, diminutive
QUIR-, QUISIT- (QUEST-)	to ask, to seek	inquire inquisition, requisition question, inquest
SEC- (SEG-), SECT-	to cut	secant segment bisect, section

II. Analyze the following italicized words and define them as they are used in the sentence or phrase.

1. . . . where the lake bottoms contain little vegetation and the water little or no plankton or the *minuscule* animal life which provides the major part of the diet of many varieties of fish. — *Atlantic Monthly*

2. The plastic first comes from the vats in a hard *granular* mass.

3. I struck him down with no more *compunction* than if he had been some foul and venomous beast. — A. Conan Doyle

4. Grey was not only calm but cheerful, talked pleasantly of horses, dogs, and field sports, and even made *jocose* allusions to the perilous situation in which he stood. — Macaulay

5. The *corpuscular* theory of light . . .

6. But politics rest on necessary foundations, and cannot be treated with *levity*. —Emerson

7. We covet no French possessions; we have no *acquisitive* appetites or ambitions in North Africa or any other part of the world. — Sir Winston Churchill

8. As the limestone of the continent consists of infinite masses of the shells of *animalcules* . . . —Emerson

9. Some dog lovers were clamoring for a law against *vivisection*.

10. But Critic Nathan — though the day had passed when he could kill a play with a quip — remained an acute and *acidulous* observer of the theater . . . *Time*

11. Her husband had to make a very *contrite* apology afterwards for the language which his wife had thought fit to employ. — Thackeray

12. . . . we and we alone of the major powers got through the Second World War without conscription of labor or any major *infringement* on the rights of free speech, free press, and assemblage. — *Harper's Magazine*

13. Instead of any *diminution,* there is need of a great increase of disinterested exertion to promote the good of others. — John Stuart Mill

14. It would be easy to accuse the two major companies . . . of taking advantage of their virtual monopoly to collect *extortionate* prices. —*Harper's Magazine*

15. Though it may rather be a *digression* from the immediate subject of this paper, I shall take occasion to mention here a supposition which has excited some alarm. — *The Federalist*

16. . . . throwing into his face the kind of *jocularity* deemed appropriate . . . on the reappearance of the newly married. — Thomas Hardy

17. In an instant, a treasure of *incalculable* value lay gleaming before us. —Edgar Allan Poe

18. This liberal-minded churchman put a room at his disposal, and allowed him to *dissect* dead bodies. —John Addington Symonds

19. Even in destitution and exile they retained their *punctilious* national pride. — Macaulay

20. In his *disquisition* on government Calhoun has expounded his theory of a constitution in a manner so profound . . . —Lord Acton

III. Distinguish in meaning between the following pairs of words:

1. choler–cholera
2. jovial–Jovian
3. mercurial–mercuric
4. sanguine–sanguinary
5. saturnine–saturnalia

LESSON XVIII Euphemism

In addition to semantic change there are various other interesting phenomena which occur in connection with words and which will be treated in the next several lessons. The first of these is euphemism, which is the substitution of a milder, less distasteful expression for one that directly refers to something unpleasant or offensive. Primitive peoples employ euphemism because they fear that uttering certain words will offend divine powers; also, since they feel that words are more than symbols and that there is a mysterious but vital connection between the word and its meaning, the mere mention of something bad will supposedly cause it to happen. In some tribes the practice of euphemism is carried to such an extreme that no one is ever called by his "real" name for fear that some enemy might be listening and that once an enemy thus got possession of the name, he would have power over the person as well. More civilized groups, however, also employ euphemism, partly because such primitive beliefs are harder to overcome than we sometimes realize and partly because there are certain subjects which we do not like to be reminded of or which we feel are improper to discuss.

One of the great sources of euphemism is death. We are all familiar with such milder expressions for dying as "pass away," "breathe one's last," "depart this life." We do not usually speak of a person as "dead," but refer to him as "the deceased" or "the late Mr. Jones." His body becomes "the remains" or "the loved one." Similarly, we have a number of euphemisms for killing, "do away with," "put out of the way," "remove," and the like.

Another area in which we do not like to "call a spade a spade" is that connected with parts or functions of the body. Thus, in the Victorian era many people felt that *leg* was an indelicate word and subsituted *limb* in the presence of ladies. *Perspiration* is often used euphemistically for *sweat*. For the same reason we have such terms as *powder room, men's lounge,* and so on. Words having to do with sex are likely to have begun as euphemisms. Thus *courtesan*, which was originally "woman attached to the court," and *mistress* acquired their present meanings.

Euphemism has often resulted in degeneration of meaning. A mild word which has been employed for a disagreeable idea tends to acquire all of the unpleasantness that it was originally used to conceal. *Undertaker* was at one time a euphemism but gradually came to be so closely associated with the unpleasantness of death that it was felt necessary to devise the new euphemisms *mortician* and *funeral director.*

The etymological meanings of some words of Latin derivation show that they were originally euphemisms. The substitution of "depart" for "die" is seen in *obituary* (*ob-* and I-, IT-, "to go"), *perish* (*per-,* "completely" and I-, IT-), and *decease* (*de-* "off," and CED-, CESS-, "to go"). *Expire* (*ex-,* "out," and SPIR-, "to breathe") meant originally "to breathe one's last." *Casualty* (CAD-, CAS-, "to befall") was formerly "a happening," as was *accident* (cf. the expression, "if anything happens to me," used instead of "if I die"). *Insane* (*in-,* "not" and SAN-, "healthy") also was probably once a euphemism, just as today in certain circles *sick* means "mentally ill."

NOUN-FORMING SUFFIXES

Learn the following suffixes and their meanings:

I. *-ance, -ancy; -ence, -ency,* "quality of —ing," "state of —ing"

			to watch			
		VIGIL-	to watch	+	*-ance*	vigilance
		HESIT-	to stick fast	+	*-ancy*	hesitancy
in-	+	FLU-	to flow	+	*-ence*	influence
		FLU-	to flow	+	*-ency*	fluency

This suffix is actually a combination of *-ant* or *-ent,* "—ing," (see Lesson X) and *-y,* "quality of," "state of" (see Lesson XV). Thus *vigilance* is literally "state of being watchful," and *hesitancy* is "state of sticking fast."

II. *-or* (in British usage often *-our*), "state of," result of"

ARD-	to burn	+	*-or*	ardor
FUR-	to rage	+	*-or*	furor
ERR-	to wander	+	*-or*	error

III. *-ary (-arium),* "place for"

LIBR-	book	+	*-ary*	library
GRAN-	grain	+	*-ary*	granary
AQU-	water	+	*-arium*	aquarium

This suffix is actually a substantive form of *-ary,* "pertaining to," etc. (see Lesson IX).

IV. *-ory (-orium),* "place for"

DORMIT-	to sleep	+	*-ory*	dormitory
LAVAT-	to wash	+	*-ory*	lavatory
AUDIT-	to hear	+	*-orium*	auditorium

This suffix is actually a substantive form of *-ory,* "serving for" (see Lesson XIII).

ASSIGNMENT

I. Learn the following bases and their meanings:

AG- (IG-), ACT-	to do, to drive	agent, agile inactive, transact
CLAM- (through French, CLAIM-)	to cry out	exclamation, proclamation declaim, proclaim
DIC-, DICT-	to say	diction, contradiction, edict
GER-, GEST-	to carry, to produce	exaggerate congestion, digest
MIT(T)-, MIS(S)-	to send, to let go	admit, transmitter missile, transmission
NASC-, NAT-	to be born	nascent native, prenatal
SON-	sound	supersonic, resonance
VAL- (through French, VAIL-)	to be strong, to be worth	value, equivalent, valid avail, prevail

II. Analyze the following italicized words and define them as they are used in the sentence or phrase.

1. . . . like a growth of fungus or any unwholesome *excrescence* produced there in neglect and impurity. — Dickens

2. During the epidemic the college *infirmary* was filled to capacity.

3. . . . that moment of astonishment and *nascent* arrogance when a beginning author discovers that he is a good writer. — *Time*

4. He was what you call a *remittance* man. He got so much a quarter . . . to keep out of England. — Norman Douglas

5. The *fervor* of these radical groups was for a time kindled . . . by the success of the Bolshevik revolution . . . —*Harper's Magazine*

6. . . . the Italian genius as it expressed itself in society, scholarship, fine art and literature, at its most brilliant period of *renascence* . . . —John Addington Symonds

7. The voting papers, and all the elements of the calculation, would be placed in public *repositories,* accessible to all whom they concerned. — John Stuart Mill

8. It recognized the South's *belligerency,* but not its national independence. — *Atlantic Monthly*

9. The words, spoken *sonorously,* with an even intonation, were heard all over the ship. — Joseph Conrad

10. He was with the battalion about two weeks when Jefferson reported to the little *dispensary* on sick call. —*Harper's Magazine*

11. This singular accident, by a strange *confluence* of emotions in him, was felt as the sharpest sting of all. — Thomas Hardy

12. The little bell giving *clamorous* notice of a visitor's approach . . . —Dickens

13. . . . the people of one English colony, and of nearly half the United States, have been *interdicted* by law from making any use whatever of fermented drinks . . . —John Stuart Mill

14. Anyone knows the sharp *dissonance* resulting from two consecutive half-tones struck simultaneously on the piano. *Atlantic Monthly*

15. Old men . . . harangued the warriors as they passed, exhorting them to *valorous* deeds.—Washington Irving

16. In Washington, U. S. officials kept up their steady pressure on Egypt to curb its *intransigence* . . . —*Time*

17. In all the thousands of words of *malediction* which have been called down upon his head, very few have made him angry. — *Harper's Magazine*

18. Von Humboldt's story, preposterous as it sounds, has a faint claim to *credence.* —*Atlantic Monthly*

19. The *refectory* was a great, low-ceiled, gloomy room; on two long tables smoked basins of something hot. — Charlotte Brontë

20. As the music came fresher on their ears, they danced to its *cadence,* extemporizing new steps. —Hawthorne

LESSON XIX   Folk Etymology

Another interesting process encountered in word study is folk etymology or, as it is sometimes called, popular etymology. This, however, affects the form of words more often than it does their meaning. Folk etymology is the attempt to make unfamiliar words resemble better-known words to which they are erroneously thought to be related, and it arises from ignorance of the true derivations of these words.

Thus, *female* is actually derived from the Latin *femella,* the diminutive of *femina,* "woman," but the English word owes its spelling to the fact that people felt it must somehow be derived from the word *male,* although there is no linguistic relationship between the two words. The *primrose* botanically has nothing to do with roses; it was originally spelled *primula* and meant "little flower of the prime or spring of the year," but popular usage gradually transformed the spelling of this foreign-sounding word to make it resemble something more familiar. Folk etymology has also caused the Spanish *cucaracha* to appear in English as *cockroach* in order to make it sound less strange. *Aecern* was altered to *acorn;* the nuts that grow on oak trees were apparently associated in the popular mind with *corn* because they can be ground into meal in the same way. Sometimes *hiccup* is spelled *hiccough.* The word arose simply as an imitation of the sound made when hiccuping, and so the first spelling is more natural; but people who do not understand this have tried to indicate some supposed resemblance to *cough.*

If a person has ever been tempted to spell or pronounce *sacrilegious* as if it were connected with *religious,* he has been influenced by the same tendency which gave rise to the previous examples of folk etymology; *sacrilegious* actually comes from the Latin *sacer*, "sacred," and *legere*, "to gather" (in the sense of "steal").

NOUN-FORMING SUFFIXES

Learn the following suffixes and their meanings:

I. *-ure*, "act of," "result of"

FRACT-	to break	+	*-ure*	fracture
PUNCT-	to prick	+	*-ure*	puncture
RUPT-	to break	+	*-ure*	rupture

II. *-(u)lence*, *-(o)lence*, "state or quality of being full of"

VI-	force	+	*-(o)lence*	violence
FRAUD-	deceit	+	*-(u)lence*	fraudulence

This suffix is a combination of *-(u)lent*, *-(o)lent*, "full of" (see Lesson IX) and *-y*, "state of," "quality of" (see Lesson XV).

III. *-or*, "one who does," "that which does"

	ACT-	to do	+	*-or*	actor
ad- +	GRESS-	to go	+	*-or*	aggressor
	TRACT-	to drag	+	*-or*	tractor
	MOT-	to move	+	*-or*	motor

IV. *-rix*, "she who does"

TESTAT-	to make a will	+	*-rix*	testatrix
AVI-	bird + *-at-*	+	*-rix*	aviatrix

This is the feminine form of the previous suffix; it occurs mainly in legal terminology.

ASSIGNMENT

I. Learn the following bases and their meanings:

ERR-	to wander	error, erratic
FER-	to bear, to carry	refer, transfer conference
JAC-, JECT-	to throw	ejaculate, inject projectile, reject

LAT-	to bear, to carry	elate, relate, translate
NOMEN-, NOMIN-	name, noun	nomenclature nominate, pronominal
SCRIB-, SCRIPT-	to write	describe, inscribe conscription, subscription
ST(A)-, STAT-	to stand	stance, circumstance station, stature
VIR-	poison	virus
VOLV-, VOLUT-	to roll	revolve, involve evolution, revolution

II. Analyze the following italicized words and define them as they are used in the sentence or phrase.

1. His landlady, Mrs. Bardel — the relict and sole *executrix* of a deceased custom-house officer . . . —Dickens

2. The woman herself was a *conjectural* creature who had little to do with the outlines presented to Sherton eyes; a shape in the gloom, whose true quality could only be approximated by putting together a movement now and a glance then . . . — Thomas Hardy

3. Do not let us add to our difficulties by any lack of clarity of thinking or any *restive* wavering in resolve. —Sir Winston Churchill

4. Wherever the sphere of action of human beings is artificially *circumscribed,* their sentiments are narrowed and dwarfed in the same proportion. — John Stuart Mill

5. When some one of his flock, nettled by his *strictures* from the pulpit, walked in dudgeon towards the church door . . . — Francis Parkman

6. This is perhaps the fullest history of those early days *extant.* — Thoreau

7. To this I was securely bound by a long strap . . . It passed in many *convolutions* about my limbs and body. —Edgar Allan Poe

8. . . . the right of Chieftainship attached to the blood of *primogeniture*, and, therefore, was incapable of being transferred. — James Boswell

9. He keeps a brass cuspidor within reachable *trajectory* of his desk . . . —*Time*

10. An office in the household, with merely *nominal* duties, had been assigned to her as a pretext for the payment of a small pension. — Hawthorne

11. A general sentiment of pity overcame the *virulence* of religious hatred. —Hawthorne

12. No humane being, past the thoughtless age of boyhood, will wantonly murder any creature which holds its life by the same *tenure* that he does. —Thoreau

13. A year ago this month, 75% of the *electorate* of Metropolitan France thunderously voted yes to de Gaulle's plan . . . —*Time*

14. We would have this wholly *aberrant* situation: namely, that comparatively poor countries would strain every nerve, and deprive themselves of essentials . . . for the sake of producing and shipping to our shores semi-luxury products which we really do not need. — *Harper's Magazine*

15. We know through what strange loopholes the human mind contrives to escape, when it wishes to avoid a disagreeable *inference* from an admitted proposition. —Macaulay

16. The sons and grandchildren of the first settlers were a race of lower and narrower souls than their *progenitors* had been. — Hawthorne

17. It is a work based on much reading and *correlation* of data in biology, psychology, aesthetics, literature, and the fine arts. — *Harper's Magazine*

18. The need for union arises not from any inherent virtues of the large state but from the *exigencies* of survival. —*Harper's Magazine.*

19. To those who support the trial it promises the first effective recognition of a world law for the punishment of *malefactors*

who start wars or conduct them in bestial fashion. — *Atlantic Monthly*

20. The whole country around Detroit was covered by a sea of fog, the *precursor* of a hot and sultry day. —Francis Parkman

III. With the aid of a dictionary determine the derivation of the following words whose forms have been influenced by folk etymology.

1. belfry (not connected with *bell*)
2. crayfish (not connected with *fish*)
3. curtail (not connected with *tail*)
4. cutlass (not connected with *cut*)
5. hangnail (not connected with *hang*)
6. headlong (not connected with *long*)
7. penthouse (not connected with *house*)
8. shamefaced (not connected with *face*)
9. sovereign (not connected with *reign*)
10. surround (not connected with *round*)

LESSON XX   Clipped Words

Another way in which the form of some words has been affected is by shortening or clipping. *Canter,* for instance, is short for *Canterbury* and originally referred to the kind of pace which was popular with pilgrims riding to the shrine of St. Thomas at Canterbury. Clipped words are usually the result of popular speech and are often labeled in dictionaries as *slang* or *colloquial,* but they are especially common in the language of college students, as may be seen from the many examples like *math, prof, exam,* and *psych.* Neverthless, despite the fact that such shortening has been frowned upon by many purists, including Jonathan Swift, the author of *Gulliver's Travels,* who deplored in particular the use of *mob* (short for *mobile vulgus,* "the movable or fickle common people"), some of our most common words represent clipped forms which have become standard English. Thus *cute* was originally *acute, drawing room* was originally *withdrawing room,* and *brandy* was *brandy-wine* (that is, "burnt or distilled wine"). *Chum* is apparently a shortened form of *chamber fellow,* while *rum* is from *rumbullion.*

VERB-FORMING SUFFIXES

Learn the following suffixes and their meanings:

I. *-ate,* "to make," "to do something with," "to subject to," "to take," etc. (This suffix has so many different senses that it is better in writing out the analysis of words to list it simply as "verbal suffix.")

		LOC-	place	+	*-ate*	locate
		NOMIN-	name	+	*-ate*	nominate
e-	+	LIMIN-	threshold	+	*-ate*	eliminate
in-	+	LUMIN-	light	+	*-ate*	illuminate

This is generally equivalent in meaning to the native English suffix *-en,* in *brighten, liven, gladden,* etc.

A. This suffix has been used most frequently in forming verbs from noun and adjective bases. Sometimes, however, it appears attached to verb bases and consequently has little effect upon the meaning. In this case *-ate* merely represents a different form of the Latin verb.

com-	+	PLIC-	to fold	+	*-ate*	complicate
inter-	+	ROG-	to ask	+	*-ate*	interrogate
		MIGR-	to pass over	+	*-ate*	migrate

B. This suffix is difficult because it is similar in form to two others which have already been considered. It is usually possible to distinguish the three *-ate* suffixes, however, if one pays attention to the part of speech of the words which they are used to form. Thus *-ate,* "possessing," "being," (see Lesson X) usually forms adjectives (though sometimes these adjectives are used as nouns, like *degenerate*); *-ate,* "office of," (see Lesson XV) forms nouns; and the suffix *-ate* treated in this lesson of course forms verbs.

II. *-esce,* "to begin," "to become"

con-	+	VAL-	to be strong	+	*-esce*			convalesce
ob-	+	SOL-	to be accus- tomed	+	*-esce*	+	*-ent*	obsolescent

ASSIGNMENT

I. Learn the following bases and their meanings:

CAPIT- (CIPIT-)	head	capital, decapitate precipitate
LOC-	place	local, dislocate
MILIT-	soldier	military, militia
PUT-	to reckon, to think	compute, reputation
RADIC-	root	radical, radish
ROG-	to ask	arrogant, derogatory
SPIR-	to breathe	spirit, conspire, inspire

II. Analyze the following italicized words and define them as they are used in the sentence or phrase.

1. The wild *effervescence* of his mood — which had so readily supplied thoughts, fantasies, and a strange aptitude of words, and impelled him to talk from the mere necessity of giving vent to this bubbling-up gush of ideas . . . —Hawthorne

2. Over it hung the *attenuated* skeleton of a chrome-yellow moon, which had only a few days to last. —Thomas Hardy

3. It was only then that the long suppression of creative energy burst forth in a second marvellous *efflorescence* . . . —*Harper's Magazine*

4. . . . the Peruvians say that the ocean left the shore and *inundated* the continent . . . —*Harper's Magazine*

5. . . . viral *respiratory* infections against which neither it nor any other antibiotic is effective . . .—*Time*

6. . . . casting myself face downwards on the earth, lay there *simulating* death. —W. H. Hudson

7. The blackness of the water was streaked with trails of light which *undulated* gently on slight ripples. —Joseph Conrad

8. Labor, naturally, claims that this bill nullifies its most precious *prerogative,* the right to strike . . . —*Harper's Magazine*

9. It proved far less easy to *eradicate* evil passions than to repeal evil laws. —Macaulay

10. But as a soldier he incurred . . . the degrading *imputation* of personal cowardice. —Macaulay

11. . . . a World Food Board with authority to store food, stabilize food production and prices, and *allocate* surpluses so as to prevent famine. —*Harper's Magazine*

12. . . . an intensification of the problems which in the past have *militated* against adequate educational experiences for the gifted. —*Atlantic Monthly*

13. . . . a green spotlight fixed immovably in the wall. Its ghastly *luminescence* flooded, from end to end, the steel bunk that was my bed. —*Harper's Magazine*

14. A thick crayon of white chalk lay on my desk for the convenience of *elucidating* any grammatical or verbal obscurity which might occur in my lesson. —Charlotte Brontë

15. The *putative* author of the anonymous letter . . .

16. At the same time, he *exculpated* himself from any part in the late hostilities, which he said had not only been conducted without his privity, but contrary to his inclination and efforts. —William Hickling Prescott

17. The division, he assured them, had been made on perfectly fair and *equitable* principles. —Prescott

18. We are also *repatriating* all French troops who were in this country, excepting those who, of their own free will, have volunteered to follow General de Gaulle. —Sir Winston Churchill

19. His record as an advocate of these principles is too well known to require more than the briefest *recapitulation* here —*Harper's Magazine*

20. . . . the *senescence* and death of a colony of wasps or bumblebees in the fall of the season in which it was founded . . . —*Harper's Magazine*

III. With the aid of a dictionary give the unshortened form from which each of the following clipped words has come.

Example: *sport*, from *disport*

1. bus
2. cab
3. cad
4. curio
5. gin (both the drink and the machine)
6. pep
7. (stage) prop
8. van (both "forefront" and "covered vehicle")
9. varsity
10. wayward
11. wig

IV. Give as many examples as you can of clipped words arising from campus life; e.g., *prof, exam, etc.*

LESSON XXI   Blends

Somewhat akin to clipped words are blends, which are produced by the combining of two words so that only a part of each remains. The meaning as well as the form is also a blend of those of the two component words. Thus *chortle*, coined by Lewis Carroll in *Through the Looking Glass*, is apparently a blend of *chuckle* and *snort*. Carroll, incidentally, called such coinages "portmanteau words," and in explaining the term he wrote, "Well, 'slithy' means 'lithe and slimy' . . . You see it's like a portmanteau — there are two meanings packed up into one word." Other examples of this kind are *smog*, formed from *smoke* and *fog*, and *Eurasia*, a blend of *Europe* and *Asia*.

VERB-FORMING SUFFIXES

Learn the following suffixes and their meanings:

I. -(*i*)*fy*, -(*e*)*fy*, "to make"

PAC-	peace	+	-(*i*)*fy*	pacify
MAGN-	large	+	-(*i*)*fy*	magnify
LIQU-	to be liquid	+	-(*e*)*fy*	liquefy

II. -(*i*)*fic*, "making," "causing"

| PAC- | peace | + | -(*i*)*fic* | pacific |
| TERR- | to frighten | + | -(*i*)*fic* | terrific |

This suffix, though it forms adjectives, is considered here because it is a form of the previous suffix. Both are related to the base FAC- (FIC)-, "to do," "to make" (Lesson XII).

III. *-igate, -egate,* "to make," "to drive"

NAV-	ship	+ *-igate*	navigate
FUM-	smoke	+ *-igate*	fumigate
VARI-	varied	+ *-egate*	variegate

This suffix is related to the base AG- (IG-), "to do," "to drive" (Lesson XVIII).

ASSIGNMENT

I. Learn the following bases and their meanings:

MEDI-	middle	median, medium, immediate
MIT-	mild, soft	mitigate
MOLL-	mild, soft	mollify, emollient
MORT-	death	mortal, mortuary
PET-, PETIT-	to seek, to assail	compete
		petition, appetite
PRED-	prey	predatory
PROL-	offspring	proletariat, proliferate
PUGN-	fight	repugnant, impugn

II. Analyze the following italicized words and define them as they are used in the sentence or phrase.

1. Today deer, protected and multiplying, are committing serious *depredations* on farmlands and gardens. —*Atlantic Monthly*

2. It is a day, however, and an age, that appears to be remarkably barren, when compared with the *prolific* originality of former times. —Hawthorne

3. . . . but what politician has a right to *deification* or posthumous respect if he has (a) been palpably wrong or (b) been proven wholly insincere? —*Harper's Magazine*

4. The odious and fleshy figure . . . fixed itself in his memory forever as the *incarnation* of everything vile and base that lurks in the world we love. —Joseph Conrad

5. "A snarling *pugnacity* will...complete no reformation."—*Time*

6. A skin *emollient* . . .

7. Cessation in his love-making had *revivified* her love. —Thomas Hardy

8. We rejected the compulsory jurisdiction of the International Court of Justice, which means that we refused to obligate ourselves even to submit our legal disputes to impartial *adjudication.* —*Harper's Magazine*

9. She obligingly consented to act as *mediatrix* in the matter. —Charlotte Brontë

10. He checked the *predatory* habits of his troops with a rigorous hand. They were forbidden, under pain of severe punishment, to molest any peaceable or unfortified towns, or any unarmed and unresisting people. —Washington Irving

11. . . . doors which were intended for *ingress* and *egress,* windows which were meant to give light . . . —John Addington Symonds

12. . . . contracts in which . . . there may have been no direct fraud or deceit, sufficient to *invalidate* them in a court of law. —*The Federalist*

13. I can furnish you with a list of *alliterative* signatures, beginning with Anne Aureole and ending with Zoë Zenith. —Oliver Wendell Holmes

14. Even Tutchin, acrimonious as was his nature and great as were his wrongs, seems to have been a little *mollified* by the pitiable spectacle. —Macaulay

15. . . . the thought of home was crowded out of the mind, all memory *obliterated* by the tyranny of the present. —Emerson

16. Upon this ground, which is evidently the true one, it will not be difficult to *obviate* the objections which have been made. —*The Federalist*

17. . . . have proposed various expedients by which the evil may be, in a greater or less degree, *mitigated*. —John Stuart Mill

18. The party leaders must *placate* and absorb as many of these minorities as possible, so that . . . they may build a compromise which will at least last until November. —*Harper's Magazine*

19. . . . a youth of restless and *impetuous* activity. —Francis Parkman

20. . . . to repent our sins, and to *mortify* ourselves with fastings, vigils, and long prayers. —Sir Walter Scott

III. With the aid of a dictionary, list the words which have been combined to produce each of the following blends:

1. Amerind
2. dumfound
3. electrocute
4. bookmobile
5. Gestapo
6. motel
7. motorcade
8. splotch
9. telecast
10. transistor

LESSON XXII Doublets

We have seen from the introduction that there were a number of different periods during which English borrowed from Latin and a number of different routes by way of which Latin words entered our language. In the Renaissance many words were borrowed directly from Latin by scholars and so more nearly preserve their original form; but in earlier times Latin words entered English generally by way of Old French or occasionally Teutonic, and often in such cases their forms became considerably altered. Thus, frequently the same Latin word has been borrowed with different spelling and often with different meaning during successive periods and so has supplied our vocabulary with two or more English words. Sometimes, also, such variations have appeared because a Latin word has entered English by way of different dialects of French. Such words which are different in spelling but are derived ultimately from the same parent word are called doublets. For example, the Latin word *dignitas* entered English as *dainty,* but was borrowed again as *dignity.* The process might be diagrammed as follows:

(Latin) *dignitas*

dainty   dignity

Sometimes doublets have completely different meanings, as in the previous example or in the case of the following:

cruise–cross (from Latin *crux,* "cross")

> When a ship cruises, it "crosses" back and forth over its previous course.

chamber–camera (from Latin *camera,* "room," as in *unicameral*)

> An early device for taking photographs was called by its inventor *camera obscura* ("dark room"), and the first part of this name came to be applied to all such devices.

ray–radius (from Latin *radius,* "spoke of a wheel")

ennui–annoy (from Latin *in odio,* "in hatred"; cf. English *odious*)

Many times, however, the meanings of doublets vary only slightly, and thus it is possible to see how the tendency to borrow has greatly increased the richness and variety of the English language. The following doublets, for instance, are fairly close in meaning but yet are not exact synonyms.

fragile–frail	*regal–royal*
abbreviate–abridge	*compute–count*

Languages other than Latin have of course supplied doublets, as, for example, *shirt–skirt,* and *ward–guard,* which are of Teutonic origin, and *cipher–zero,* from Arabic.

Sometimes a single parent word has given our language three or more different words, as in the following instances:

ratio–ration–reason

capital–cattle–chattel (from Latin *caput, capitis,* "head")
> Cattle at one time formed a very important item of "capital" (literally, "chief property").

gentle–gentile–genteel–jaunty

Words which are the reverse of doublets are called homonyms, that is, words similar in form or at least in pronunciation, but of different origin and meaning, as, for example, in the assignment of the previous lesson *van*, "the forefront" and *van*, "a covered vehicle," or *gin*, "an alcoholic beverage," and *gin*, "a machine for removing the seeds from cotton." In the formation of homonyms there is nothing that can be described as a process; generally the similarity between the two words is due purely to chance.

ASSIGNMENT

I. Learn the following bases and their meanings:

GRAT-	pleasing, grateful	gratitude, gratuitous
MISC-	to mix	promiscuous, immiscible
MOV-, MOT-	to move	movement, remove motion, remote
NEG-	to deny	negative, renegade
PURG-	to clean	purge, purgative
TEND-, TENS-, TENT-	to stretch, to strive	tend, contend tense, intense extent, intent
VULG-	common	vulgar, vulgate

II. Analyze the following italicized words as they are used in the sentence or phrase.

1. ... the solemn pledge we had already signed agreeing not to *divulge* classified information we might acquire ... —*Harper's Magazine*

2. Hitting hard at *pretentious* commencements, big time football ... Conant snorts that all such status seeking is utterly without "sound educational reason." —*Time*

3. *Miscegenation* may now be handled discreetly, but anything inciting hatred among peoples is taboo. —*Time*

4. A tortured and complicated character, full of *ambivalences* and utter contradictions ... —*Harper's Magazine*

5. To justify their jobs, bureaucrats *proliferate* their duties.—*Time*

6. The man shook his fist and gnashed his teeth as he uttered these words *incoherently*. —Dickens

7. . . . Hoover endured not only the *emotional* torment of the Depression, but two decades of obloquy in which his name was equated with economic disaster and social injustice.—*Time*

8. On a large centre table a number of artistic objects were lying together in a *promiscuous* jumble. —W. H. Hudson

9. Every eye and every tongue affected to express their sense of the general happiness, and the veil of ceremony and *dissimulation* was drawn for a while over the darkest designs of revenge and murder. —Edward Gibbon

10. ". . . *impugned* the motives, actions, and conduct of the officers and directors of the newspaper and have otherwise attacked their probity and imputed improper purposes to them . . ." —*Time*

11. Nor is it possible to plead, in *extenuation* of his guilt, that he was misled by inordinate zeal for the public good.—Macaulay

12. . . . keeping a constant fire, they could pass a winter . . . though smoke, filth, vermin, bad air, the crowd, and the total absence of privacy would make it a *purgatory* to any civilized white man. — Francis Parkman

13. The last thing I would advocate would be a return to the *militant* tactics of some of the early feminists. —*Harper's Magazine*

14. We all know what *specious* fallacies may be urged in defence of every act of injustice yet proposed for the imaginary benefit of the mass. — John Stuart Mill

15. Many of the translations, they complain, are *expurgated* Victorian versions . . . — *Time*

16. Debate could be protracted interminably, and an active minority, by *dilatory* motions and filibustering, could create preposterous delays. — Allan Nevins

17. . . . air assault, which Hitler was led to believe would shatter our industries and reduce us to *impotence* and subjection. — Sir Winston Churchill

18. "Our life has been a vain attempt at self-delight. But self-*abnegation* is the higher road. We should mortify the flesh." — Thomas Hardy

19. He was kind, cordial, open, even *convivial* and jocose, would sit at table many hours, and would bear his full share of festive conversation. — Macaulay

20. We have seen with what sagacious policy the French had labored to *ingratiate* themselves with the Indians. —Parkman

21. The two liquids were *immiscible*.

22. The principal *exponent* of this theory . . . —*Time*

23. It must indeed be a *captious* critic who can find a pretext to make a quarrel out of that. —Churchill

24. When he refused to lend his car in return, he was regarded as an *ingrate*.

25. . . . when belligerent nations, under the impossibility of making acquisitions upon us, will not lightly hazard the giving us *provocation*. —Washington

III. With the aid of a dictionary give the doublet of each of the following:

Example: *feat*–fact

> On looking up *feat* you will find that it is derived from the Latin *factum,* "that which is done." The form *factum* should suggest the obvious derivative which is the doublet, *fact*.

1. aggrieve	6. parcel
2. antic	7. pity
3. coy	8. poignant
4. loyal	9. sample
5. naïve	10. sure

IV. With the aid of a dictionary determine the derivations of the following homonyms:

1. cashier (to dismiss with disgrace)   cashier (one who has charge of money)

2. junk (a type of sailing vessel)   junk (useless material)

3. policy (course of action)   policy (insurance contract)

4. quarry (an object of pursuit)   quarry (excavation from which stone is obtained)

5. school (an educational institution)   school (a large number of fish)

6. tattoo (markings on the skin)   tattoo (a signal on a drum or a bugle call)

LESSON XXIII   Uncommon Usages of Words

One of the reasons why modern readers have difficulty appreciating older writers is that they encounter many obsolete words or words used in a sense different from that of today. College students find this type of difficulty most frequently perhaps in the works of Shakespeare. In *Henry V,* for instance, the line occurs, "By my troth, I will speak my conscience of the king." *Conscience* (SCI-, "to know") here does not mean, however, "knowledge of right and wrong," the modern meaning, but "inmost thoughts," "mind." In *Hamlet* Ophelia, who has become insane, is described as "a document in madness," *document* (DOC-, "to teach") here being "lesson" rather than "written proof."

These two examples are instances of words which have since become specialized, although used in a generalized sense in Shakespeare's time. Likewise Shakespeare sometimes employs words in a literal sense whereas the modern meaning is figurative (e.g., *extravagant* in the third of the quotations listed below, where it means "wandering outside"). Often a knowledge of bases combined with careful attention to the context will enable a student to determine more precisely the meaning of a word as it occurs in one of Shakespeare's plays.

I. On the basis of your knowledge of bases, prefixes, and suffixes, give the meanings of the italicized words as they occur in the following quotations from Shakespeare.*

1. The people love me, and the sea is mine;
   My powers are *crescent* . . .
   — *Antony and Cleopatra*

2. . . . an excellent play, well *digested* in the scenes . . .
   — *Hamlet*

3.   . . . and at his warning,
   Whether in sea or fire, in earth or air,
   the *extravagant* and *erring* spirit hies
   To his confine. (VAG-, to wander)
   — *Hamlet*

4.   . . . falling in the land,
   Have every pelting river made so proud,
   That they have overborne their *continents*.
   — *A Midsummer Night's Dream*

5. The Turk with a most mighty preparation makes for Cyprus.
   Othello, the *fortitude* of the place is best known to you.
   — *Othello*

6. Whose white *investments* figure innocence . . .
   — *Henry IV*

7.   . . . and of the truth herein
   This present object made *probation*.
   — *Hamlet*

8. Abate the edge of traitors, gracious Lord,
   That would *reduce* these bloody days again.
   — *Richard III*

9. If you have hitherto conceal'd this sight,
   Let it be *tenable* in your silence still.
   — *Hamlet*

---

*Many of these examples have been taken from Edith F. Claflin, "The Latinisms in Shakespeare's Diction," *Classical Journal*, 16 (1920–21), pp. 346-59, and C. C. Hower, "Importance of a Knowledge of Latin for Understanding the Language of Shakespeare," *Classical Journal*, 46 (1950–51), pp. 221-7.

II. Give the meanings of the following italicized obsolete or archaic words as they are used in the passages below:

1. Let it stamp wrinkles in her brow of youth;
   With *cadent* tears fret channels in her cheeks.

   — King Lear

2. Then weigh what loss your honour may sustain,
   If with too *credent* ear you list his songs.

   — Hamlet

3. The presence of a king engenders love
   Amongst his subjects and his loyal friends,
   As it *disanimates* his enemies.

   — Henry VI

4. For ever should they be *expulsed* from France,
   And not have title of an earldom here.

   — Henry VI

5. What *propugnation* is in one man's valour,
   To stand the push and enmity of those
   This quarrel would excite?

   — Troilus and Cressida

6. . . . stubbornly he did *repugn* the truth.

   — Henry VI

7.   Now, the next day
   Was our sea-fight; and what to this was *sequent*
   Thou know'st already.

   — Hamlet

8. Thou perjured, and thou *simular* man of virtue . . .

   — King Lear

9. As knots, by the conflux of meeting sap,
   Infect the sound pine and divert his grain
   Tortive and errant from his course of growth.

   — Troilus and Cressida

ASSIGNMENT

I. Learn the following bases and their meanings:

CORD-	heart	cordial, accord, record
FLECT-, FLEX-	to bend	deflection, reflection flexible, reflex

MAN(U)-	hand	manicure, manipulate
		manual, manuscript
PORT-	to carry	portable, deport, report
STRU-, STRUCT-	to build	instrument
		structure, instruct
TERMIN-	boundary, end	terminal, determine
VINC-, VICT-	to conquer	convince, evince
		victor, convict

II. Analyze the following italicized words and define them as they are used in the sentence or phrase:

1. They made a mad attempt to follow us in the factured canoe, but finding it useless, again vented their rage in a series of hideous *vociferations.* —Edgar Allan Poe

2. They exclaimed that they were betrayed, and that the truce had been only an *artifice* to secure their inactivity until the arrival of the expected succours. — William Hickling Prescott

3. . . . laying his finger on his lip, drew his companions back again, with the greatest caution and *circumspection.* —Dickens

4. His stern features expressed *inflexible* resolution; his brows were puckered, and his lips compressed, with deep and settled purpose. — Dickens

5. . . . rightly *construed* this as an acquiescence in his proposition. — Dickens

6. The claims of the rival nations were in fact so *discordant* that any attempt to reconcile them must needs produce a fresh quarrel. — Francis Parkman

7. Men, seeing the nature of this man like that of the brute, think that he has never possessed the *innate* faculty of reason. — Thoreau

8. . . . would cling with an *invincible* tenacity of grip to any purpose which he might espouse. — Parkman

9. The town, seeing the castle in the hands of the Christians, and the garrison routed and destroyed, readily *capitulated.* — Washington Irving

10. His will made provision for the *manumission* of his slaves.

11. Plays and poems, hunting and dancing, were *proscribed* by the austere discipline of his saintly family. — Macaulay

12. The resolution was, of course, carried with loud *acclamations,* every man holding up both hands in favour of it. — Dickens

13. He refused to *retract* his statement.

14. ... his face expressive of pain and care, — not *transitory,* but settled pain, of long and forcedly patient endurance. — Hawthorne

15. Therefore, I hope the debate when it ends may leave the impression that there has been no *derogation* from the authority and freedom of Parliamentary institutions. — Sir Winston Churchill

16. Yet the spirit can ... *transmute* what in form is the grossest sensuality into purity and devotion. — Thoreau

17. As it proved, science has achieved the possibility of that *emancipation* from want ... —*Harper's Magazine*

18. ... had sunk into a chair, with an expression of the most *abject* and hopeless misery that the human mind can imagine portrayed in every lineament of his expressive face.—Dickens

19. He failed to grasp the full *import* of her words.

20. It was the report of a trial for breach of promise of marriage, giving the testimony in full, with fervid extracts from both the gentleman's and lady's *amatory* correspondence. —Hawthorne

21. The audience ... were ineffably delighted and gave way to such a tumult of *approbation,* that, just as the story closed, the benches broke beneath them. — Hawthorne

22. After a week of soulless dissipation, I invited a small party of the most *dissolute* students to a secret carousal in my chambers. — Poe

23. ... hearty *extroverts* with the ever-ready smile, the big hello, the manly handshake, the surefire memory for first names. *Harper's Magazine*

24. There is an *indeterminacy* about all the events of the atomic universe which refinements of measurement and observation can never dispel. — *Harper's Magazine*

25. Let us examine the point of the story . . . . We will introduce it by an *apposite* anecdote. —Charles Lamb

LESSON XXIV   Uncommon Usages of Words

Many other writers besides Shakespeare have of course used familiar words with meanings not found today. On the basis of your knowledge of bases, prefixes, and suffixes, give the meanings of the italicized words as they occur in the following passages, most of which have been taken from the *Oxford English Dictionary*.

1. In order to lighten the crown still further, they *aggravated* responsibility on ministers of state.   — Burke (1790)

2. The moste *comfortable* Sacrament of the body and bloud of Christe . . .   — Ordre of Communion (1547–8)

3. There is no *convenience* between Christ and Belial.
          —Sampson (1554)

4. The *conversion* of Jupiter about his own axis . . .   (1655–6)

5. At length *convinced* with the heavinesse of sleep . . . he turned him to the wall.   — Munday (1633)

6. The insatiable Appetites of a *decimating* Clergy . . .
          — Penn (1670)

7. Venice was a Colonie *deducted* and drawne from thence.
          — Holland (1600)

8. . . . to be exiled and *dejected* from those high mansions.
          — Mede (1638)

9. The drapery . . . that *depends* from his shoulders . . .
          — Hogarth (1753)

10. An *excursion* of land shooting out directly . . . —Browne (1682)

11. An accessory before the *fact* . . .

12. All these afflictions . . . they knowingly did *object* themselves to.   — Barrow (1677)

13. God . . . had *pretended* a remedie in that behalfe which was . . . Manna.   — Carew (1594)

14. Love is more *prevalent* in obtaining what you desire than fear.
           — King (1711)

15. The fortunate soil assisted, and even *prevented,* the hand of cultivation.   — Gibbon (1776)

16. An insect with the extremity of its abdomen *produced* into a sharp point . . .   —Darwin (1877)

17. . . . and have *punctuated* unto me so many remarkeable things and novelties . . .   —Tirwhyte (1634)

18. Morley, made at first bishop of Worcester, and soon after . . . *translated* to Winchester . . .   —Burnet (1683)

ASSIGNMENT

I. Learn the following bases and their meanings:

AUD-, AUDIT-	to hear	audience audit, auditorium
NUNCI- (through French, -NOUNCE)	to announce	annunciation, denunciation denounce, pronounce
PRESS-	to press	pressure, compression
PROPRI-	one's own, fitting	proprietary, appropriate
SAT(IS)-	enough	satiate satisfy

II. Analyze the following italicized words and define them as they are used in the sentence or phrase.

 1. He found the country was pouring forth its legions from every quarter, and perceived that there was no safety but in *precipitate* flight. —Washington Irving

 2. . . . Russia's two great *expatriates* — one of whom had not set foot in his homeland for half a century, the other for better than 35 years . . . — *Time*

3. All honour to those who can abnegate for themselves the personal enjoyment of life, when by such *renunciation* they contribute worthily to increase the amount of happiness in the world. — John Stuart Mill

4. Under cover of the rustle of the tracings, he murmured . . . in a low voice *inaudible* to the other two. —Thomas Hardy

5. A *prescient* analyst of Far East development in the 1930's, Close predicted Japanese war aims and the rise of Red China. — *Time*

6. Under the ruins were human skeletons and a great mass of pottery, clay figurines and other *artifacts*. —*Time*

7. . . . drew up an address to Dr. Johnson on the occasion, *replete* with wit and humour, but which it was feared the Doctor might think treated the subject with too much levity. — James Boswell

8. I do this with no desire to make *invidious* comparisons or rouse purposeless rivalries with our greatest ally, the United States. — Sir Winston Churchill

9. It seemed worth putting down among the noblest sentiments *enunciated* by the best of men. —Dickens

10. Thou lovest; but ne'er knew love's sad *satiety*. —Shelley

11. I would not, at twenty years, be a preaching missionary of abstemiousness and sobriety; and I should let other people do as they would, without formally and *sententiously* rebuking them for it. — Lord Chesterfield

12. It looked like an infirmary for decayed and *superannuated* furniture, where everything diseased or disabled was sent to nurse or to be forgotten. — Washington Irving

13. He *comported* himself with great dignity. —Joseph Conrad

14. Here was the priest in the *vestments* of his office. —Francis Parkman

15. The great landed properties were *expropriated* by the state a generation ago and parcelled out among the indigent peasantry. — *Atlantic Monthly*

16. Never was there a sweeter-tempered, a better-mannered member of that often *contentious* and not infrequently acrimonious body. — Samuel Hopkins Adams

17. Increasingly *repressive* legislation — certain to limit and restrict our civil liberties — would certainly result . . . — *Harper's Magazine*

18. . . . watching the monotony of everyday occurrences with a kind of *inconsequential* interest and earnestness. —Hawthorne

19. . . . that morbid condition of the *auditory* nerve which rendered all music intolerable to the sufferer. —Edgar Allan Poe

20. . . . the vista of that noble street, stretching into the *interminable* distance between two rows of lofty edifices. —Hawthorne

21. His nostrils were *distended* with anger.

22. He seemed to think I had committed an *impropriety* in proposing to accompany him unmarried. — Charlotte Brontë

23. . . . observed a vow of *continence,* and imposed on his appetites a perpetual *abstinence* from wine and flesh. —Edward Gibbon

24. He cared little for wine or for beauty; but he desired riches with an ungovernable and *insatiable* desire. —Macaulay

25. The occasional heave of the wind became the sigh of some immense sad soul, *conterminous* with the universe in space, and with history in time. — Thomas Hardy

LESSON XXV   Latin Words in English

Some words have entered English from Latin without becoming completely anglicized; thus they still retain their Latin endings and consequently have a foreign, un-English appearance. In some cases the plurals of such words are formed in the Latin fashion; in other cases the regular English plural *-s* or *-es* is used; while in still other cases both English and Latin plural forms are to be found. One can only be certain by consulting a dictionary.

There are a number of different Latin plural endings for nouns, too many in fact to attempt to classify fully here. For our purposes it is enough to learn the most frequently occurring Latin singular endings,

-us, -a, and *-um,* with their corresponding plurals, *-i* (usually), *-ae,* and *-a.* Thus:

alumnus–alumni
alumna–alumnae
medium–media

Also might be mentioned words ending in *-ix* and *-ex,* with plurals in *-ices.* Thus:

appendix–appendices
vortex–vortices

Note that some of the words in the assignment usually appear in the plural form, for example, *agenda* and *minutiae.* Also, many borrowed Latin words were originally not nouns but verbs, and consequently have Latin verbal endings which indicated tense and the person of the speaker. Thus *credo* meant in Latin, "I believe," and *tenet,* "he holds."

ASSIGNMENT

I. The following italicized words contain bases which have already been studied. Define each word as it is used in the sentence or phrase, and give the base and its meaning.

1. The committee was unprepared for the proposal since it had not been listed in the *agenda.*

2. It will be all the easier for us to conduct ourselves as belligerents in a high spirit of right and fairness because we act without *animus,* not in enmity towards a people . . . —Woodrow Wilson

3. . . . pillared on three sides, a proud *ante-bellum* house. — William Allen White

4. . . . a *congeries* of brilliant passages in support of an untenable thesis. — *Harper's Magazine*

5. The *consensus* is that the trial will not be concluded before May at the earliest. — *Atlantic Monthly*

6. The following errors have not been listed in the *corrigenda* of the book.

7. Early councils were primarily concerned with combating heresy and defining the truths that form the *credo* of most believing Christians . . . — *Time*

8. This effort of the Germans to secure daylight mastery of the air over England is, of course, the *crux* of the whole war. — Sir Winston Churchill

9. . . . an addled old clerk who has sandbagged his office with 67 filing cabinets full of senselessly duplicated *detritus* dating from 1939 . . . — *Time*

10. Men still quoted with approval Jefferson's *dictum* that government is best when governing least. — *Atlantic Monthly*

11. An indescribable and complicated smell, made up of damp earth below, of the taint of dried fish and of the *effluvia* of rotting vegetable matter, pervaded the place.— Joseph Conrad

12. They are so natural that they seem to be the *extempore* conversations of two people of wit, rather than letters. — Lord Chesterfield

13. The cave-in wrote *finis* to his attempt to build a tunnel.

14. It is inconsistent to pay the one, and accept the service of the other *gratis*. —Thomas Paine

15. As an *interim* measure, before the full scientific treatment can be given to this procedure . . . — Churchill

16. . . . her features, of so distinctive a kind, but which her character, though developing so fast, had not yet fully carved out of the soft *matrix* of childhood. — *Atlantic Monthly*

17. Cortés established a control over his band of bold and reckless adventurers, such as a pedantic martinet, scrupulous in enforcing the *minutiae* of military etiquette, could never have obtained. — William Hickling Prescott

18. A report-drafting committee gathers memoranda from the economists and co-ordinates the stuff into a kind of *omnibus* draft embodying the suggestions. — *Harper's Magazine*

19. The bottle, as the doctor had reason to know, contained a *placebo* — sugar pills. —*Time*

20. A written *prospectus* of this issue of stock will be sent upon request.

21. Neither the *regalia* of his office nor the elaborate uniforms he occasionally affected could give dignity to his irresolute stance . . . — *Atlantic Monthly*

22. . . . an unknown energy which played with all his generation as a cat plays with mice. The *simile* is none too strong. — Henry Adams

23. The religious *tenets* of his family he had early renounced with contempt. — Macaulay

24. . . . Duluth, the western *terminus* of the St. Lawrence Seaway . . . — *Time*

25. As he walked up the Treasury stairs on his return, he was siezed with *vertigo* and fell heavily. —Allan Nevins

II. Give the plural or plurals of each of the following singular forms:

1. apex
2. apparatus
3. arena
4. cactus
5. campus
6. crux
7. curriculum
8. focus
9. formula
10. genus
11. index
12. memorandum
13. species
14. stadium

LESSON XXVI Latin Phrases in English

Besides having carried on wholesale borrowing of individual words from the Latin language, English has adopted many Latin phrases in their original form. Some of these are so familiar that we scarcely think of them any longer as belonging to a foreign tongue, *post mortem* (literally, "after death"), for instance, and *vice versa* (literally, "the alternation or order being turned about"). Others are less familiar but are not infrequently found in literary and legal language.

Perhaps the biggest problem in connection with Latin phrases in English is pronunciation (and this holds true as well for Latin words like those listed in the preceding lesson). Dictionaries often give an anglicized pronunciation for such phrases and words, but many people who have studied Latin prefer to use the system of pronunciation taught in most schools in this country, where Latin is pronounced as nearly as possible in the manner of the ancient Romans. Thus, although some dictionaries give the pronunciation of *per diem* as "per-DYE-em," one is probably more likely to hear it as "per DEE-em." Likewise, the pronunciation of *antennae* (the plural of *antenna*) is given in dictionaries as "antenn-EE," but many, including some zoologists, say "antenn-EYE." We are not justified in insisting that one system is correct and the other incorrect, or even that one system is better than the other. (As a matter of fact, there is still a third system of Latin pronunciation, which in this country is used principally in the Roman Catholic Church.) We can only observe the way these phrases are pronounced by educated users with whom we are acquainted and, when in doubt, rely upon the dictionary.

ASSIGNMENT

The following Latin phrases in English are listed together with the literal meaning of the Latin. Define them as they are used in the accompanying sentences. Note that some are regarded as belonging to a foreign language and are consequently italicized.

1. ad hoc (with regard to this)
   . . . responsibility for the study and its findings fell on an *"ad hoc* citizens committee of 22 . . ."* — Time*

2. ad nauseam (to nausea)
   My friend of the pit repeated it *ad nauseam* during the performance. — Thackeray

3. ad valorem (according to value)
   . . . the British Board of Trade announced the application of a 75 per cent ad valorem tax against foreign film-earnings in the United Kingdom. — *Harper's Magazine*

4. alter ego (another I)
   The Governor sits in on many of these discussions and is usually represented by his alter ego . . . when he cannot attend.—*Harper's Magazine*

5. casus belli (occasion for war)
   He stabbed him, accordingly, in the midst of the Algonquin chiefs, who in requital killed the murderer. Here was a *casus belli* involving most serious issues for the French. — Francis Parkman

6. de facto (from the fact)
   A growing problem in every big Northern city, *de facto* segrega-

tion results from slum housing, racial ghettos and rigid school zoning laws. — *Time*

7. de jure (from right)

   It was not until late in 1940 that the Allies gave *de jure* recognition to the Czechoslovak government-in-exile . . . — *Harper's Magazine*

8. deus ex machina (a god from a machine)

   The strength of the enemy was so great that without some *deus ex machina* in the form of a secret weapon victory was impossible.

9. ex cathedra (from the chair)

   He advanced with a very doctorial air, placed himself behind a chair, on which he leaned as on a desk or pulpit, and then delivered, ex cathedra, a mock solemn charge. — Washington Irving

10. ex officio (from the office)

    At the top, of course, are the officers of the Corps of Engineers, who are ex officio members of the Rivers and Harbors Congress. — *Harper's Magazine*

11. ex post facto (from what is done afterwards)

    Ex post facto laws are prohibited by our constitution and are rightfully considered contrary to good morals and natural law. — *Atlantic Monthly*

12. in toto (in the whole)

    For example, a supersonic beam may be reflected almost *in toto* by a brick wall, but only partially by a privet hedge. — *Atlantic Monthly*

13. ipso facto (by the very fact)

    As the Army expanded, everyone managed to have some innocent fun with the idea that the officer was *ipso facto* a gentleman. — *Harper's Magazine*

14. modus operandi (manner of operating)

    But for the present the committee has decided to seek with the New York publishers a voluntary *modus operandi* under which both courts and newspapers would endeavor to protect the rights of defendants. — *Harper's Magazine*

15. modus vivendi (way of living)

    This government at last even considered offering the Japanese a "modus vivendi" calling for a three months' truce . . . — *Harper's Magazine*

16. ne plus ultra (no more beyond)
All those works of scholarship, which seemed to our ancestors the *ne plus ultra* of refinement, are now relegated to the lumber-room of erudition that has been superseded. — John Addington Symonds

17. non sequitur (it does not follow)
. . . evade the law by patching together a rat's nest of innuendo, *non sequitur* and irrelevancy. — *Time*

18. per capita (by heads)
New England still produces some lumber, but well below the national average per capita . . . —*Harper's Magazine*

19. per diem (by the day)
. . . generous per diem allowances for employees trapped by high hotel expenses. — *Harper's Magazine*

20. per se (by himself or itself)
No man was either great or good per se, but as compared with others not so good or great. — James Boswell

21. persona non grata (a person not acceptable)
The embassy official was declared *persona non grata* by the Cuban government.

22. prima facie (on the first appearance)
If anyone does an act hurtful to others, there is a prima facie case for punishing him, by law, or, where legal penalties are not applicable, by general disapprobation. — John Stuart Mill

23. pro tempore, pro tem. (for the time being)
He was elected President of the Senate pro tem.

24. reductio ad absurdum (reduction to an absurdity)
In this unlucky chapter the argument of the book confutes itself by a *reductio ad absurdum*. — Arnold Toynbee

25. sine die (without a day)
Amid confusion the legislature adjourned sine die. —Allan Nevins

26. sine qua non (without which not)
. . . an enlightened electorate is a *sine qua non* for success in our kind of government. —*Harper's Magazine*

LIST OF SUFFIXES (LATIN)

The Roman numerals in parentheses following the meanings indicate the lesson in which each suffix is to be found.

-able, -ible, able to be, etc. (XI)

-acious, tending to, etc. (XI)

-acity, quality of being inclined to (XV)

-acy, quality of being or having (XIV)

-al (-ial, -eal), pertaining to, etc. (VIII)

-an, see -ane

-ance, -ancy; -ence, -ency, quality of ——ing, etc. (XVIII)

-ane, -an (-ian), pertaining to, etc. (VIII)

-ant, -ent (-ient), present participial ending (X)

-ar, pertaining to, etc. (VIII)

-ary, pertaining to, etc. (IX)

-ary, (-arium), place for (XVIII)

-ate, possessing, etc. (X)

-ate, office of, etc. (XV)

-ate, verbal suffix (XX)

-cle, see -cule

-cule, -cle, little (XVII)

-egate, see -igate

-el, little (XVII)

-ence, -ency, see -ance

-ent, see -ant

-esce, to begin, etc. (XX)

-(i)fic, making, etc. (XXI)

-(i)fy, -(e)fy, to make (XXI)

-ible, see -able

-ic, -tic, pertaining to, etc. (IX)

-id, tending to, etc. (XII)

-igate, -egate, to make, etc. (XXI)

-il, little (XVII)

-il, see -ile, pertaining to

-ile, -il, pertaining to, etc. (IX)

-ile, able to be, etc. (XI)

-ine, pertaining to, etc. (X)

-ion, act of, etc. (XVI)

-itude, quality of, etc. (XIV)

-itious, tending to, etc. (XII)

-ity (-ety, -ty), quality of, etc. (XIV)

-ive, tending to, etc. (XIII)

-le, see -ole

-(u)lence, -(o)lence, state or quality of being full of (XIX)

-(u)lent, -(o)lent, full of, etc. (IX)

-men, result of, etc. (XVI)

-ment, result of, etc. (XVI)

-(i)mony, quality of (XV)

-ole, -ule, -le, little (XVII)

-or, one who does, etc. (XIX)

-or (-our), state of, etc. (XVIII)

-ory, tending to, etc. (XIII)

-ory (-orium), place for (XVIII)

-ose (-iose), full of (VIII)

-ous (-ious, -eous), full of, etc. (VIII)

-rix, she who does (XIX)

-tic, see -ic

-ule see -ole

-ulous, tending to, etc. (XII)

-uous, tending to, etc. (XIII)

-ure, act of, etc. (XIX)

-y, quality of, etc. (XV)

LIST OF BASES (LATIN)

The Roman numerals in parentheses following the meanings indicate the lesson in which each base is to be found.

A

ACR-, see AC(U)-
ACT-, see AG-
AC(U)-, ACR-, sharp (XII)
AG- (IG-), ACT-, to do, to drive (XVIII)
ALIEN-, of another (II)
AM-, to love (XIV)
ANIM-, mind, feeling, life (VII)
ANN(U)-, ENNI-, year (VII)
AQU(A)-, water (VIII)
ART-, art, skill (II)
AUD-, AUDIT-, to hear (XXIV)
AUDIT-, see AUD-

B

BELL-, war (IX)
BENE-, well, good (VII)
BENIGN-, kind (VII)
BI-, BIN-, two, twice (VI)
BIN-, see BI-

C

CAD- (CID-), CAS-, to fall, to befall (XII)
CALC-, limestone, pebble (XVII)
CAP- (CIP-), CAPT- (CEPT-), to take, to seize (XII)
CAPIT- (CIPIT-), head (XX)
CAPT-, see CAP-
CARN-, flesh (VIII)
CAS-, see CAD-
CED-, CESS-, to go, to yield (III)
CEIV-, see CAP-
CELER-, swift (XIV)
CENT-, hundred (VI)
CEPT-, see CAP-
CERN-, CRET-, to separate, to distinguish (XIII)
CESS-, see CED-
CEST-, see CAST-
CID-, see CAD-
CID-, CIS-, to kill, to cut (XV)
CIP-, see CAP-
CIPIT-, see CAPIT-
CIS-, see CID-
CLAIM-, see CLAM-
CLAM- (CLAIM-), to cry out (XVIII)
CLOS-, see CLUD-
CLUD-, CLUS- (CLOS-), to shut (V)
CLUS-, see CLUD-
CORD-, heart (XXIII)
CORP-, see CORPOR-
CORPOR-, CORP- (CORPUS-), body (VIII)
CORPUS-, see CORPOR-
COURS-, see CUR(R)-
CRE-, CRESC-, CRET-, to grow (XVI)
CRED-, CREDIT-, to believe, to trust (XI)
CRESC-, see CRE-
CRET-, see CERN-
CRET-, see CRE-
CRUC-, a cross (IV)
CUB-, see CUMB-

CULP-, blame, fault (XI)
CUMB-, CUB-, to lie down (X)
CUR (R)-, CURS-, (COURS-),
  to run, to go (V)
CURS-, see CUR(R)-

D

DE-, DIV-, a god (XIV)
DECI-, DECIM-, tenth (VI)
DIC-, DICT-, to say (XVIII)
DICT-, see DIC-
DIV-, see DE-
DOC-, DOCT-, to teach (XI)
DOCT-, see DOC-
DU-, two (VI)
DUC-, DUCT-, to lead (III)
DUCT-, see DUC-

E

ENNI-, see ANN(U)-
EQU-, equal, even (VII)
ERR-, to wander (XIX)

F

FA-, FAT-, to speak (XI)
FAC- (FIC-), FACT- (FECT-),
  to do, to make (XII)
FACT-, see FAC-
FALL-, FALS-, to deceive (XI)
FALS-, see FALL-
FAT-, see FA-
FECT-, see FAC-
FER-, to bear, to carry (XIX)
FERV-, to boil, to bubble (XII)
FIC-, see FAC-
FID-, faith (X)
FIDEL-, faithful (X)
FIN-, end, limit (II)
FIRM-, firm, strong (II)

FLECT-, FLEX-, to bend
  (XXIII)
FLEX-, see FLECT-
FLOR-, flower (XII)
FLU-, FLUX-, to flow (XII)
FLUX-, see FLU-
FORT-, strong (II)
FOUND-, see FUND-
FRACT-, see FRANG-
FRANG- (FRING-), FRACT-,
  to break (XVII)
FRING-, see FRANG-
FUND-, FUS-, (FOUND-), to
  pour, to melt (XIII)
FUS-, see FUND-

G

GEN-, GENIT-, to produce, to
  give birth to (XIII)
GEN-, see GENER-
GENER-, GEN-, race, kind
  (IX)
GENIT-, see GEN-
GER-, GEST-, to carry, to
  produce (XVIII)
GEST-, see GER-
GRAD-, GRESS-, to step, to go
  (V)
GRAN-, grain (XVII)
GRAND-, great (II)
GRAT-, pleasing, grateful
  (XXII)
GRAV-, heavy (II)
GREG-, flock, herd (IV)
GRESS-, see GRAD-

H

HER-, HES-, to stick (X)
HES-, see HER-

I

I-, IT-, to go (XVI)
IG-, see AG-
IT-, see I-

J

JAC-, JECT-, to throw (XIX)
JECT-, see JAC-
JOC-, joke (XVII)
JOIN-, see JUNCT-
JUDIC-, judgment (VIII)
JUNCT- (JOIN-), to join
  (XVI)
JUR-, to swear (III)

L

LAT-, to bear, to carry (XIX)
LATER-, side (IX)
LECT-, see LEG-
LEG- (LIG-), LECT-, to
  choose, to pick out, to read
  (XVI)
LEV-, light (in weight) (III)
LIG-, see LEG-
LINE-, line (II)
LITER-, letter, literature (XIV)
LOC-, place (XX)
LOCUT-, see LOQU-
LOQU-, LOCUT-, to speak (III)
LUC-, light, to shine (XIV)
LUD-, LUS-, to play, to mock
  (III)
LUMIN, light (IX)
LUS-, see LUD-

M

MAGN-, great (VII)
MAL(E)-, MALIGN-, bad (VII)
MALIGN-, see MAL(E)-

MAN(U)-, hand (XXIII)
MATERN-, see MATR-
MATR-, MATERN-, mother
  (XV)
MEDI-, middle (XXI)
MILIT-, soldier (XX)
MILL-, thousand (VI)
MINOR-, MINUS-, MINUT-,
  small, smaller (XVII)
MINUS-, see MINOR-
MINUT-, see MINOR-
MISC-, to mix (XXII)
MIS(S)-, see MIT(T)-
MIT-, mild, soft (XXI)
MIT(T)-, MIS(S)-, to send,
  to let go (XVIII)
MOLL-, mild, soft (XXI)
MON-, MONIT-, to warn,
  to advise (XVI)
MONIT-, see MON-
MORT-, death (XXI)
MOT-, see MOV-
MOV-, MOT-, to move (XXII)
MULT-, many VII)
MUT-, to change (XI)

N

NASC-, NAT-, to be born
  (XVIII)
NAT-, see NASC-
NEG-, to deny (XXII)
NOMEN-, NOMIN-, name,
  noun (XIX)
NOMIN-, see NOMEN-
-NOUNCE, see NUNCI-
NUL(L)-, nothing (II)
NUNCI- (-NOUNCE), to
  announce (XXIV)

O

OCT-, eight (VI)
OCTAV-, eighth (VI)
OMN-, all (VIII)
ORDIN-, order (X)
OUND-, see UND-

P

PART-, part (II)
PASS-, see PATI-
PATERN-, see PATR-
PATI-, PASS-, to endure,
 to suffer (XII)
PATR-, PATERN-, father (XV)
PATRI-, fatherland, country
 (XV)
PECUNI-, money (IX)
PED-, foot (IV)
PEL(L)-, PULS-, to drive,
 to push (XIII)
PEND-, PENS-, to hang, to
 weigh, to pay (V)
PENS-, see PEND-
PET-, PETIT-, to seek,
 to assail (XXI)
PETIT-, see PET-
PLAC-, to please, to appease (X)
PLE-, PLET-, to fill (V)
PLEN-, full (XV)
PLET-, see PLE-
PLEX-, see PLIC-
PLIC-, PLICIT-, PLEX-,
 (PLY-), to fold, to interweave,
 to tangle (VII)
PLICIT-, see PLIC-
PLY-, see PLIC-
PON-, POSIT-, (POUND-),
 (-POSE), to place, to put
 (XIII)

PORT-, to carry (XXIII)
-POSE, see PON-
POSIT-, see PON-
POT-, to have power (X)
POUND-, see PON-
PREC-, prayer (III)
PRED-, prey (XXI)
PRESS-, to press (XXIV)
PRIM-, first (VI)
PROB- (PROV-), good, to test
 (XIV)
PROL-, offspring (XXI)
PROPRI-, one's own, fitting
 (XXIV)
PROV-, see PROB-
PUGN-, fight (XXI)
PULS-, see PEL(L)-
PUNCT-, see PUNG-
PUNG-, PUNCT-, to prick,
 point (IV)
PURG-, to clean (XXII)
PUT-, to reckon, to think (XX)

Q

QUADR(U)-, four (VI)
QUART-, fourth (VI)
QUEST-, see QUIR-
QUINT-, fifth (VI)
QUIR-, QUISIT- (QUEST-),
 to ask, to seek (XVII)
QUISIT-, see QUIR-

R

RADIC-, root (XX)
RECT-, right, straight (VIII)
RECT-, see REG-
REG- (RIG-), RECT-, to
 straighten, to rule (XII)
RIG-, see REG-

ROG-, to ask (XX)
RUPT-, to break (XVI)

S

SACR- (SECR-), sacred (IV)
SAL- (SIL-), SALT- (SULT-),
  to leap (X)
SALT-, see SAL-
SANCT-, holy (XV)
SANGUIN-, blood (IX)
SATI(S)-, enough (XXIV)
SCI-, to know (XIII)
SCRIB-, SCRIPT-, to write
  (XIX)
SCRIPT-, see SCRIB-
SEC- (SEG-), SECT-, to cut
  (XVII)
SECR-, see SACR-
SECT-, see SEC-
SECUT- see SEQU-
SED- (SID-), SESS-, to sit,
  to settle (X)
SEG-, see SEC-
SEMI-, half, partly (VI)
SEN-, old (IX)
SENS-, see SENT-
SENT-, SENS-, to feel, to think
  (IV)
SEPT-, SEPTEM-, seven (VI)
SEPTEM-, see SEPT-
SEQU-, SECUT-, to follow
  (XV)
SERV-, to serve, to save (IX)
SESS-, see SED-
SEXT-, sixth, six (VI)
SID-, see SED-
SIL-, see SAL-
SIMIL-, SIMUL-, like (VIII)
SOL-, alone (XV)
SOLUT-, see SOLV-

SOLV-, SOLUT-, to loosen,
  to free (XVI)
SON-, sound (XVIII)
SPEC- (SPIC-), SPECT-,
  to look (V)
SPECT-, see SPEC-
SPIC-, see SPEC-
SPIR-, to breathe (XX)
ST(A)-, STAT-, to stand (XIX)
STAT-, see STA-
STRAIN-, see STRING-
STRICT-, see STRING-
STRING-, STRICT-,
  (STRAIN-), to draw tight
  (XIII)
STRU-, STRUCT-, to build
  (XXIII)
STRUCT-, see STRU-
SULT-, see SAL-

T

TACT-, see TANG-
TAIN-, see TEN-
TANG- (TING-), TACT-,
  to touch (XI)
TEMPOR-, time (VIII)
TEN- (TIN-), TENT- (TAIN-),
  to hold (XI)
TEND-, TENS-, TENT-, to
  stretch, to strive (XXII)
TENS- see TEND-
TENT-, see TEN- or TEND-
TENU-, thin (VIII)
TERMIN-, boundary, end
  (XXIII)
TIN-, see TEN-
TING-, see TANG-
TORQU-, TORT-, to twist
  (XIII)
TORT-, see TORQU-

TRACT-, to drag, to draw (XI)
TRI-, three (VI)
TRIT-, to rub, to wear (XVI)
TRUD-, TRUS-, to push,
   to thrust (III)
TRUS-, see TRUD-
TURB-, to disturb (IV)

U

UN-, one (VI)
UND- (OUND-), wave (V)

V

VAIL-, see VAL-
VAL- (VAIL-), to be strong,
   to be worth (XVIII)
VEN-, VENT-, to come (III)
VENT-, see VEN-
VER-, true (XIV)

VERB-, word, verb (II)
VERS-, see VERT-
VERT-, VERS-, to turn (IV)
VEST-, garment (II)
VI-, way, road (IV)
VICT-, see VINC-
VID-, VIS-, to see (V)
VINC-, VICT-, to conquer
   (XXIII)
VIR-, poison (XIX)
VIS-, see VID-
VIV-, to live (XV)
VOC- (VOK-), voice, to call (V)
VOK-, see VOC-
VOL-, to wish (VII)
VOLUT-, see VOLV-
VOLV-, VOLUT-, to roll (XIX)
VOR-, to devour (VIII)
VULG-, common (XXII)

PART TWO
WORD ELEMENTS FROM GREEK

INTRODUCTION

IN GENERAL, Greek has not exerted so continuous nor so extensive an influence upon English as Latin has. In many specialized areas of study, however, Greek has furnished the majority of technical terms and even more than Latin has become the language of science. Since we live in a scientific age, therefore, the study of the Greek elements in our language will be found as useful as the study of the Latin elements. Furthermore, compound words of Greek origin tend to be more self-explanatory than those of Latin, so that a knowledge of bases, prefixes, and suffixes is often even more helpful in the case of the former.

Words of Greek origin have generally entered English in one of three ways: (1) they have come indirectly by way of Latin; (2) they have been borrowed directly from Greek writers; (3) especially in the case of scientific terms, they have been formed in modern times by combining Greek elements in new ways.

I. Until the Renaissance there was little direct contact between Greek and English; Greek was known to only a handful of scholars in Western Europe during the Middle Ages. But, as we have seen from the Introduction to Part I (pp. 8-9), there was considerable borrowing from Latin by English during the early periods, and many Greek words had become part of the Latin language.

The reason why Latin was greatly influenced by Greek is not difficult to see. When Rome was little more than a collection of shepherds' huts beside the Tiber, Greece possessed a great and flourishing civilization. Eventually, of course, Roman armies conquered Greece, but the conqueror was in turn taken captive by

136

Greek culture. Greek poetry and drama provided the models for Roman literature; Greek statues adorned the homes of Roman statesmen; Roman students flocked to Athens to complete their education by studying Greek philosophy and oratory. It was only natural, then, that many Greek words should have been introduced into Latin.

Thus, on the various occasions when Latin words were being borrowed by English, words of Greek were entering as well. Some of the products, for instance, which Roman civilization introduced to the primitive Teutonic tribes who later brought their language to the British Isles (see p. 8) bore Greek names; e.g., *butter* (Greek, *boutyron*), *dish* (Greek, *diskos*), and *mint* (Greek, *mentha*). Christianity arose in an area where Greek served as the common language and, when the new religion reached Rome, it brought with it a number of Greek words. These were in turn introduced into English when Roman missionaries converted the Angles and Saxons (see p. 8). Such Greek words as *alms, anthem,* and *deacon* were borrowed in this fashion by our language.

II.   The great majority of words from Greek, however, have been borrowed in a more direct fashion. With the Renaissance (see pp. 9-10) came a revival of interest in classical antiquity. The study of Greek began to flourish again, and terms were borrowed from the works of the great Greek writers by men who were almost as familiar with the language of Plato and Aristotle as with their own and who regarded the ancient authors as the supreme thinkers and models of literary expression.

III.   Once a considerable number of Greek words were to be found in English, these began to be combined and recombined in ways never known to the Greeks, and among many of the sciences today this has become the accepted practice in forming words to designate new discoveries. Such modern medical terms as *antibiotic, leukemia, allergy, poliomyelitis,* and *electrocardiograph* were coined in this way from Greek elements, while in other biological sciences have appeared terms like *chromosome, protoplasm* and *chlorophyll,* also formed in recent times from the Greek. In psychology the same process has given us *schizophrenia, psychiatry, kleptomania,* and *psychoneurosis.*

ASSIGNMENT

The words which came from Greek before the Renaissance were generally popular borrowings, that is, they were adopted by the common people, who knew no Greek, rather than by scholars. Furthermore, such words often entered English indirectly, not only by way of Latin, but sometimes by way of Old French, or even, in some cases, through Arabic. They therefore usually show considerable divergence in form from the Greek original. Sometimes the same Greek word was later reborrowed with a different meaning and in a form more closely resembling the Greek.

I. The following words have come from Greek. With the aid of a dictionary give the Greek word from which each is derived and the meaning of the Greek word; also give another English derivative more closely resembling the original Greek form. (In most cases this will be a doublet; see p. 107).

Examples: *dish* (Greek, *diskos,* "quoit," "discus") — *disk* (or *discus*)
treasure (Greek, *thesauros,* "a treasure") — *thesaurus*

1. bishop	6. glamour
2. blame	7. palsy
3. chair	8. parole
4. desk	9. priest
5. devil	10. story

II. With the aid of a dictionary trace the route of each of the following words from Greek to Modern English:

1. alms	5. elixir
2. box	6. pew
3. chimney	7. prow (of a ship)
4. church	

III. The following common English words are also derived from Greek. In the case of each give the Greek original and its meaning.

1. almond	7. lantern
2. cherry	8. licorice
3. date (fruit)	9. place
4. fancy	10. surgeon, surgery
5. frantic	11. truck (vehicle)
6. guitar	

LESSON I Words from Greek Mythology

Many words in our language have been derived from proper names, the names of people, cities, etc. One obvious purpose in the formation of such words is to designate scientific or technical processes and inventions. For example, the verb *pasteurize* is derived from the name of the celebrated scientist who discovered the process, Louis Pasteur. A grimmer example of this type is seen in the French instrument of execution, the guillotine, which is called by the name of the man who proposed its use during the Reign of Terror. (He was not himself executed by this device, as is often supposed). The origins of many terms, however, are more obscure although they are just as interesting; for example, the word *derrick,* which now has a quite commonplace meaning, comes from the surname of a well-known 17th century hangman of Tyburn Prison in London.

Frequently a product is named from the place where it was first produced. This is particularly true with types of cloth and clothing. Thus, *calico* was originally imported from Calicut, a city in India; *muslin,* from *Mosul,* a city in what is now Iraq. *Jean,* a cloth used in blue jeans, was first made in Genoa, and *denim* is short for *serge de Nîmes,* "serge of Nîmes," a city in Southern France. Also, this practice of naming products after places seems almost invariable in the case of European wines, *port,* for instance, coming from Oporto, in Portugal, and *sherry,* from Xeres (Jerez), a Spanish town near Cadiz.

In other cases, the name of an individual famous in history, literature, or legend has become proverbial for some particular characteristic. Thus, we speak of a traitor as a *Judas;* and an uncultured, unenlightened person is a *Philistine.* Both of these examples are, of course, taken from the Bible, which has given us many other terms including *babel, Nimrod, doubting Thomas,* and *good Samaritan.* Along with the Bible, Greek culture has also greatly enriched the vocabulary of our language in this fashion. The mythology of the Greeks especially has impressed itself upon European literature and art, as is shown by the following passage from Shakespeare, where Hamlet describes his dead father:

> See what a grace was seated on this brow;
> Hyperion's curls, the front of Jove himself,
> An eye like Mars to threaten and command;
> A station like the herald Mercury
> New-lighted on a heaven-kissing hill.

The legends of Greece, with their gods and heroes, have consequently provided English with more words derived from proper names than perhaps any other single source, and many of these words have extremely interesting backgrounds.

The following are some of the words which Greek mythology has contributed to English together with examples of their use and brief descriptions of their origins. You will find that a knowledge of the background of such words will make them more vivid and will often give them added significance. Note that some of these words are still capitalized, while others have been used as common nouns to such an extent that they are generally written with a small initial letter.

1. *Achilles' heel,* "a single vulnerable spot"

Lack of oil was the *Achilles' heel* of Japan's wartime economy.

Achilles was the greatest of the Greek heroes who took part in the Trojan War, and in this war he was killed. His mother, a goddess, was aware that her son was fated to die in battle, and she did everything in her power to protect him. When he was a baby, she dipped him in the River Styx (see below), the waters of which rendered his body invulnerable. But she held Achilles by his heel, which the water consequently did not touch. During the siege of Troy he received a fatal wound from an arrow that struck this one unprotected part.

2. *Adonis,* "an extremely handsome young man"

The casting director's office was full of *Adonises* waiting for screen tests.

Adonis was a very beautiful youth, so beautiful in fact that the goddess Aphrodite (or Venus) fell in love with him. When Adonis was killed while hunting a wild boar, Aphrodite was inconsolable and obtained from Zeus, king of the gods, the promise that her beloved might leave the Underworld to spend part of each year with her.

3. *aegis,* "sponsorship or protection"

Rome remained inviolable beneath the *aegis* of her ancient prestige.
—John Addington Symonds

In Greek mythology the aegis was a piece of armor or shield worn by Zeus and later by the goddess Athena. It was not only an awesome defense but filled with horror those against whom it was shaken.

4. *aeolian,* "produced by the wind"

There was never yet such a storm, but it was *aeolian* music to healthy and innocent ears. —Thoreau

Aeolus was appointed by the gods to rule the winds, which he kept imprisoned in a vast cavern on an island in the Mediterranean. For those whom he liked he would release favorable winds, but against those who had incurred his wrath or the wrath of the gods he would send wild storms. When Odysseus (see below) was trying to sail back to Greece after the Trojan War, he put in at Aeolus' island and appealed to the king for help. Aeolus gave him a leather bag which contained all of the unfavorable winds, so that only favoring breezes were free to drive his ship homeward. But when Odysseus had almost reached his goal, while he was asleep, the members of his crew opened the bag thinking that it was full of gold and silver. Immediately the adverse winds rushed forth and blew Odysseus' ship back to its starting point.

5. *amazon,* "a powerful, masculine woman"

. . . the professional women, the emancipated *amazons* of Marxist society. —*Time*

The Amazons were a legendary race of female warriors who supposedly lived in the region of the Black Sea and often fought the Greeks. In the Trojan War they were allies of Troy, and their queen was slain by Achilles. The great river in South America received its name from the fact that early Spanish explorers, during battles with the Indians along its banks, observed women fighting beside the men.

6. *atlas,* "a collection of maps"

Atlas, one of the Titans (see below), was condemned to support the world on his shoulders. Apparently because early books of maps so frequently pictured Atlas performing this task, they came to bear his name. In anatomical terminology *atlas* refers also to the first vertebra of the neck, which supports the skull as the giant supposedly did the world.

7. *Cassandra,* "a person who warns of coming evil but whose prophecies are disregarded"

I have, as you know, long foretold the now approaching catastrophe; but I was *Cassandra.* —Lord Chesterfield

Cassandra was a Trojan princess with whom the god Apollo fell in love. To win her favors, he bestowed on her the gift of prophecy, but when she resisted his advances, instead of taking back his gift, he decreed a far worse punishment, that no one should believe her warnings. Thus Cassandra was condemned to the frustration of prophesying in vain the fall of Troy, while her hearers not only failed to heed her but regarded her dire predictions as the ravings of an insane person.

8. *chimera,* "a foolish or idle fancy"

All those alarms which have been sounded . . . must be ascribed to the *chimerical* fears of the authors of them. —*The Federalist*

The Chimera was a fire-breathing monster with the head of a lion, the body of a goat, and the tail of a dragon. It was so fantastic a hybrid that it became the symbol of vain imaginings.

9. *Elysium,* "place or state of blissful happiness"

Again you say, you much fear that that *Elysium* of which you have dreamed so much is never to be realized. —Abraham Lincoln

In Greek mythology the Elysian Fields or Elysium was the abode after death of those who had led good lives; it was a region of ideal happiness, to some extent the equivalent of the Christian heaven.

10. *halcyon,* "calm, peaceful"

During those *halcyon* years before the invasion of Charles VIII, it seemed as though the peace of Italy might last unbroken. —Symonds

The expression *halcyon days,* meaning a period of calm and tranquility, takes its origin from the ancient belief that the kingfisher, called *halcyon* by the Greeks, hatched its young in a nest floating on the sea. During its nesting period the bird supposedly calmed the weather by means of a magic charm so that the waves were quiet and it could brood undisturbed.

According to myth, the kingfisher, whose Greek name was also spelled *alcyon,* had once been a woman, Alcyone, wife of Ceyx, the king of Thessaly. Alcyone had mourned so piteously for her husband who was drowned in the ocean that the gods changed both into sea birds so that they might be reunited.

11. *herculean,* "very powerful"

He was short in stature . . . but his limbs were of *Herculean* mold. —Edgar Allan Poe

Hercules, the son of Zeus and a mortal mother, was of course the strongest of all the heroes of Greek fable. In particular, he was renowned for a series of mighty deeds, the "labors of Hercules," imposed upon him by the goddess Hera, who hoped that he would be killed in the performance of them.

12. *hydra,* "a persistent evil, one difficult to eradicate"

Thirteen independent courts of final jurisdiction over the same causes . . . is a *hydra* in government from which nothing but contradiction and confusion can proceed. —*The Federalist*

One of the labors of Hercules was to slay the Hydra, a poisonous water serpent with nine heads whose very breath was fatal. The difficulty of this task was increased by the fact that, when one of the heads was cut off, two more grew in its place; but Hercules solved the problem by having an assistant sear the neck with a hot iron after each head had been severed.

13. *labyrinth,* "a complicated arrangement of passageways or roads, a maze"

We rattled with great rapidity through such a *labyrinth* of streets, that I soon lost all idea where we were. —Dickens

The original labyrinth was a huge structure full of intricate passageways, which was built at the order of King Minos of Crete as a place of confinement for the Minotaur, a monster half bull and half man. Those whom the King wished to destroy were placed in the labyrinth, from which they were unable to find an exit, and where they wandered until they were discovered and eaten by the Minotaur or died of starvation.

14. *mentor,* "a wise counselor"

Had she been brought up by any sterner *mentor* than that fond father . . . she might perhaps have saved herself from this great fault. —Anthony Trollope

Mentor, a word usually found nowadays in the sports section of newspapers where it refers to a football coach, comes from the name of the faithful adviser to whom Odysseus entrusted the education of his son when he sailed away to fight at Troy.

15. *Midas,* "a very rich man"

You could feel just as certain that he was opulent as if he had exhibited his bank account, or as if you had seen him touching the twigs of the Pyncheon Elm, and, *Midas*-like, transmuting them to gold.—Hawthorne

Midas was a legendary king of Asia Minor, whose desire for riches was apparently exceeded only by his lack of intelligence. Once he had performed a service for one of the gods and in return was granted the fulfillment of a wish. Without thinking, Midas asked to be given the power of turning into gold whatever he touched. To his dismay, however, he discovered that not only the roses in his garden and the tables in his palace were changed to gold, but also the food and drink which he tried in vain to swallow. So he was the richest and hungriest king in all the world until the god had pity on him and told him to rid himself of this fatal gift by bathing in the River Pactolus, whose sands were ever after rich in gold.

16. *myrmidon,* "a subordinate who obeys orders unquestioningly and often cruelly"

The best hotel, and all its culinary *myrmidons,* were set to work to prepare for the feast. —*Dickens*

The Myrmidons were the troops led by Achilles in the Trojan War, and were the fiercest and best disciplined of all the Greek contingents. According to one legend, Zeus had created the Myrmidons by transforming ants (Greek, *myrmex*) into human beings.

17. *narcissism,* "abnormal attachment to one's own appearance and personality"

Psychologists set forth that anyone who becomes an actor in the first place must be a *narcissist,* yearning for ever-new romantic mirrors to provide adoration. —*Time*

Narcissus was a beautiful youth whom the nymph Echo loved. When he did not return her affection, Echo pined away from grief until nothing was left of her but her voice. Aphrodite, however, punished Narcissus for his cruel neglect. One day, as he leaned down to drink from a clear pool, he spied his own reflection in the water and at once fell in love with it. Unable to tear himself away, he was consumed by his longing for this figure which he saw in the pool and finally was changed into the flower which bears his name.

18. *nemesis,* "retribution, one who inflicts retribution"

The fantastic valuation which we put upon youthful beauty in women, for example, brings its *nemesis* in bedizened crones. —*Atlantic Monthly*

Nemesis was a goddess, the personification of righteous anger. She hated every transgression of the proper order of things and visited upon the wicked punishment for their sins.

19. *Nestor,* "a wise old counselor, an elder statesman"

One morning we were summoned to the lodge of an old man, the *Nestor* of his tribe. —Francis Parkman

Nestor was the oldest of the Greek kings who took part in the Trojan War. At the councils of the leaders his voice carried great weight because of his vast experience and wisdom, and his advice was always asked regarding important decisions.

20. *odyssey,* "a long series of wanderings"

He made his way on foot from Cairo to South Africa, and on his return to America he described his *odyssey* in a long article.

Homer's epic poem, the *Odyssey,* tells of the wanderings of the Greek hero Odysseus in attempting to return to his home and family at the conclusion of the Trojan War. After being driven by adverse winds and by the anger of the gods over the wide reaches of the Mediterranean, and after encountering many strange adventures and misfortunes, Odysseus finally reached his native land ten years after he had set sail from Troy.

21. *Oedipus* (complex), "an abnormal attachment to one's parent of the opposite sex with corresponding hostility to the other."

Also, Freud's unusual family setting, with a young mother, but a father old enough to be his grandfather, led to overemphasis on *Oedipal* feelings. — *Time*

Like the story of Narcissus, the myth of Oedipus has suggested to modern psychologists the name for a mental state. Oedipus, the subject of a famous tragedy by Sophocles, learned of a prophecy that he would one day kill his father and marry his mother. He did all in his power to avoid this dreadful fate, only to discover, after he had risen to greatness, that despite his efforts the prophecy had come true, whereupon he blinded himself and went into exile.

22. *Olympian*, "exalted, majestic"

He, the ruler of that minute world, seldom descended from the *Olympian* heights — Joseph Conrad

The most familiar of the Greek gods are those who dwelt on Mt. Olympus, Zeus, or Jupiter, to give him his Roman name, Hera or Juno, Aphrodite or Venus, and the rest. Though there are many stories about their scandalous behavior, *Olympian* today refers to the calm, imposing, majestic natures of these divine beings in their better moments, as they are represented, for instance, in classical Greek sculpture.

23. *paean*, "a song of thanksgiving or praise"

For the press received the news of Gordon's mission with a *paean* of approbation. — Lord Elton

Paean came to be a name of the god Apollo, one of whose attributes was the power of healing. Many hymns of thanksgiving for recovery from illness and for averting evil were addressed to him under this title, and eventually *paean* was used to designate any hymn of thanksgiving or praise.

24. *Procrustean*, "forcing rigid conformity"

He was disposed to place all their separate and individual charters on a *Procrustean* bed, and shape them all into uniformity simply by reducing the whole to a nullity. — John Lothrop Motley

Procrustes was a legendary highwayman who possessed a grim sense of humor. He forced his victims to lie in an iron bed. Those who were too short he stretched; the limbs of those who were too long he lopped off with his sword, so that one way or the other all who fell into his hands were killed by being made to fit exactly his famous bed.

25. *protean,* "extremely changeable"

Man, being a *Protean* animal, swiftly shares and changes with his company and surroundings. — Robert Louis Stevenson

Proteus, the herdsman of the sea in Greek mythology, was able to change his shape at will. In the *Odyssey* an incident is described where one of the Greek heroes attempted to capture him. Trying to escape, Proteus turned himself first into a lion, then a snake, finally into running water and even into a tree.

26. *siren,* "an alluring but dangerous woman, seductive"

The *siren* cries of nothing down, easy credit and pay later have made the installment plan an essential part of the U. S. economy. — *Time*

The Sirens were nymphs, part woman and part bird, who sat on an island surrounded by the bones of sailors whom they had lured to destruction by the magic of their singing. Odysseus in his wanderings sailed past this island but stuffed the ears of his crewmen with wax so that they were immune to the charms of the Sirens' song. Leaving his own ears unplugged, however, he had himself bound to the ship's mast so that he could hear and yet not be enticed to his death.

27. *stentorian,* "very loud"

In another second or two the nightcap was thrust out of the chaise-window, and a *stentorian* voice bellowed to the driver to stop. — Dickens

Stentor, who was the herald of the Greek army at Troy, was reputed to have a voice as loud as the voices of fifty ordinary men.

28. *Stygian,* "dark, gloomy"

His debauched and reprobate life cast a *Stygian* gloom over the evening of his father's days. — Samuel Johnson

The Styx, as we saw in connection with Achilles, was a river of the Underworld; across it the souls of the dead were ferried by the grim old boatman Charon. To the ancients the Underworld was generally a place of darkness and gloom.

29. *tantalize*

There lives no man who at some period has not been tormented, for example, by an earnest desire to *tantalize* a listener by circumlocution. —Edgar Allan Poe

Tantalus was admitted to the friendship of the gods, but then tried to deceive them. As punishment they decreed that he should stand eternally in a pool of water in Hades over which hung fruit-laden boughs. Whenever he leaned down for a drink, however, the water receded, and whenever he tried to pick the fruit, the branches were blown out of his reach. Thus Tantalus stood, suffering forever the pangs of hunger and thirst which were made all the keener by the nearness of food and drink.

30. *titanic,* "of enormous size and power"

General Smith does not expect that Stalin's death will precipitate a *titanic* struggle such as followed Lenin's. — *Atlantic Monthly*

The Titans were a race of primeval giants, the children of Earth and Heaven, who ruled the universe before the Olympian gods with whom they fought long and bitterly. Finally the Titans were overthrown by the thunderbolts of Zeus in a war that lasted for ten years and almost destroyed the world.

Not included here are the innumerable botanical and zoological names drawn from classical mythology. Some of these names have little or no connection with their source, but others were bestowed because the organism thus designated has some characteristic of the person after whom it was named. Thus *Hydra* also refers to a genus of fresh-water polyps, so called by Linnaeus because cutting apart the bodies of these animals only serves to increase their numbers.

To cite a few more examples, Atropos was one of the Three Fates, the grim sisters who were thought of by the Greeks as spinning out the destiny of each man's life in the form of a thread and who cut it at the appointed time. Her name has provided the scientific designation for the deadly nightshade, *Atropa belladonna,* the source of the highly poisonous alkaloid atropine. Lachesis, another of the Fates, has given her name to the bushmaster, *Lachesis mutus,* the deadliest snake in the Western Hemisphere.

The Polyphemus moth (*Telea polyphemus*) was named for the grotesque giant Polyphemus, who had a single huge eye in the middle of his forehead. (He tried to eat Odysseus and was blinded by the hero.) The scientific use of the name is an allusion to the fact that the moth has a large eye-shaped marking on its wings.

PRONUNCIATION EXERCISE

I. Indicate the pronunciation of the following:

1. The **ae** of *aegis* is pronounced like (1) the **i** in *bite* (2) the **a** in *gate* (3) the **e** in *equal* (4) the **e** in *tent*.

2. The **g** of *aegis* is pronounced like the **g** in (1) *get* (2) *gem* (3) *tongue*.

3. The **ch** of *chimera* is pronounced like (1) the **c** in *certain* (2) the **c** in *can* (3) the **sh** in *shell* (4) the **ch** in *chair*.

4. The **i** of *chimera* is pronounced like the **i** in (1) *bite* (2) *sanity* (3) *tin*.

5. The **c** of *halcyon* is pronounced like (1) the **c** in *certain* (2) the **c** in *can* (3) the **sh** in *shell* (4) the **ch** in *chair*.

6. The **a** of *labyrinth* is pronounced like the **a** in (1) *gate* (2) *father* (3) *about* (4) *land*.

7. The **y** of *labyrinth* is pronounced like the **i** in (1) *bite* (2) *sanity* (3) *tin*.

8. The **i** of *Midas* is pronounced like the **i** in (1) *bite* (2) *sanity* (3) *tin*.

9. The **y** of *myrmidon* is pronounced like (1) the **e** in *here* (2) the **i** in *tin* (3) the **i** in *bite* (4) the **u** in *urge*.

10. The **oe** of *Oedipus* is pronounced like the **e** in (1) *equal* (2) *agent* (3) *tent*.

11. The **u** of *Oedipus* is pronounced like the **u** in (1) *sue* (2) *put* (3) *cube* (4) *up*.

12. The **ae** of *paean* is pronounced like (1) the **i** in *bite* (2) the **a** in *gate* (3) the **e** in *equal* (4) the **e** in *tent*.

13. The **e** of *siren* is pronounced like the **e** in (1) *equal* (2) *agent* (3) *tent*.

14. The **y** of *Stygian* is pronounced like the **i** in (1) *bite* (2) *sanity* (3) *tin*.

II. Circle the syllable on which the primary accent falls in each of the following:

1. aeolian
2. chimera
3. herculean
4. labyrinth

5. narcissism
6. nemesis
7. Procrustean
8. stentorian

LESSON II   Words from Greek History and Philosophy

At a time when a thorough acquaintance with classical culture was the mark of an educated man, a number of words from the names of persons, or places, or institutions connected with Greek history and philosophy entered our language. In fact, by tracing the origins of many of these words, one can see reflected some of the great events of Greek life and thought. Thus, the long race known as a *marathon* received its designation from the Plain of Marathon, the site of a historic victory by the Athenians over the Persian invaders, because the messenger who reported the good news to Athens ran so swiftly. The modern race of approximately 26 miles represents the distance between Athens and Marathon. *Solon,* a term generally seen nowadays in newspapers with reference to a senator, was originally the name of a statesman who was commissioned to reform the laws of Athens and whose wise measures marked perhaps the beginning of Western democracy.

I. The following are some of the words which Greek culture and history have contributed to English together with examples of their use and brief descriptions of their origins.

1. *academy,* "a school or learned society"

The financially successful painters were the *academicians* who perpetuated the mannerisms of the past. — *Harper's Magazine*

Near Athens was a grove of olive trees sacred to the hero Academus. In this grove the philosopher Plato and his successors taught, and this school of philosophy was consequently known as the *Academy*. Because of the school's vast influence upon European thought, the name passed into the language to designate various types of educational institutions or learned groups.

2. *Arcadian,* "simple, peaceful, rustic"

We had in this region, twenty years ago, among our educated men, a sort of *Arcadian* fanaticism, a passionate desire to go upon the land and unite farming to intellectual pursuits. — Emerson

The region of Greece known in classical times as Arcadia is quite mountainous. It was therefore rather inaccessible and so was proverbial for its peaceful, rustic way of life.

3. *Croesus,* "a very rich man"

You are aware that my father — once reckoned a *Croesus* of wealth — became bankrupt a short time previous to his death. —Charlotte Brontë

Croesus, like Midas, was a very wealthy king of Asia Minor. Croesus, however, was a historical figure, while Midas was legendary. In an age of barter Croesus' kingdom had been one of the first nations to mint coins of precious metal; it had, so to speak, invented money. (This was actually before Croesus' time, however.) Also, Croesus sent magnificent offerings to the temples of Greece, and these likewise impressed the Greeks with his wealth and luxury. Later his kingdom was conquered by the Persians, and his life was consequently regarded as furnishing the supreme example of a disastrous change of fortune.

4. *cynic,* "one who sarcastically doubts human motives"

To every remonstrance he listened with a *cynical* sneer, wondering within himself whether those who lectured him were such fools as they professed to be, or were only shamming. — Macaulay

A *Cynic* was originally a member of a Greek philosophical school noted for its exaggerated contempt of social conventions and institutions. The most famous of the Cynics, Diogenes, since he wished to show the uselessness of civilized customs, lived in a large earthenware tub; and, to demonstrate his scorn for the rest of society, he went about in broad daylight with a lantern looking, as he said, for an honest man.

5. *Draconian,* "extremely severe"

Thanks to Macmillan's *Draconian* measures, Britain stood a good chance of staving off fiscal disaster . . . —*Time*

In the seventh century B.C. Draco was given special authority by the Athenians to codify and systematize their laws. In the resulting code certain minor offenses, such as stealing a cabbage, were made punishable by death, and the laws of Draco thus gained a reputation for severity that caused one Greek orator to describe them as having been written not in ink but in blood.

6. *epicure,* "a person of refined taste in matters of food and drink"

Only an *epicure* would be willing to pay so much for these delicacies.

Epicurus was the founder of a school of philosophy which held that the supreme goal of life should be pleasure. He carefully elaborated this doctrine, however, and taught that the most effective way to achieve pleasure is through the avoidance of pain, by living temperately and righteously so as to avoid the anxieties caused by immoral acts and unnecessary desires. Actually, then, the man who led a blameless life would find the greatest amount of pleasure in the long run. Unfortunately, many people, including some who claimed to be Epicurus' followers, failed to note his restriction of the idea of pleasure, and so his name has unfairly become associated with the doctrine of "eat, drink, and be merry," and in particular has reference to the delights of the table.

7. to cut the *Gordian* knot, "to solve a difficult problem by direct and drastic means"

Never was such a tangled knottiness,
But this authority cuts the *Gordian* through. — Browning

According to legend, a king named Gordius once tied an extremely intricate knot, whereupon a prophecy arose that whoever untied it would rule Asia. Many tried and failed, and the knot remained on public display until Alexander the Great, on being shown it and finding himself unable to penetrate its intricacies, whipped out his sword and cut it, thus turning the prophecy to his advantage by showing that he would become ruler of Asia with the sword. The whole story is highly improbable but it has given our language an expressive phrase.

8. *helot,* "a slave or serf"

A *Helot* feeling, compounded of awe and hatred, is but too often discernible in the children of the vanquished. — Macaulay

When the Spartans (see below) conquered the area of Greece where they dwelt in historical times, they reduced the original inhabitants to the status of serfs, who were called *Helots*. Now slavery was a universal practice in ancient Greece, but the life of the Helots was perhaps worse than that of most slaves. They were the property not of individual owners but of the state, and a systematic terrorism at the hands of a secret police kept them in subjection. Each year the government of Sparta went through the formality of declaring war on them so that any of their number who seemed at all likely to cause trouble might be summarily executed.

9. *laconic,* "brief, pithy, concise"

He seemed to be of a *laconic* disposition, and merely said — "How goes it?" — Dickens

Laconia was another name for Sparta. (Actually it was the district of Greece in which the city of Sparta was located.) The Spartan citizens were trained from childhood to be soldiers and little else; everything in their upbringing was aimed at making them perfectly disciplined war-riors. They consequently acquired the reputation of being blunt and decisive men of few words. There is a story that an enemy, threatening war, sent the Spartans an ultimatum that if he invaded Laconia, he would raze Sparta to the ground, whereupon the Spartans sent back the reply, "If —."

10. *mausoleum,* "a large tomb"

He saw the house was occupied and animated — if animation might be talked about in a place which had hitherto answered to his idea of a magnificent *mausoleum.* — Henry James.

When King Mausolus of Caria died, his wife was inconsolable. She built a magnificent tomb in his honor called the Mausoleum, which was numbered among the Seven Wonders of the World.

11. *meander,* "to follow a winding course"

Among their smooth trunks a clear brook *meandered* for a time in twin-ing lacets before it made up its mind to take a leap into the hurrying river. —Joseph Conrad

The Meander, now called Menderes, is a river in Turkey which was proverbial in ancient times for its crooked, wandering course.

12. *ostracism,* "exclusion from society"

After having been sentenced to a perpetual *ostracism* from the esteem and confidence and honors and emoluments of his country, he will still be liable to prosecution and punishment in the ordinary course of the law. — *The Federalist*

This word is not strictly speaking derived from a proper name, but it has been included here since the civilization of Greece gave it to our language. Ancient Athens was one of the first democracies in the world and contributed many of its political ideals to later ages, but the Athenians had one rather peculiar governmental institution. They greatly feared the rise of a dictator and, to prevent this, on occasion held a special election in which each voter inscribed on a broken piece of pottery (called *ostrakon* in Greek and hence the term *ostracism*) the name of the man whom he considered most dangerous to the state. If 6000 ballots were cast, the person who received the greatest number of votes was sent into exile for ten years, without incurring any disgrace, however, unlike the modern form of ostracism.

13. *philippic,* "a bitter denunciation"

Savonarola added withering *philippics* on the tyranny of Lorenzo the Magnificent . . . —*Time*

Philip of Macedon, the father of Alexander the Great, determined to gain control of all Greece, but he carefully concealed his designs, playing the apathetic and complacent Greek city-states one against the other. The Athenian statesman Demosthenes, however, clearly realized the true intentions of Philip and, denouncing him in a series of bitter orations, sought to arouse the other Greek states against the common danger. These orations were named from the object of their attack *Philippics.* Though the Greeks failed to check Philip and were conquered by the Macedonians, Demosthenes' ideals lived on. When the Roman orator Cicero delivered a series of invectives against Mark Antony, he likewise called these *Philippics,* and the term has now come to refer to any bitter verbal attack.

14. a *Pyrrhic* victory, "a victory won at too great a cost"

His victory in securing the nomination could only be described as *Pyrrhic,* for the bad feeling caused by the struggle cost him the election.

Pyrrhus, King of Epirus and second cousin of Alexander the Great, was a skillful military commander; when he was exiled from his native land, he became a soldier of fortune. On one occasion he accepted the invitation of the Greeks in Southern Italy to lead their armies against the Romans. The Roman generals were no match for Pyrrhus, who won several battles against them. But the Roman infantrymen showed great courage; they refused to retreat and died where they stood, inflicting such heavy losses on Pyrrhus' troops that after the Battle of Asculum Pyrrhus is reported to have said as he surveyed the gaps in the ranks of his armies, "One more such victory and we are undone."

15. *solecism,* "a substandard usage of language, a social blunder"

Ladies highly born, highly bred, and naturally quick witted, were unable to write a line in their mother tongue without *solecisms* and faults of spelling. — Macaulay

The Greeks sent many colonists to other lands in the Mediterranean, to Southern Italy, the Black Sea region, and the coast of Asia Minor. At one such colony, Soli, the last outpost so to speak of Greek civilization, the inhabitants had developed such a barbarous dialect that the name of the town became proverbial for grammatical mistakes. By extension *solecism* has come to mean "social error" as well as "incorrectness of speech."

16. *sophistry,* "clever but fallacious argumentation designed to mislead"

But he had one of those happily constituted intellects which, across labyrinths of *sophistry,* and through masses of immaterial facts, go straight to the true point. — Macaulay

The Sophists were originally early teachers of Greece; their name means "wise man" (*sophos,* "wise," as in *philosophy,* which is literally "love of wisdom"). They traveled about the country giving lessons in public speaking, politics, and mathematics, and many of them were virtuous, learned men. Some, however, rejected any sort of objective moral standards and counseled that the only consideration should be worldly success. In teaching public speaking, they emphasized winning one's case without regard for the truth, and they trained their pupils in all the tricks of obscuring the facts. These men ruined the reputation of the whole group and gave the word *sophistry* its unpleasant meaning.

17. *Spartan,* "rigorous, austere, disciplined"

They were in no sense elaborate or pretentious, but designed on simple functional lines, not for luxurious but for rather *Spartan* living. —*Harper's Magazine*

The Spartans were famed as the bravest and hardiest warriors of Greece. Everything about their training from earliest childhood was designed to make them able to endure the rigors of military service and to instill in them a single-minded devotion to their country. At the age of seven, boys were taken from their mothers and sent to train in barracks, where they were made to do without any of the usual comforts. They were forced to wear thin clothing and go barefoot in winter, to sleep without covering, and to forage for their food. So that they would have nothing to distract them from their dedication to the state, Spartan citizens were forbidden to own private property, and their family life was rigidly restricted. All this resulted in an admirable simplicity and singleness of purpose, and *Spartan* is generally a complimentary term, but this austere discipline was unfortunately directed to one end alone, military might.

18. *stoic,* "impassive"

He looked around him in agony, and was surprised, even in that moment, to see the *stoical* indifference of his fellow-prisoners. —Scott

One of the teachings of Stoicism, a Greek philosophical school, was that the universe is governed by a divine providence, and so whatever happens, if viewed properly, is for the best. Consequently, it was felt, pain and death are not evil, and one should bear them with equanimity. The feats of the Stoics in enduring pain were legendary, and it is for this that they are best known.

19. *sword of Damocles,* "a constantly threatening danger"

The German Air Force was a *sword of Damocles* hanging over all of the nations within its range.

Damocles, seeing the power and magnificence of Dionysius, tyrant or dictator of Syracuse, constantly referred to him as the happiest of men; whereupon Dionysius determined to show this deluded member of his court what a tyrant's life is really like. He invited Damocles to a delicious dinner; when in the midst of his enjoyment Damocles looked up, however, he saw a sword suspended over his head by a single thread, illustrating the ever-present danger in which a dictator lives.

20. *sybarite,* "one devoted to luxury and pleasure"

He led the life of a *sybarite* in the famous palace and gardens of Azahara, surrounding himself with all that could excite the imagination and delight the senses. —Washington Irving

Sybaris was a Greek colony in Southern Italy famed for its wealth and luxurious living. It was, of course, destroyed by a less wealthy, but also less self-indulgent, neighbor.

II. The names of people and places in other ages have also greatly enriched the English vocabulary. For instance, the eighteenth-century Earl of Sandwich was so addicted to gambling that, according to report, he could not bring himself to leave the gaming table long enough for meals, but had food brought to him. In order to eat and at the same time hold his cards, he resorted to the practice of putting meat between two slices of bread and thus gave his name to the article of food which is so common today.

ASSIGNMENT

The following are some additional examples of words derived from proper names. With the aid of a dictionary identify the persons or places whose names they represent, and determine their meanings.

1. bedlam

Immediately after the explosion the hall became a *bedlam*.

2. boycott

"They are being ostracized, their shops . . . are completely *boycotted,* their children without a school." —*Time*

3. dunce

Only a *dunce* would fail to see that this is so.

4. Frankenstein

In arming China the Russians are creating a *Frankenstein*.

5. jeremiad

The government paid no attention to Churchill's *jeremiads* provoked by the appeasement of Hitler at Munich.

6. maudlin

He burst into tears of *maudlin* pity for himself. —Dickens

7. quixotic

What wonder, then, if the Spaniard of that day, feeding his imagination with dreams of enchantment at home, and with its realities abroad, should have displayed a *Quixotic* enthusiasm! —William Hickling Prescott

8. simony

He did not scruple to become a broker in *simony* of a peculiarly discreditable kind, and to use a bishopric as a bait to tempt a divine to perjury. —Macaulay

9. tawdry

History is what happened, it is not what fits some scriptwriter's *tawdry* idea. —*Harper's Magazine*

10. utopia

It is often said that an ideal state — an *Utopia* where there is no folly, crime, or sorrow — has a singular fascination for the mind. —W. H. Hudson

PRONUNCIATION EXERCISE

I. Indicate the pronunciation of the following:

1. The **oe** of *Croesus* is pronounced like (1) the **oi** in *oil* (2) the **o** in *tone* (3) a combination of the **o** in *tone* and the **e** in *equal* (4) the **e** in *equal*.

2. The first **a** of *Draconian* is pronounced like the **a** in (1) *land* (2) *gate* (3) *father* (4) *about*.

3. The **o** of *Draconian* is pronounced like the **o** in (1) *pot* (2) *tone* (3) *wisdom*.

4. The **e** of *helot* is pronounced like the **e** in (1) *equal* (2) *agent* (3) *tent*.

5. The **o** of *helot* is pronounced like the **o** in (1) *pot* (2) *tone* (3) *wisdom*.

6. The **a** of *laconic* is pronounced like the **a** in (1) *land* (2) *about* (3) *gate* (4) *father*.

7. The **o** of *laconic* is pronounced like the **o** in (1) *pot* (2) *tone* (3) *wisdom*.

8. The **e** of *mausoleum* is pronounced like (1) the **e** in *tent* (2) the **i** in *tin* (3) the **a** in *gate* (4) the **e** in *equal*.

9. The **y** of *Pyrrhic* is pronounced like the **i** in (1) *bite* (2) *fir* (3) *tin*.

10. The **o** of *solecism* is pronounced like the **o** in (1) *pot* (2) *tone* (3) *wisdom*.

11. The **c** of *solecism* is pronounced like (1) the **c** in *can* (2) the **sh** in *shell* (3) the **c** in *certain*.

12. The **y** of *sybarite* is pronounced like the **i** in (1) *bite* (2) *sanity* (3) *tin*.

13. The **ei** of *Frankenstein* is pronounced like (1) the **i** in *tin* (2) the **i** in *bite* (3) the **e** in *equal* (4) the **e** in *tent*.

14. The **i** of *simony* is pronounced like the **i** in (1) *bite* (2) *sanity* (3) *tin*.

15. The **o** of *simony* is pronounced like the **o** in (1) *pot* (2) *tone* (3) *wisdom*.

II. Circle the syllable on which the primary accent falls in each of the following:

1. Damocles	7. philippic
2. Draconian	8. quixotic
3. jeremiad	9. simony
4. laconic	10. solecism
5. mausoleum	11. sophistry
6. meander	12. sybarite

LESSON III   Greek Bases

Most of the English words derived from Greek are compounds formed from several different elements: prefixes, bases, and suffixes, which are used repeatedly in various combinations. In this lesson we shall consider Greek bases, that is, Greek words as they appear in English derivatives, without the characteristic Greek endings, *-os, -e, -on,* etc. (These are sometimes called roots, or stems, or combining forms, as well as bases.) As in the case of Latin bases, these will be printed in capital letters followed by a dash, e.g., CYCL-, PYR-, SPHER-. Later we shall see how, by the addition of various prefixes and suffixes, many English words have been formed from a single base. For example, from PSYCH-, "mind," "soul," have come:

PSYCH-IATR-y	PSYCH-osis
PSYCH-o-ana-LY-sis	PSYCH-o-SOMAT-ic
PSYCH-o-logy	PSYCH-o-tic
PSYCH-o-NEUR-osis	met-em-PSYCH-osis
PSCHY-o-PATH	

The meaning given for a base will in general represent its significance in the various compounds and combinations in which it appears in English. Language, however, is an extremely changeable and flexible instrument; consequently, in the course of the many centuries during which the process of forming new words has been going on, it is only to be expected that certain variations in the meanings of bases should have appeared. For example, from the base PYR- "fire," have been formed, among others, the following words:

pyromania   a psychopathic impulse to set fires

pyrometer   an instrument for measuring extreme temperatures

pyrogenic   produced by heat

pyrosis   a disorder of the stomach accompanied by a burning sensation

pyretic   pertaining to fever

pyre   a pile of combustible material on which a dead body is burned

In all of these words PYR- represents the basic idea of "fire," yet the concept of a literally blazing heap of fuel will not apply in many of these cases. One must therefore keep a flexible mind and be prepared for the different shades and nuances of meaning which are encountered everywhere in connection with language.

Frequently Greek bases appear in English without the addition of any prefix or suffix.

I. Sometimes a base by itself forms an English word.

Greek Base	*English Derivative*
ORGAN- instrument	organ
ANGEL- messenger	angel
GRAPH- to write	graph

II. In other cases a final silent *e* is added when the base appears in English. (This *e* is not a suffix and has no meaning.)

PYR- fire	pyre
CYCL- circle, wheel	cycle
SPHER- ball	sphere

Dictionaries, in describing the origin of an English word derived from Greek, will give the actual Greek word; e.g., *angel* is listed as coming from the Greek *angelos, organ* from the Greek *organon.* If one keeps in mind the English word, however, the base ANGEL- or ORGAN- can be readily seen. In this book we will be primarily concerned with Greek bases as they appear in English words.

Often, besides the addition of an ending, one will find a difference in spelling between the actual Greek word as it is transliterated in a dictionary and its English derivatives; e.g., *cycle* is listed as coming from the Greek *kyklos,* and *sphere* from *sphaira.* Such differences are due to the fact that originally Greek words entered English by way of Latin and thus acquired a Latinized spelling. Even though later borrowing from Greek has mostly been direct, the practice of Latinization has generally, but not always, been continued. These differences in spelling between the Greek and the English (or Latinized) form are summarized below. It will be useful to remember them, for one will thus be able to recognize more easily words which have been brought from Greek into English without first receiving a Latinized spelling, as, for example, *kaleidoscope.*

Greek	*English*
k (*kyklos, konos*)	c (*cycle, cone*)

(Occasionally the *k* is kept; for example, from the Greek word *kinein,* "to move," has come *kinetic* as well as *cinema,* also *leucocyte* but *leukemia.*)

ai (*sphaira, phainomenon*)	e (*sphere, phenomenon*)

(Sometimes this appears in English as *ae;* for example, from *aisthetikos* "perceptive," comes *aesthetics* as well as *anesthetic.* In British usage *ae* is more frequent than *e,* as, for example, in the British spellings *anaesthetic* and *haemorrhage* [instead of *hemorrhage*].)

ei (*eidolon, eikon*)   i (*idol, icon*)

(Occasionally the *ei* is kept as an alternate spelling; e.g., both *chirography* and *cheirography* are given by dictionaries, though the former is more usual.)

oi (*oikonomia, amoibe*)   e, oe (*economy, amoeba*)

(Note that dictionaries usually give *ameba* as a variant spelling. Also, in older books *economy* is sometimes spelled *oeconomy*.)

ou (*mousike, Ouranos*)   u (*music, Uranus*)

Greek words were of course originally written with different characters from those used for English, but since these words have been transliterated in dictionaries, the Greek alphabet has been omitted from consideration in this book. Note, however, that the names of the Greek letters have provided English with such words as *iota, delta, alpha* and *omega,* and *alphabet* itself, as well as having given such technical terms as *sigmoid* ("curved like the letter *s*"), *chiasma* ("a crossing, as in the Greek letter *chi*"), and *lambdacism* ("difficulty in pronouncing the letter *l*"). A listing of the Greek alphabet, along with the Russian and Hebrew, can be found in a good dictionary. (In *Webster's New Collegiate Dictionary* see under or near *alphabet;* in *The American College Dictionary* and in *Webster's New World Dictionary* see the inside of the back cover.)

ASSIGNMENT

I. Learn the following bases and their meanings. Study each base so that you can recognize it in a long compound word.

BIBLI-	book
CANON-	a rule
CRYPT-, CRYPH-	hidden, secret
CYCL-	circle, wheel
GLOSS-, GLOT(T)-	tongue, language
ICON-	image
MIM-	to imitate
OD-	song, poem
PYR-	fire
TOM-	to cut

II. The foregoing bases all appear as English words by themselves or with the addition of a final *e* (with a slight exception in the case of BIBLI-). Without using a dictionary, list as many additional words formed from them as you can. Then check these words in your dictionary to make sure that they actually contain the particular Greek base. For example, *odious* has nothing to do with OD-, "song, poem," but is formed from the Latin base ODI-, "hatred."

III. List the base and its meaning in each of the following italicized words and define the word as it is used in the sentence or phrase.

Example: *monody;* base, OD-, "song," "poem;" a song in which one voice carries the melody.

1. He discovered that there were few *bibliographical* aids in the subject about which he was writing a term paper.

2. They determined to propose that, in the public services of the Church, lessons taken from the *canonical* books of Scripture should be substituted for the lessons taken from the *Apocrypha.* —Macaulay

3. . . . a code unbreakable by any known *cryptographic* method. — *Time*

4. We have only to stand on the eminence of the hour, and look out thence into the *empyrean*. —Thoreau

5. . . . despite his *encyclopedic* knowledge and amazing breadth and power of his intellect, he was using little more than half his brain . . .—*Time*

6. It is a significant fact, stated by *entomologists* . . . that "some insects, in their perfect state, though furnished with organs of feeding, make no use of them." — Thoreau

7. . . . the Kremlin nonetheless kept up the momentum of its demolition of Stalin and, with that, of the *iconography* of the Communist way of life for the past 30 years. — *Time*

8. He used to amuse the company by his talent at story-telling and his powers of *mimicry,* giving capital imitations of . . public characters of the day. — Washington Irving

9. *Parody* obviously demands that the original parodied should be well known to the reader . . . —*Time*

10. . . . Singapore was in reality a defenseless, *polyglot* commercial town of Chinese, Japanese, Indians, Jews and British . . . — *Time*

IV. Define the following italicized words as they are used in the sentence or phrase. These represent various Greek words borrowed by English without prefixes or suffixes.

1. He did not at this time profess the *austere* devotion which, at a later period, gave his court the aspect of a monastery. —Macaulay

2. Or that the Everlasting had not fix'd
   His *canon* 'gainst self-slaughter! —Shakespeare

3. Within the wall thus exposed by the displacing of the bones, we perceived a still interior *crypt* or recess, in depth about four feet. —Edgar Allan Poe

4. It has long . . . been a common saying, that if a good *despot* could be ensured, despotic monarchy would be the best form of government. — John Stuart Mill

5. . . . an old lady buys, without even haggling, a few lilies to take to the sacred *icon* of the Most Holy Virgin in a neighborhood church. — *Atlantic Monthly*

6. Walden Pond was already . . . covered with *myriads* of ducks and geese. — Thoreau

7. But the *nomad* instinct, as I said, persists to drive us to fresh fields and pastures new. — Emerson

8. . . . but the Iroquois had slept off the effect of their *orgies* and were again on the alert. — Francis Parkman

9. I pause with reverential awe, when I contemplate the ponderous *tomes,* in different languages, with which they have endeavored to solve this question. — Irving

10. I have spent many an hour, when I was younger, floating over its surface as the *zephyr* willed. —Thoreau

LESSON IV   Combinations of Bases

Although, as we saw in the previous lesson, Greek bases are sometimes used by themselves, usually they occur in combination with other elements. Frequently two bases have been combined.

TELE-	far	+ PHON-	sound			telephone
PSYCH(o)-	mind	+ SOMAT-	body	+ ic		psychosomatic
THERM(o)-	heat	+ DYNAM-	power	+ ics		thermodynamics

Note that often an *o* is used as a connective between bases, usually when the second base begins with a consonant. Some dictionaries, in listing such Greek word elements (which they call "combining forms") as separate entries, include the *o*, giving PSYCHO-, THERMO-, etc. There are numerous instances, however, where this *o* does not appear, in *psychiatry, psychic,* and *thermal,* for example.

Sometimes Greek bases are combined with elements from other languages to form hybrids (see Part I, Lesson VII). Thus Latin and Greek have been combined in *dehydrate* (Latin, *de-,* "from," *-ate,* verbal suffix, and Greek, HYDR-, "water"), *automobile* (Greek, AUT(o)-, "self," and Latin, *mobilis,* "movable"), and *claustrophobia* (Latin, CLAUSTR-, "bar," "bolt," and Greek, PHOB-, "to be afraid").

PREFIXES

Often Greek bases appear in English with the addition of prefixes, that is, elements placed in front of the base which modify its meaning. Most of the prefixes were originally Greek prepositions or adverbs.

dia-	through, across	+ GRAM-	writing	diagram
epi-	upon	+ GRAM-		epigram
pro-	before	+ GRAM-		program

Most Greek prefixes end in a vowel which usually disappears before an initial vowel or *h* in a base.

parà-graph and *para-site,* but *par-ody*

cata-strophe and *cata-logue,* but *cat-holic*

hypo-dermic and *hypo-thesis,* but *hyp-hen*

A base may be preceded by more than one prefix.

a-, not + *sym-,* with + METR-, measure + *-ic* + *-al* asymmetrical
par-, beside + *en-,* in + THE-, to place + *-sis*   parenthesis

Learn the following prefixes and their meanings:

a- (an- before vowels or *h),* not, without
    examples: abyss, amoral
             anarchy, anemia

amphi-, both, on both sides of, around
    examples: amphitheater, amphibious

ana- (an- before vowels or *h),* up, back, again
    examples: analysis, anatomy
             anode

anti- (ant- before vowels or *h),* against, opposite
    examples: antiseptic, antiaircraft
             antarctic, antagonist

apo- (ap- before vowels or *h),* from, off
    examples: apology, apostle
             aphelion

cata- (cat- before vowels or *h),* down, against, very. (In many English words it is difficult to see the force of this prefix.)
    examples: cataract, catastrophe
             cathode, catholic

dia- (di- before vowels or *h),* through, across, between
    examples: diameter, diagnosis
             diocese

ASSIGNMENT

I. Learn the following bases and their meanings:

Base	Meanings	English Derivatives
ALG-	pain	neuralgia, nostalgia
BI-	life	biology, biography
CHRON-	time	chronic, chronicles
DEMON- (DAEMON-)	spirit, evil spirit	demon

GE-	earth	geography, geology

LOG-, -LOGUE	speech, word, pro-
	    portion, reasoning
		apology
		    epilogue, prologue

LY-	to loosen	analysis, paralysis
MNE-	to remember	amnesia

PAN-, PANT-	all, every	Pan-American,
		    panorama
		    pantomime

POD-	foot	podium, tripod
THE-	god	theology, monotheism
TROPH-	to nourish, to grow	atrophy

II. Define the following words in such a way that you indicate the force of the prefix:

Examples: *diagonal,* "at an angle *across"*
　　　　　 abyss, "a pit *without* bottom"

1. anonymous	7. amphitheater
2. antarctic	8. anesthetic
3. apostle	9. diameter
4. catastrophe	10. amoral
5. aseptic	11. catapult
6. antiseptic	12. anarchy

III. List the base or bases and prefixes (if any), together with their meanings, in each of the following italicized words. Define each word as it is used in the sentence or phrase. In this and in similar exercises the bases contained in the words are ones assigned in the lesson or in previous lessons. If you cannot remember the meaning of a particular base, however, refer to the section at the end of Part II, where all bases are listed which students are expected to learn.

Example: *apology; apo-,* "off," and LOG-, "speech;" acknowledgment of improper conduct

1. I confess I was a little dubious at first whether it was not one of those *apocryphal* tales often passed off upon inquiring travellers like myself. —Washington Irving

2. The *analytical* power should not be confounded with simple ingenuity. —Edgar Allan Poe

3. Inactivity is the patients' worst enemy; their muscles *atrophy* and tendons shrink. — *Time*

4. If rightly made, a boat would be a sort of *amphibious* animal, a creature of two elements, related by one half its structure to some swift and shapely fish, and by the other to some strong-winged and graceful bird. — Thoreau

5. Neither scholar, *mnemonic* freak nor gambler, Elfrida has hit the top in what is still the most demanding and sophisticated of all quiz shows. — *Time*

6. The whole Aztec *pantheon* partook more or less of the sanguinary spirit of the terrible war-god who presided over it. — William Hickling Prescott

7. Physically beautiful men — the glory of the race when it was young — are almost an *anachronism* now. —Thomas Hardy

8. . . . her face enacting a vivid *pantomime* of the criticisms passing in her mind. — Thomas Hardy

9. There is no reasonable objection to examining an *atheist* in the evidences of Christianity, provided he is not required to profess a belief in them. — John Stuart Mill

10. The delegate of a country *antipodal* to Greece, New Zealand . . . —*Atlantic Monthly*

11. . . . it gives preliminary promise that a partial separation of the *analgesic* and addicting properties may have been achieved. — *Time*

12. There is an unmistakable *analogy* between these wicked weeds and the bad habits and sinful propensities which have overrun the moral world. — Hawthorne

13. The discovery of *antibiotics* greatly reduced the number of deaths from infection.

14. The depth of his knowledge of *anatomy* has no parallel among the artists of modern times. — Emerson

15. When I think of the benefactors of the race, whom we have *apotheosized* as messengers from heaven, bearers of divine gifts to man . . . —Thoreau

16. Chancellor Adenauer's problem . . . is therefore to find a way of becoming a *catalytic* agent for normalizing relations between the Soviets and the whole West . . . —Dorothy Thompson

17. . . . its scripts are full of insight and nicely caught *dialogue* — *Time*

18. When night came, it brought with it a *pandemonium* of dancing and whooping, drumming and feasting. — Francis Parkman

19. A full *amnesty* for past offenses was granted to the citizens. — Macaulay

20. (a) When the Explorers' orbits were carrying them near the earth, they both reported reasonable numbers of cosmic rays . . . but as they climbed up towards their *apogees* the count became faster. — *Time*

    (b) In the book as in history, John Adams emerges as the *apogee* of moral courage . . . —*Time*

LESSON V   Prefixes

Learn the following prefixes and their meanings:

dys-, bad, disordered, difficult
   examples: dysentery, dysfunction

ec-, (ex- before vowels or *h*), out, out of
   examples: eccentric, ecstasy
             exodus

en- (em-, el-), in, into
   examples: energy, enthusiasm
             emblem, emphasize
             elliptical

endo-, ento- (end-, ent- before vowels or *h*), within
   examples: endocrine, endogamy
             entophyte
             endamoeba

epi- (*ep-* before vowels or *h*), upon, to, in addition to
  examples: epidemic, epidermis
            epode

eu- (*ev-* before vowels), good, well
  examples: eugenics, euphony
            evangelist

exo-, ecto-, outside, external
  examples: exogamy, exotic
            ectoparasite

ASSIGNMENT

I. Learn the following bases and their meanings:

Base	Meanings	English Derivatives
AGON-	struggle, contest	agony, protagonist
ANGEL-	messenger, message	angelic
CENTR-	center	concentric
DEM-	people	democracy, demagogue
GAM-	marriage	bigamy, polygamy
HEM- (HAEM-), HEMAT- (HAEMAT-)	blood	hemorrhage, hemoglobin hematology leukemia

(This base usually appears as EM- if preceded by a prefix or another base; e.g., *anemia, leukemia.*)

Base	Meanings	English Derivatives
HEMER-	day	ephemeral, Decameron
OD-, HOD-	way, road	odometer, electrode cathode
STOL-, STAL-, -STLE	to send, to draw	epistolary peristalsis epistle
TAPH-	tomb	cenotaph, epitaph
THANAT- (THANAS-)	death	thanatopsis

II. Define the following words in such a way that you indicate the force of the prefix.

1. exoskeleton
2. dysentery
3. embryo
4. dysfunction
5. enthusiasm
6. exotic
7. ectoparasite
8. epidermis
9. eugenics
10. endocrine

III. List the base or bases and prefixes (if any), together with their meanings, in each of the following italicized words. Define each word as it is used in the sentence or phrase.

1. (a) Uttering a low querulous growl, the speaker, whose harsh countenance was the very *epitome* of selfishness . . . — Dickens

(b) Such, in very brief *epitome,* are the salient points in this lamentable and also memorable episode of which no doubt a much fuller account will be given by history. — Sir Winston Churchill

2. Precisely because the tyranny of opinion is such as to make *eccentricity* a reproach, it is desirable, in order to break through that tyranny, that people should be eccentric. — John Stuart Mill

3. Diseases which are *endemic* in Egypt include worms and other parasites, amoebic dysentery, malaria . . . —*Harper's Magazine*

4. Between it and ourselves is the Race — a place where *antagonistic* currents meet and form whirlpools — a spot which is rough in the smoothest weather, and terrific in a wind. — Thomas Hardy

5. The serious reader will be materially aided by an exceptionally complete index, a *glossary* of military terms and abbreviations, and a running commentary on world affairs . . . — *Atlantic Monthly*

6. Just as a man may not consent to *euthanasia* because religious law forbids him from doing away with himself . . . —*Time*

7. Nearly all the labourers . . . intended flight, and early in the morning there was a general *exodus* in the direction of the town. — Hardy

8. He had fallen a victim to that terrible *epidemic,* the small-pox, which was now sweeping over the land like fire over the prairies. — William Hickling Prescott

9. Finally, in 1918–19, it erupted in a global *pandemic,* one of the worst disease disasters in history, which claimed at least 15 million dead . . . *—Time*

10. The practice of *exogamy* among the northern tribes . . .

11. The *epitaph* composed by Lascaris for his own tomb in Santa Agata touchingly expresses the grief of an exile. — John Addington Symonds

12. A dull and *anemic* style . . .

13. Last week, in the sixth *encyclical* of his reign, Pope John XXIII called on a Christianity surrounded by the forces of Communism and secularism to join together . . . *—Time*

14. Muscular *dystrophy,* a progressive wasting of muscle power for which neither cause nor cure is known . . . *—Time*

15. But what he seemed to be saying with the evanescent words of his music . . . was that life is *ephemeral* and let us make the most of it. — *Atlantic Monthly*

16. Something of the ancient prophetic and *apostolic* fire needs to be rekindled in the piety of peace of mind . . . *—Atlantic Monthly*

17. I can imagine that at the end of ten years we might have a very pleasant correspondence. I shall have matured my *epistolary* style. —Henry James

18. . . . and there poured out such a *eulogy* upon her children's qualities as fond mothers know how to utter. — Thackeray

19. I owe to their spontaneous, genuine, genial compassion, as large a debt as to your *evangelical* charity. —Charlotte Brontë

20. The hero's old age was described in an *epilogue.*

LESSON VI Prefixes

Learn the following prefixes and their meanings:

hyper-, over, excessive
examples: hypercritical, hypersonic, hypertension

hypo- (*hyp-* before vowels or *h*), below, less than normal
examples: hypodermic, hypothesis
hyphen

meta- (*met-* before vowels or *h*), after, changed
examples: metabolism, metamorphosis
method

para- (*par-* before vowels or *h*), beside, disordered
examples: paralysis, parasite
parenthesis, parody

peri-, around, near
examples: perimeter, periscope

pro-, before, in front of
examples: program, prologue

pros-, toward, in addition to
examples: proselyte, prosthetic

syn- (*sym-, syl-, sy-, sys*), with, together
examples: syndicate, synonym, synthetic
sympathy, symphony
syllable
systole, system

ASSIGNMENT

I. Learn the following bases and their meanings:

Base	Meanings	English Derivatives
BALL-, BOL-, BLE-	to throw, to put	ballistics symbol emblem, problem
DERM-, DERMAT-	skin	epidermis, pachyderm dermatologist, dermatitis

DOX-, DOG-	opinion, teach-ing	heterodox, orthodox dogma
GNO-	to know	agnostic, diagnosis
HOM-, HOME-, (H)OMAL-	same, similar regular	homogenized, homosexual homeopathy
MORPH-	form, shape	morphology metamorphosis
ONYM-	name, word	anonymous, synonym
PHER-, PHOR-	to bear, to go	periphery phosphorescent, sema-phore
TACT-, TAX-	to arrange, to put in order	tactics taxonomy, taxidermy

II. Define the following words in such a way that you indicate the force of the prefix:

1. hypersonic
2. parallel
3. syllable
4. hypertension
5. hypothyroidism
6. proscenium
7. periscope
8. sympathy
9. paranoia
10. perimeter
11. symphony
12. prosthetic

III. List the base or bases and prefixes (if any), together with their meanings, in each of the following italicized words. Define each word as it is used in the sentence or phrase.

1. He knew . . . how America's illiterate and half-educated citizenry spoke, and mispronounced, foundered on *syntax,* floundered among clichés . . . —*Time*

2. The King's printing house . . . was — to use a coarse *metaphor* which then, for the first time, came into fashion — completely gutted. —Macaulay

3. A *hypodermic* injection . . .

4. . . . the moral *anomaly* of punishing the accessory, when the principal is (and must be) allowed to go free. — John Stuart Mill

5. *Paradoxical* as the assertion may be, the conscious ability to do without happiness gives the best prospect of realising such happiness as is attainable. — Mill

6. Moral insanity is often nothing more than the *hypertrophy* of some vulgar passion — lust, violence, cruelty, jealousy, and the like. — John Addington Symonds

7. At the Roman Catholic University of Santa Clara, students formed a group to invite *agnostic,* anticlerical speakers to the campus. — *Time*

8. His optimism has no religious source but derives from youth, from the *euphoria* given by the joy of living under a bright sun and a clear, diaphanous sky. — *Atlantic Monthly*

9. . . . eventually they die from a swift and general collapse of the body's *metabolic* processes. —*Time*

10. The hope that truth and wisdom would be found in the assemblies of the orthodox clergy induced the Emperor to convene, at Constantinople, a *synod* of one hundred and fifty bishops. — Edward Gibbon

11. The forests have departed, but the old customs of their shades remain. Many, however, linger only in *metamorphosed* or disguised form. — Thomas Hardy

12. The satirist strikes more directly; he either attacks manners, customs, institutions, and persons without disguise or he does so under a thin veil of *parable.* —Symonds

13. This victory, more complete than even the sanguine temper of Cortés had *prognosticated,* proved the superiority of the Spaniards. — William Hickling Prescott

14. At its highest point (apogee), the orbit rises to 1,700 miles above the earth, descending to about 200 miles (*perigee*). — *Time*

15. . . . its numerous and spacious apartments, which Cortés, with enthusiastic *hyperbole,* does not hesitate to declare superior to anything of the kind in Spain. — Prescott

16. The *antonym* of "attack" is "defend."

17. They forgot even the rules of *prosody,* and, with the melody of Homer yet sounding in their ears, they confound all measure of feet and syllables. —Gibbon

18. . . . it was anomalous that Russia, also on the *periphery* of modern Europe, should have been the theater of Marxist revolution. — *Time*

19. Two thirds of the people of America could not long be persuaded, upon the credit of artificial distinction and *syllogistic* subtleties, to submit their interests to the management and disposal of one third. — *The Federalist.*

20. "Bore" and "boar" are *homonyms.*

IV. By changing (or omitting) the prefix, form the antonym of each of the following:

Example: *apogee — perigee*

1. exoskeleton
2. sympathy
3. aphelion
4. proslavery
5. atheism

6. anabolism
7. ectoparasite
8. epilogue
9. hypertonic
10. euphoria

LESSON VII   Suffixes

Along with bases and prefixes, suffixes have often been used in word formation. Suffixes are word elements attached to the end of a base which modify the meaning of the base. Thus:

a-	+	THE-	god	+	*-ism*	belief in	atheism
amphi-	+	BI-	life	+	*-ous*	having the character of	amphibious
ec-	+	CENTR-	center	+	*ic*	pertaining to	eccentric

Suffixes not only affect the meaning of a base, but they also determine the part of speech of the word thus formed. In the last two examples, for instance, suffixes attached to noun bases have formed adjectives. We shall be dealing in the following lessons with three types of suffixes, adjective-forming, noun-forming, and verb-forming.

More than one suffix is sometimes found in a single word. For example:

CANON- rule + -ic pertaining to + -al pertaining to   canonical

a- + THE- god + -ist one who   + -ic pertaining to   atheistic
                  believes in

Learn the following suffixes and their meanings:

I. *-ic* (*-ac* after the letter *i*), *-tic,* "pertaining to," "like"

	DESPOT-	absolute ruler	+ -ic	despotic
epi- +	DEM-	people	+ -ic	epidemic
	CARDI-	heart	+ -ac	cardiac
	STA-	to stand	+ -tic	static

II. *-ics, -tics,* "art, science, or study of"

ETH-	custom	+ -ics	ethics
PHYS-	nature	+ -ics	physics
GENE-	to be produced	+ -tics	genetics

This was originally the plural form of the previous suffix and meant "things pertaining to," but words which exhibit this suffix are usually treated as singular; e.g., "Modern physics is a rapidly advancing science."

III. *-oid,* "like," "having the shape of"

ADEN-	gland	+ -oid	adenoid
SPHER-	ball	+ -oid	spheroid

ASSIGNMENT

I. Learn the following bases and their meanings:

Base	Meanings	Derivatives
AESTHE-, ESTHE-	to feel, to perceive	aesthete anesthetic
ANTHROP-	human being, man	anthropology, philanthropy
ARCHA(E)- (ARCHE-)	ancient, primitive, beginning	archaeology Archeozoic

AST(E)R-	star	astronomy
		asterisk, disaster
GEN(E)-, GON-	to be produced, to originate, to produce	hydrogen genesis, gene theogony
GER-, GERONT-	old age, old people	geriatric gerontocracy
HOL-	whole	holocaust
IATR-	physician, medicine	psychiatric, pediatric
PEP(T)-	to digest	peptic, pepsin
TECHN-	art, skill, craft	technical, polytechnic

II. List the prefixes, bases, and suffixes, together with their meanings, in the following italicized words. Define each word as it is used in the sentence or phrase.

Example: *endemic; en-,* "in," "on"; DEM-, "people"; *-ic,* "pertaining to"; "peculiar to a certain district"

1. When Galileo peered through his telescope four centuries later and saw a heliocentric rather than a *geocentric* universe . . . —*Time*

2. . . . a polemic against polytheism . . . as regards the *anthropomorphic* conception of deity prevalent in Greece. —John Addington Symonds

3. A scientific knowledge of *genetics* has greatly improved the breeding of cattle.

4. She murmurs *cryptic* remarks about life and love . . . —*Time*

5. . , . whenever Vishinsky howls and Molotov roars that Democracy is a fraud because it doesn't repress the activities of the *anthropoid* element in our population. —*Harper's Magazine*

6. "*Geriatrics* and mental disease are the two biggest problems in the U. S. . . ." —*Time*

7. . . . Composer Poulenc abandoned . . . the brassy *pyrotechnics* which once made him the rage of the Left Bank. —*Time*

8. To say of an ancient literary composition that it has anti-quarian interest, often means that it has no distinct *aesthetic* interest for the reader of today. —Walter Pater

9. In her *anthropocentric* indifference to Heaven and Hell . . .
—*Time*

10. Most *asteroids* stay on the far side of Mars, but at least twelve are known whose eccentric orbits carry them near the earth. —*Time*

11. With all this, however, the Moslem empire in Spain was but a brilliant *exotic,* that took no permanent root in the soil it embellished. —Washington Irving

12. *Dyspeptic* individuals bolted their food in wedges; feeding not themselves, but broods of nightmares, who were continually standing at livery within them. —Dickens

13. . . . a magnificent panorama, only slightly spoiled by the odors bred by the *archaic* drainage system . . . —*Harper's Magazine*

14. The next thirty years were years of *chronic,* smothered war, disguised, but never quite at rest. —Francis Parkman

15. The hunter still kept his place and listened to the hounds. Still on they came, and now the near woods resounded through all their aisles with their *demoniac* cry. —Thoreau

16. The President headed west . . . on his congressional-election tour in such a cheerful, *eupeptic* and thoroughly nonpolitical mood . . . —*Time*

17. With these exceptions, I can read almost anything. I bless my stars for a taste so *catholic,* so unexcluding. —Charles Lamb

18. The physician administered an *anesthetic.*

19. The basic principles of *eugenics* are violated by the practice of war, which kills off the strongest and fittest.

20. Does reason constrain us to believe . . . in a *cyclic* movement of human history? —Arnold Toynbee

III. Distinguish in meaning between the following pairs of words:

1. amnesia — anamnesis
2. anesthesia — paresthesia
3. anti-Christian — ante-Christian
4. antiseptic — aseptic
5. hypocritical — hypercritical

6. immoral — amoral
7. supersonic — hypersonic
8. symbolism — embolism
9. sympathy — empathy
10. synonym — homonym

LESSON VIII   Word Analysis

Read the section on word analysis in Chapter IX of Part I (pp. 52-53).

ADJECTIVE-FORMING SUFFIXES

The suffixes treated in this lesson are actually of Latin origin (see Part I, Lesson VIII), but are frequently attached to Greek bases, so that it will be useful to study them again here.

I. -al, "pertaining to," "like," "belonging to," "having the character of"

		IDE-	idea				-al	ideal
dia-	+	GON-	angle			+	-al	diagonal
		ETH-	custom	+	-ic	+	-al	ethical

II. -an (-ian), "pertaining to," "like," "one concerned with"

amphi-	+	BI-	life			+	-an	amphibian
		BARBAR-	foreign			+	-ian	barbarian
		THE(o)-	god	+	-logy	+	-an	theologian

III. -ous (-ious), "full of," "pertaining to," "like"

		BARBAR-	foreign	+	-ous	barbarous
amphi-	+	BI-	life	+	-ous	amphibious
an-	+	ONYM-	name	+	-ous	anonymous

ASSIGNMENT

I. Learn the following bases and their meanings:

CHROM-,	color	chromosome
CHROMAT-		chromatic

CRI-	to judge, to decide, to separate	critic, crisis, endocrine
ETHN-	race, cultural group	ethnology, ethnography
LOG(UE), LECT-	to speak, to choose	anthology eclogue, prologue dialect, analects
PHA(N)-	to show, to appear	phantom, epiphany phase, emphasis fantasy
PHIL-	to love	philharmonic, philosophy
PHON-	sound, voice	phonetic, telephone
POLY-	many, much	polyglot, polygamy
TAUT-	the same	tautology, tautomerous
THERM-	heat	thermometer, thermodynamics

II. Analyze the following italicized words and define them as they are used in the sentence or phrase.

Example: *anthropomorphic;* ANTHROP(o)-, "human being"; MORPH-, "form"; *-ic,* "like"; "represented with human characteristics or form"

1. The season was that period in the autumn when the foliage alone of an ordinary plantation is rich enough in hues to exhaust the *chromatic* combinations of an artist's palette. —Thomas Hardy

2. The orchestra played in a web of complicated *polyphony,* and the chorus sang in as many as twelve parts. —*Time*

3. Leaving things to the government, like leaving them to Providence, is *synonymous* with caring nothing about them. —John Stuart Mill

4. The ancient Hellenes were an *ethnic* mixture of prehistoric Mediterranean peoples and of northern invaders who, in successive waves, overran the country in the millennium before Christ. —*Atlantic Monthly*

5. Among other achievements, *Bibliophile* Ransom has made the university one of the country's richest repositories of rare manuscripts. —*Time*

6. He mingled with his reverence for the Supreme, the *astral* worship which existed among the Toltecs. —William Hickling Prescott

7. "It was her father that I got acquainted with first. And through getting acquainted with him, you see — why — I got acquainted with her," said Plornish *tautologically*. —Dickens

8. *Panchromatic* film . . .

9. It was a lovely May sunset, and the birch trees which grew on this margin of the vast Egdon wilderness had put on their new leaves, delicate as butterflies' wings, and *diaphanous* as amber. —Hardy

10. . . . cloaked in the gobbledygook of Marxist *dialectic* . . . —*Time*

11. At the extremely low temperature of liquid helium, *thermal* motions almost stop . . . —*Time*

12. The most important and serious essay in this direction is a little book of great interest and almost *hypercritical* acumen published recently in Naples. —John Addington Symonds

13. The war is, perhaps, severest between the males of *polygamous* animals, and these seem oftenest provided with special weapons. —Darwin

14. To convey these directions, Laderman relies on musical notes together with music's *diacritical* markings; staccatos, rests, accents . . . —*Time*

15. Master of an elegantly involuted style . . . James sometimes carried it to the point of "*euphonious* nothings." —*Time*

16. Most societies naturally entertain strongly *ethnocentric* views.

17. His account of that celebrated collection of books . . . cannot fail to impress all his readers with admiration of his *philological* attainments. —James Boswell

18. I never heard of a *philanthropic* meeting in which it was sincerely proposed to do any good to me, or the like of me. —Thoreau

19. What she wrote had never satisfied her; it was dull, labored, hampered, *amorphous,* as she knew. *—Harper's Magazine*

20. The main case that can be made against his music is that it is *eclectic* . . . *—Time*

III. Separate the following into syllables:

1. amorphous	6. euphonious
2. astral	7. polygamous
3. diacritical	8. synonymous
4. diaphanous	9. tautological
5. eclectic	10. thermal

LESSON IX   Place Names

Up to now we have been concentrating on the analysis of words. There is more to vocabulary study, however, than simply breaking words down into their component parts. As we have seen from Lessons I and II, many terms which do not lend themselves to analysis of this sort or which are not derived from the classical languages at all have extremely interesting backgrounds, and in the next lessons we shall study some of these, for one of the purposes of this book is to develop an interest in words without which vocabulary study becomes mere meaningless drill.

Among the words whose origins and meanings many people find a fascinating study are place names. The names of cities and lakes and mountains and other locations are not usually mere counters or arbitrary designations selected at random; in the language of those who first applied it, a name often had a significance which may tell us something about the history of the place or at any rate may arouse our curiosity as to why the name was used.

The study of place names is difficult, however, for many are of great antiquity. New races which occupied the land, usually as the result of conquest, did not often change the names which they found there, but usually modified the pronunciation to resemble that of their own language. As a result, the earliest form of a place name may have little resemblance to later forms, and this causes difficulty in tracing its history. Thus *York* in the language of the ancient Britons was *Eburacon,* probably coming from the name of a man *Eburos.* When the Anglo-Saxon invaders displaced the Celts of Britain, this word became *Evuroc* and later *Eofor;* to it the suffix *wic,* meaning "dwelling place," was added. Under the influence of the invading Danes, the name *Eoforwic* acquired the pronunciation *Iorvik,* and eventually *York* was the result.

Since this book is primarily concerned with words derived from Greek and Latin, it might be well to start our consideration of place names with those which the early Greeks and Romans gave to settlements outside their homeland. Naples was originally a Greek colony, and its name is a contraction of *Neapolis,* literally "New City." (See NE- and POLIS in the list of bases for this lesson.) Other places which were once settled by the Greeks and contain the Greek word for city, *polis,* are *Tripoli* (*Tripolis,* "Triple City"), Gallipoli (*kallos,* "beauty" and *polis*), and *Constantinople* ("Constantine's City"). Here also might be mentioned modern names like our own Annapolis (for Queen Anne), Indianapolis, and Arkopolis, which fortunately was discarded in favor of *Little Rock;* also the Russian Sevastopol (*sebastos,* "august").

The extent of the Roman Empire is likewise reflected by the names of some familiar cities. *Cologne* comes from *Colonia Agrippina,* an early Roman colony in Germany; the last part of *Lincoln,* the city in England, was also once *colonia,* i.e., "colony at Lindum." *Xeres,* or *Jerez,* in Spain, from which sherry takes its name, was originally (*Urbs*) *Caesaris,* "City of Caesar." The many English towns whose names end in *-chester* and *-caster,* such as *Winchester* and *Lancaster,* were once merely Roman military camps, the Latin word for which is *castra.*

In addition to the Romans, of course, each of the various other national groups which at one time or another invaded England (see Introduction, pp. 7-8) contributed its share of place names. A Celtic word for "river" is *avon,* and this is found today as the name of many English streams. The word *dun* in Celtic indicated a hill fortress, so names like *Dunstable, Dumbarton,* and *Dundee,* not to mention the French *Verdun,* belong to this early stratum. The Angles and the Saxons contributed, among others, the place names ending in *-ton, -ham, -bury, -burgh,* and the like, all conveying the idea of enclosure or protection. The towns settled by the Danish invaders a few centuries later are distinguished by such suffixes as *-thorp* and *-by,* originally "single farm" and later "village," e.g., *Derby* and *Rugby.**

In our own country the place names which have perhaps the most universal appeal are those of the fifty states. These, like many other words in our language, reflect the varied national backgrounds of the early explorers and settlers. The majority (twenty-six) of the names of the states are of course Indian; eleven are of English origin; six are from Spanish, and three from French. Two (*Indiana* and *Washington*) might be described as genuine American, while Dutch has perhaps provided us with one name, and the designation of one of our newest states, Hawaii, comes from a Polynesian language.†

Many of the states whose names have come from England were called after important persons. Virginia, for instance, was named by Sir Walter Raleigh for Elizabeth I, the Virgin Queen; Georgia, after King George II; Delaware, after Lord de la Ware, the first governor-general of Virginia; and the Carolinas, for King Charles I (*Carolus* being the Latin form of *Charles*).

Some of the most interesting names are those from Spanish. Florida, meaning "flowery," was discovered by Ponce de Leon shortly after Easter Sunday and was consequently named for that day, which in Spanish is called *Pascua Florida,* "Feast of the Flowers." The explorer meant also to indicate the fertility of this green land rich with the promise of spring flowers. *California* was originally the name of an imaginary land of gold and jewels, an island inhabited by Amazons, described in one of the Spanish romances of chivalry. The name was bestowed on this section of the New World (at first referring only to the peninsula of Lower California, which was thought to be an island) when one of Cortez's captains sent back a report from some Indians that such a very rich country was to be found to the northwest of Mexico. The name perhaps has no meaning at all and may simply have been coined by the writer of the popular romance in the same way as names of places in modern science-fiction stories.

---

* Isaac Taylor, *Words and Places,* abridged and edited by Beatrice S. Snell, London, 1925

†Based on Frederick Lawrence, "The Origin of American State Names," *National Geographic,* Aug. 1920, pp. 105–143.

Nevada in Spanish means "snowy," this name having been given to the state from the lofty Sierra Nevada range. *Colorado* (a cognate of English *colored*), meaning "red," was a term originally applied to the river because its waters contained so much reddish mud (cf. Red River and River Rouge); eventually the name was used for the state which is one of its sources. *Montana* means "mountainous."

French has given us *Vermont* (literally "Green Mountain"), *Louisiana* (after Louis XIV), and perhaps *Maine* (named for a province of France). The only Dutch contribution is Rhode Island. Apparently the name was originally spelled "Roode Eyland," meaning in Dutch "reddish island" from the color in the soil of an island nearby; when the English disputed the Dutch holdings in the New World, they gave a similar but more English-sounding name to the region.

The names given by the Indians, which usually refer to some natural feature of the land, likewise have significance in their languages; thus, for example, *Connecticut* (originally spelled "Quinetucquet" and applied to the river) meant "long estuary;" *Arizona*, "little spring;" and *Minnesota*, "cloudy water," describing a river at flood stage.

Hundreds of thousands of less important place names in the United States are of course impossible to classify. But to give some idea of the manifold ways in which they have come to appear on the map, a few miscellaneous examples of more than usual interest have been included here.*

Baton Rouge

A group of Frenchmen exploring the Mississippi River came to a place called in the Choctaw language *Istrouma*, which means "red post," because such a marker was used to indicate the boundary between the lands of two tribes. The French simply translated this into their own tongue as Baton Rouge.

Sedalia

The founder of Sedalia, Missouri, had a daughter named Sarah, whom he called by the pet name of "Sed." He therefore decided to name the new town in her honor *Sedville,* until a friend persuaded him that -*ville* was not a very dignified suffix and that a more impressive sounding name would be *Sedalia.*

The Bronx

In the early days of New York, just north of Manhattan was a farm

---

*Taken from George R. Stewart, *Names on the Land,* New York, 1945

owned by a Danish settler named Jonas Bronck. The stream which flowed past his property was known as Bronck's river, and the region came to be called "the Broncks" (later "Bronx") just as people say "the Smiths" to mean "where the Smiths live."

Berkeley

When a name was being sought for what is now Berkeley, California, several prominent officials were one afternoon inspecting the site of the proposed city and could see in the distance the ships sailing out through the Golden Gate. One of their number happened to quote the line from Bishop Berkeley's writings, "Westward the course of empire takes its way," which seemed so appropriate that the name of its author was at once chosen for the new city.

NOUN-FORMING SUFFIXES

Learn the following suffixes and their meanings:

I. *-ician,* "specialist in," "practitioner of"

TECHN-	art, skill	+	*-ician*	technician
ELECTR-	electricity	+	*-ician*	electrician
TACT-	to arrange	+	*-ician*	tactician

This suffix is actually a compound of *-ic,* or *-ics* (see Lesson VII) and *-ian* (see Lesson VIII).

II. *-ism,* "belief in," "practice of," "condition of"

		COMMUN-			+	*-ism*	Communism
		DESPOT-	absolute ruler		+	*-ism*	despotism
ant-	+	AGON-	struggle		+	*-ism*	antagonism
		ALCOHOL			+	*-ism*	alcoholism

III. *-ist,* "one who believes in," "one engaged in"

		COMMUN-		+	*-ist*	communist
ant-	+	AGON-	struggle	+	*-ist*	antagonist

IV. *-ite,* "one connected with," "inhabitant of" (also used to denote chemicals, minerals, etc.)

SYBAR-		+	-ite	sybarite
ISRAEL-		+	-ite	Israelite
DYNAM-	force	+	-ite	dynamite

A. If this is followed by an additional suffix, the *e* disappears.

SYBAR- + -*ite* + -*ic*   sybaritic

ASSIGNMENT

I. Learn the following bases and their meanings:

AGOG-, -AGOGUE	to lead	demagogic
		synagogue
CHIR- (CHEIR-)	hand	chiropractor
COSM-	universe, order	cosmic, cosmetic
HETER-	other, different	heterogeneous
		heterosexual
NE-	new, new and different form of	neon, neoclassic
		Neoplatonism
ODONT-	tooth	orthodontia
		mastodon
OP-, OPT-	eye, to see	optic, autopsy
ORTH-	straight, correct	orthodox
PED- (PAED-)	child (-PEDIA, education)	pediatrician
		encyclopedia

(Do not confuse this with the Latin base PED-, "foot," as in *pedal* and *pedestrian*.)

POL-, POLIS	city, state	politician, policy
		Annapolis

II. Analyze the following italicized words and define them as they are used in the sentence or phrase.

1. Foot doctors began to be called *chiropodists* in the 18th century — just why is not certain. —*Time*

2. William, however, with *politic* clemency, abstained from shedding the blood even of the most culpable. —Macaulay

3. Frequently in the practice of *orthopaedic* surgery there is need for bone, either to pack an area from which diseased bone has been removed or to supply bone where bone has never grown . . . —*Harper's Magazine*

4. I cannot open my lips at home on the subject we have been discussing, and I am looked at coldly here, in my own village, on account of my *heterodox* opinions. —W. H. Hudson

5. (a) . . . Ikhnaton set aside the prevailing *pantheism* in which the God Amon and Amon's priests ruled over a motley array of other deities. —*Time*

   (b) His original attitude — a purely sensuous worship of nature . . . — became steadily more spiritualized until it reached that of a wholly mystical *pantheistic* worship of the natural world. —*Atlantic Monthly*

6. He began to lecture his followers with the . . . air of a *pedagogue*, and sought out occasions to worry them with small discipline. —Henry Adams

7. The *polytheistic* system of the Indians, like that of the ancient Greeks, was of that accommodating kind which could admit within its elastic folds the deities of any other religion, without violence to itself. —William Hickling Prescott

8. Many children go through a period when they wear braces placed upon their teeth by an *orthodontist*.

9. Moreover, he is a polished gentleman, — a citizen of the world — yes, a true *cosmopolite;* for he will speak like a native of each clime and country on the globe. —Hawthorne

10. He was referred by his dentist to an *exodontist* for the removal of the tooth.

11. He did not disdain the low arts of a *demagogue* to gain the favor of the populace. —Prescott

12. It is not for nothing that Shakespeare was the greatest *neologist* who ever wrote in English . . . —*Harper's Magazine*

13. He went to an *optician* to have the frames of his glasses straightened.

14. ... has set up widespread village nurse and sanitation pro-
grams, instructed village women in pregnancy and *pediatrics*.
—*Time*

15. The strategy of the Nazis was generally dictated by considera-
tions of *geopolitics*.

16. "... the *synoptic* vision of an Augustine or St. Thomas
Aquinas ..." —*Time*

17. The hunter took the animal which he had shot to a *taxidermist*.

18. A police *ballistics* expert examined the bullet.

19. *Orthodox* believers regarded his ideas as godless.

20. Last week the National Association of Chiropodists changed
its name to American Podiatry Association, hoped that victims of corns, calluses and ingrown toenails would begin
calling the nation's 8,000 foot doctors "*podiatrists*." —*Time*

III. The following are common nouns formed from place names (see
Lesson I). List the place from which each has been derived and,
in the case of cities and districts, give the location.

Example: *canter*, from *Canterbury*, England

1. bantam	9. milliner
2. bayonet	10. peach
3. bungalow	11. spaniel
4. bunk (nonsense)	12. spruce
5. currant	13. tarantula
6. dollar	14. turquoise
7. gypsy	15. tuxedo
8. magenta	

LESSON X Expressions*

Not only individual words but also common phrases and expressions
often have unusual histories, and many people find the explanation of
their origins a most interesting study. Thus the expression "sold down

---

*The examples in this lesson have been taken from Charles E. Funk, *A Hog
on Ice and Other Curious Expressions*, New York, 1948.

the river" takes us back to the days of slavery in this country. In the nineteenth century the sugar and rice plantations of Louisiana were rapidly expanding, while agriculture in the upper South was declining. It therefore became a frequent and tragic practice to sell slaves from the plantations of Virginia and Kentucky, where they were used to less exhausting labor, to dealers "down river" in New Orleans. From here they were often shipped to the cane fields, where the climate was unwholesome and the work brutal.

The origin of the phrase "to look a gift horse in the mouth," meaning to be critical of something which one has been given, is not so apparent in modern times as it was in horse and buggy days, when the customary way of judging a horse's age was to examine its teeth. Thus it was impolite to show concern about the age of an animal which one had received as a present.

The sources of several expressions are to be found in absurd and long forgotten beliefs about the habits of certain animals. "Crocodile tears" owes its origin to a notion, once actually held, that the crocodile, after it had devoured its prey, shed tears over the fate of its victim. "Swan song," a last book or farewell speech, comes from the belief that the swan, which was unable to sing throughout its life, gave forth glorious melodies when it felt the approach of death. "To lick into shape" reflects the erroneous idea that, when a bear cub was first born, it was merely a formless lump of flesh, and that only by the assiduous licking of its mother did it acquire its characteristic shape.

Another expression taken from animal lore is "show the white feather," that is, to play the coward. This actually comes from the so-called sport of cockfighting. At one time the belief was current that, if a gamecock had any white feathers in its tail, it was of an inferior breed and would immediately turn its back on an opponent and run.

Several curious phrases have undergone changes in form suggested by their meaning but actually reflecting a misunderstanding of their source (see Folk Etymology, p. 96); and so, while picturesque, they only make literal sense in terms of their actual origin. Thus the "favor" of "to curry favor" was once spelled *fauvel* or *favel* (meaning in French "chestnut horse"), and in a famous medieval French allegory such a horse appeared as a symbol of deceit (somewhat like Reynard the Fox). Perhaps as a result of this poem, then, "to curry Fauvel," meant to gain a person's friendship by cunning flattery; but, because of the meaning of the expression, and since "Fauvel" sounded unfamiliar, the word was eventually transformed into the more recognizable "favor." In the saying "to eat humble pie," *humble* was originally *umble* or *numble,* the numbles being an old term for the entrails of a deer or other animal, which were given to the servants, while the choicer parts were reserved for the nobles. "Forlorn hope" is simply the way in which the Dutch military expression *verloren hoop,* the equivalent of "lost battalion" (*verloren,* "lost," "abandoned;" *hoop,* "troop") sounded to English ears. The Dutch phrase referred to a small detachment of soldiers who undertook some especially dangerous mission. Since many such enterprises had little chance of success, the pronunciation of the words suggested in English "forlorn hope" and came to have the meaning of a desperate venture which will more than likely fail.

"Flash in the pan" likewise comes from military language. On the old flintlock musket there was a small pan containing gunpowder, which received the spark from the flint and was ignited. This in turn exploded the charge of powder in the barrel. Sometimes, however, although the powder in the pan was ignited, the main charge failed to fire, so that the only result of the long and laborious task of loading such a weapon was an ineffectual "flash in the pan."

Finally, a "red-letter day" was originally a holy day, one in honor of some saint or on which a church festival took place, so called from the custom of marking such days on the calendar in red. Now the expression means a day memorable because of some personal experience.

NOUN-FORMING SUFFIXES

Learn the following suffixes and their meanings:

I. *-ast, -st,* "one who does"

		GYMN-	naked	+	*-ast*	gymnast
en-	+	THUS(i)- (THEOS-)	god	+	*-ast*	enthusiast
ana-	+	LY-	to loosen	+	*-st*	analyst

II. *-t, -te,* "he who," "that which"

		POE-	to make	+	*-t*	poet
pro-	+	PHE-	to speak	+	*-t*	prophet
		ATHLE-	to contend	+	*-te*	athlete
		PIRA-	to attempt	+	*-te*	pirate

III. -y, -ia, "quality of," "state of," "act of"

AGON-	struggle + -y	agony
PHIL- to love + ANTHROP- man	+ -y	philanthropy
an- + (H)EM-	blood + -ia	anemia

ASSIGNMENT

I. Learn the following bases and their meanings:

ALL-	other	allegory, parallel
CAC-	bad	cacogenics, cacophony
CAU-, CAUS-	to burn	cauterize
CLA-	to break	iconoclast
DO-	to give	dose, antidote
DYN-, DYNAM-	force, power	dynasty dynamic, dynamo
ERG-, URG-	work	erg, energy metallurgy
LAT(E)R-	to worship excessively, to be fanatically devoted to	idolater idolatry
PATH-	to feel, to suffer, disease	sympathy, telepathy, pathology
PHY-	to grow; PHYSI-, nature	neophyte physics physiology
STA-	to stand, to stop	static
THE-	to place, to put	thesis, theme synthetic

II. Analyze the following italicized words and define them as they are used in the sentence or phrase.

1. . . . but the punishment of death is inflicted upon the *apostates* who have professed and deserted the law of Mahomet. —Edward Gibbon

2. The camera watches this grisly operation so closely that the moviegoer, with a little *empathy,* can feel the cold blade as it glides across the neck. —*Time*

3. The truths which are ultimately accepted as the first principles of a science, are really the last results of *metaphysical* analysis. —John Stuart Mill

4. Great generals with armies at their backs start into being from apparent nothingness ... found ephemeral *dynasties,* and pass away like mists. —John Addington Symonds

5. I can think of no *epithet* but snaky to describe this man. —W. H. Hudson

6. Churchill was determined to avoid the *holocaust* of great casualties and long stalemate. —*Atlantic Monthly*

7. The skin eruption was due to an *allergy.*

8. In former times old women were sometimes accused of *demonolatry.*

9. (a) But the Henry Ford of the earlier Model T days was an *iconoclast* attacking in the name of morality and science the established order of J. P. Morgan. —*Harper's Magazine*

   (b) ... cleared the way for Western experts to remove the plaster and paint that pious, *iconoclastic* Moslems had daubed over the great Christian mosaics. —*Time*

10. Nothing is more essential than that permanent, inveterate *antipathies* against particular nations and passionate attachments for others should be excluded. —Washington

11. ... the error commonly made by *neophyte* students of political science: that you can pass a law to stop almost everything, including sin. —*Harper's Magazine*

12. In quite the same way as the *thermostat* manipulates the fuel supply to maintain a prearranged temperature in the house ... —*Harper's Magazine*

13. In dark nights, when your thoughts had wandered to vast and *cosmogonal* themes in other spheres ... —Thoreau

14. Her favorite strong blues and purples would have struck painfully on the refined colour-sense of an *aesthete*. —Hudson

15. Thirty years' observation of Roman society had sharpened her wit and given her an inexhaustible store of *anecdote*. —Henry James

16. Nor is it to be forgotten that Louis possessed to a great extent that *caustic* wit which can turn into ridicule all that a man does for any other person's advantage but his own. —Sir Walter Scott

17. These things are rank image-worship; and where *iconolatry* enters, the faith is dying. —*Harper's Magazine*

18. In the federal capital of Lagos . . . where gleaming buildings rise among the slums, the streets are a *cacophony* of honking autos and a torrent of heedless jaywalkers. —*Time*

19. Some stood aghast and bewildered at the fatal blow; others were sunk in the *apathy* of despair. —Francis Parkman

20. There is no better *antidote* against entertaining too high an opinion of others, than having an excellent one of ourselves at the very same time. —Scott.

LESSON XI Words and Religion

Our vocabulary, as we have seen, has come from many different geographical sources, Greece, Rome, France, Arabia, India, etc. But there is another way of classifying the sources of numerous English words and expressions, and that is to consider them according to the various spheres of activity which have contributed them to our language. Thus, religion, farming, sport, seafaring, all have greatly enriched our speech with their distinctive terminology which has passed into general usage; but often we are no longer aware of the origins of such words and so are not conscious of their one-time connection with a particular activity. *Adept* (Latin *adeptus,* "one who has arrived at"), for instance, was originally a term from alchemy and referred to a person who claimed to have "arrived at" the secret of transmuting base metals into gold. *Average* (French *avarie,* "damage to a ship or goods") is derived from the language of the sea, where it came to mean in maritime law the equitable division of such loss among the backers of the voyage, and through this step it acquired its current meaning. In tracing the histories of words contributed to our language in this fashion, we shall meet many examples which will illuminate the life and culture of the past and so serve as landmarks in the history of human progress.

In considering some of the areas from which words have become the common property of our speech, we might start with religion. The Bible has of course provided us with many such terms, and the sources of these are generally familiar to anyone acquainted with the Scriptures. Nevertheless, several are worth mentioning here if only because they are so common that their origin is often overlooked. *Scapegoat,* for instance, was originally *escape goat,* and referred in the Old Testament (see Lev. 16: 10) to an animal over which the high priest of the Jews confessed the sins of the people; then the goat was allowed to "escape," and it wandered off into the wilderness symbolically carrying away upon itself all the wickedness of the Children of Israel.

The expression "the handwriting on the wall" comes from the Book of Daniel (5), where at the feast of King Belshazzar in Babylon the figure of a hand mysteriously appeared and wrote on the wall that Belshazzar had been weighed in the balance and found wanting, and that his rule was at an end. That very night Belshazzar was killed and his kingdom divided among the Medes and the Persians.

In New Testament times *talent* meant a weight of gold or silver and therefore referred to an amount of money. It acquired its modern meaning of "native ability" when Christ in a parable (Matt. 25: 14–30) described three servants who had each been entrusted by their master with a certain number of talents of silver which he expected them to invest wisely. What Christ meant by the parable was that our inborn abilities, like the money given to the servants, is a trust from God to be used in His service, and from this passage *talent* acquired its figurative meaning.

To cite a less common example, *shibboleth,* a phrase or watchword which is the distinctive formula of a particular group, comes from the Book of Judges (12: 6), where it was used as a test word to distinguish friend from foe, since the enemy could not pronounce the sound "sh."

Not so well known are the origins of certain words which have developed in the later ages of Christianity. Many have perhaps wondered what the connection was between "the Orient" and "Orientation," a course which modern college freshmen often take. Both words come from the Latin *oriri,* "to rise," and originally referred to the rising sun, that is, the east; when first used the verb *orient* meant to place a church in the proper position, with its altar at the east end, to allow the congregation to face Jerusalem. Gradually the term became generalized to refer to the placing of anything in its proper position.

Bead comes from the Old English *bed,* "prayer" (related to Modern English *bid*), its present meaning having arisen from the use of strings of prayer beads. *Gossip* is a combination of *God* and Anglo-Saxon *sibb,* "relative" (cf. *sibling*), and at first meant "godparent." From the fact that godparents were usually elderly people, who are often much given to discussing the shortcomings of others, *gossip* acquired its current meaning. The color *chartreuse* by a rather devious route goes back to the name of a monastery in France *La Grande Chartreuse,* the former headquarters of the Carthusian Order. Here the monks manufactured a pale green liqueur called, as is customary, after the place, and this name has come to designate a color similar to that of the liqueur.

Dirge represents the first word of the Latin hymn for the burial of the dead, *Dirige, Domine, Dominus meus, in conspectu tuo viam meam,* "Direct, O Lord, my God, my way in thy sight." *Adieu* is from the French, meaning "to God" (cf. Spanish *adios*) and is roughly equivalent to the English *good-bye,* which is a contraction of "God be with ye." Originally *carnival* was specifically the festival of merrymaking just before Lent; it is derived from the Latin *carnem levare,* "to remove meat" (CARN-, "flesh," Part I, Lesson VIII), from the religious practice of abstaining from meat during that period.

NOUN-FORMING SUFFIXES

Learn the following suffixes and their meanings:

I. *-ma, -m, -me,* "result of"

		DRA-	to do, to act	+	*-ma*	drama
pro-	+	BLE-	to put	+	*-m*	problem
dia-	+	DE-	to bind	+	*-m*	diadem
		THE-	to place	+	*-me*	theme

A. If this is followed by an additional suffix, it usually becomes *-mat-*.

		DRA-	to do, to act	+	*-mat-*	+	*-ic*	dramatic
pro-	+	BLE-	to put	+	*-mat-*	+	*-ic*	problematic
		THE-	to place	+	*-mat-*	+	*-ic*	thematic

II. *-sis, -se, -sy, -sia,* "act of," "state of," "result of"

ana-	+	LY-	to loosen	+	*-sis*	analysis
dia-	+	GNO-	to know	+	*-sis*	diagnosis
		DO-	to give	+	*-se*	dose
AUT(o)- self		+ OP-	to see	+	*-sy*	autopsy
a-	+	MNE-	to remember	+	*-sia*	amnesia

A. The adjectival form of this suffix sometimes appears as *-tic* and sometimes as *-stic*.

| ana- | + | LY- | to loosen | + | *-tic* | analytic |
| dia- | + | GNO- | to know | + | *-stic* | diagnostic |

ASSIGNMENT

I. Learn the following bases and their meanings:

ANDR-	man, male	androgenous philander
KINE-, CINE-	to move	kinetic cinema
GEN(E)-	kind, race	genocide genealogy
GYN(E)-, GYNEC- (GYNAEC-)	woman, female	gynarchy gynecology
IDI-	one's own, peculiar	idiot, idio-syncrasy
LITH-, -LITE	stone	lithograph phonolite
MIS-	hatred	misanthrope
PHE-, PHA- (PHEM-, voice)	to speak	prophet aphasia
SCHIZ-, SCHIS-	to split	schizophrenia schism
STERE-	solid, three-dimensional	stereophonic stereopticon
TYP-	stamp, model	typographical typical

II. Analyze the following italicized words and define them as they are used in the sentence or phrase.

1. She haunted the San Francisco *Chronicle* city room for six months before penetrating the conventional *misogyny* of the craft and persuading the weekly news review to hire her. — *Time*

2. The *cinematic* art has greatly progressed since the days of silent pictures.

3. In the ruins of Hacilar, an ancient Anatolian town . . . Mellaart has discovered the remains of a culture so sophisticated as to shatter all previous notions about Late *Neolithic* man. — *Time*

4. It was a *heterogeneous* assemblage of people of all ranks and countries, who had arrived in all kinds of vehicles. —Washington Irving

5. In some of the tribes where men outnumber women *polyandry* is a common practice.

6. (a) There are those to whom this particular kind of biography is *anathema,* no matter who does it or how good it is . . . —*Harper's Magazine*

   (b) A dire *anathema* was thundered against them and their posterity if they should dare to renew the same freedom of choice. —Edward Gibbon

7. . . . it makes no difference to the *prognosis* whether treatment is given or not . . . —*Atlantic Monthly*

8. It involves what the experts call "vulnerability reduction" — a polite military *euphemism* to describe the relocation of populations, the decentralization of industry . . . —*Harper's Magazine*

9. He was in an *ecstasy* of fear, for he shivered from head to foot. — A. Conan Doyle

10. The *schism* which was then appearing in the nation, and which has been from that time almost constantly widening, had little in common with those schisms which had divided it during the reigns of the Tudors and the Stuarts. — Macaulay

11. The House of Commons, the *archetype* of all the representative assemblies which now meet, either in the old or in the new world . . . —Macaulay

12. The picture presents two hours and 25 minutes of continuously colossal spectacle in CinemaScope, Technicolor and *stereophonic* sound. —*Time*

13. The young man's reply marked him as a foreigner, not by any variation from the *idiom* and accent of good English, but because he spoke with more caution and accuracy, than if perfectly familiar with the language. — Hawthorne

14. Television is not just the latest and most miraculous of these media. It is a *synthesis* of them all. —*Harper's Magazine*

15. Without committing ourselves to the *dogmatism* of a theory, we are led to certain general conclusions. —John Addington Symonds

16. Even France, possessed of one of the most *homogeneous* communities in the world, is finding it a herculean task to draft a constitution which will satisfy conflicting class interests. — *Harper's Magazine*

17. Hence when experiments showed that light can travel in a vacuum, scientists evolved a *hypothetical* substance called "ether" which they decided must pervade all space and matter. — *Harper's Magazine*

18. . . . useless ornamentation is the *antithesis* of beauty. —*Harper's Magazine*

19. The doctor's *misanthropic* mistrust of mankind (the bitterer because based on personal failure) . . . —Joseph Conrad

20. ". . . that *stereotype* of the Communist Russian which is too prevalent in American thinking." — *Time*

LESSON XII   Words and Religion

In continuing our discussion of words which have arisen in connection with religious beliefs and practices, we shall consider in this lesson some words coming from non-Christian sources. One important element in the religion of the ancient Greeks and Romans was the prediction of the future by means of omens, that is, by means of some unusual occurrence, such as a bolt of lightning, which could be regarded as a sign from heaven; and this practice has given us words like *ominous* and *abominate* (literally, "to regard as a bad omen"). Before any important course of action was decided upon at Rome, it was customary for certain priests called *augurs* to search for some omen which would indicate whether or not the gods looked with favor upon the enterprise; thus the word *inaugurate* meant (formerly) "to make a formal beginning by consulting the omens." One of the most usual ways of foretelling the future was to observe the flight of birds, and this practice was called in Latin *auspicium* (*avis*, "bird," and SPIC-, "to look"); so originally an *auspicious* occasion was one which had begun with some such good omen as the appearance of a flock of six white doves. *Monster,* as the root of the word indicates (MON-, "to warn," "to show"; cf. *demonstrate*), likewise owes its origin to this type of belief; an abnormally formed animal was regarded as a portent of evil.

Another religious belief of the Greeks and Romans is reflected in the word *enthusiasm,* literally, "state of having a god within" (Greek, *en-,* "in," and THE-, "god"), which indicates that a person in religious ecstasy was regarded as actually having been taken possession of by a divinity. But this is not a belief peculiar to the Greeks, as is shown by the original meaning of *giddy,* "god-possessed," which is of Teutonic ancestry (apparently from Germanic *gud-,* "god"). Likewise, when we speak of a statement as *oracular* in the sense of solemn and wise, we are recalling the oracles of the ancient world, the shrines at which were priests or priestesses who served as mediums through whom the gods foretold the future and who consequently spoke with the voices of the gods.

The religions of more distant lands have also contributed terms to the English language. Perhaps we should add that in some cases it is an erroneous idea of other beliefs which has been responsible for the appearance of such words in English. Westerners have not always understood the faiths of other peoples. Somehow Christians of the Middle Ages got the notion that the Mohammedans worshiped a deity by the name of *Tervagant* or *Termagant,* which of course they do not. In the religious dramas of the times Termagant was represented as a violent, quarrelsome bully, naturally one of the villains of the piece. From this characterization the name came to mean a woman of violent temper. *Juggernaut* is a distorted version of *Jagannath,* one of the avatars of the Hindu god Vishnu. At the festival in his honor a large image of this god is drawn through the streets in a wagon, and the erroneous belief arose among Europeans that his devotees in a frenzy of religious fervor threw themselves in front of the vehicle to be crushed by its wheels. Hence today *juggernaut* refers to an irresistible force which blindly runs over whatever gets in its way.

In one instance, unfortunately, the reputation of an Indian sect has been all too deserved. Until they were suppressed by the British, the *Thugs* (Hindi *thag,* "thief"), a secret religious group who worshiped Kali, the Hindu goddess of destruction, made it a practice to murder and rob in the service of the goddess. They usually selected as their victims wealthy travelers, whom they invariably killed, generally by strangulation, in honor of Kali; part of the proceeds from such activities were also devoted to the deity. The word *thug* has come into our language reminding us of their brutality.

The term *mufti* in reference to civilian clothes worn by soldiers apparently represents the Arab word for an expounder of Mohammedan religious law. (At the present time the Grand Mufti is often mentioned by newspapers in connection with the Arab nations.) This use of the word may have come from the resemblance between the costume of such a priestly official and the dressing gown and tasseled cap which so many British officers of the nineteenth century wore when off duty.

From the West African religions has come *fetish* (Portuguese *feitico,* "charm"), a term applied by the early explorers from Portugal to idols and amulets which the natives regarded as possessing magical powers because of an indwelling supernatural spirit. From Polynesia has come *taboo,* referring originally to religious prohibitions placed upon certain objects or words or actions, the violation of which would release evil magical forces, although the term today is often used simply to mean the restrictions enforced by social custom.

NOUN-FORMING SUFFIXES (COMBINING FORMS)

The following are not strictly speaking suffixes, but have been formed from bases. Thus *-logy* is an adaptation of LOG-, "speech," "word." Since these occur so frequently as the final element of compound words, however, they are more conveniently treated as suffixes. Learn the following combining forms and their meanings:

I. *-logy,* "science of," "systematic study of"

BI(o)-	life	+	*-logy*	biology
THE(o)-	god	+	*-logy*	theology
ASTR(o)-	star	+	*-logy*	astrology

II. *-nomy,* "science of," "system of laws governing"

ASTR(o)-	star	+	-*nomy*	astronomy
EC(o)-	house, community	+	-*nomy*	economy
AGR(o)-	field	+	-*nomy*	agronomy

A. When the two preceding suffixes are followed by additional elements, the final *y* disappears.

BI(o)-   life + *-logy* + *-ist*   biologist
ASTR(o)- star + *-nomy* + *-ic* + *-al* astronomical

III. *-cracy,* "rule by," "type of government"

DEM(o)-	people	+	*-cracy*	democracy
ARIST(o)-	the best	+	*-cracy*	aristocracy
BUREAU-		+	*-cracy*	bureaucracy

IV. *-crat,* "one who advocates or practices rule by"

DEM(o)-	people	+	*-crat*	democrat
ARIST(o)-	the best	+	*-crat*	aristocrat

ASSIGNMENT

I. Learn the following bases and their meanings:

AUT-	self	automobile, automatic
GASTR-	stomach	gastric, gastrointestinal
HELI-	sun	helium, heliocentric
IDE-	thought, idea	ideal, ideation
MANC-, MANT-	to divine by means of	bibliomancy, pyromancy mantic
MICR-	small, one millionth part of	microphone, microscope microgram
NECR-	the dead, corpse, dead tissue	necrosis, necropolis
PALE- (PALAE-)	old	paleontology paleography
PSEUD-	false	pseudoscientific pseudointellectual
PSYCH-	mind	psychology, psychosis
TROP-	to turn	tropic, phototropic

II. Analyze the following italicized words and define them as they are used in the sentence or phrase.

1. Christ was to be considered the Head of the State. This step at once gave a *theocratic* bias to the government which determined all the acts of the monk's administration. — John Addington Symonds

2. I again felt rather like an individual of but average *gastronomical* powers sitting down to a feast alone at a table spread with provisions for a hundred. — Charlotte Brontë

3. Suntan oils may cause inflammation at the very time they are protecting the skin against sunburn, warned *Dermatologist* Wiley M. Sams of Miami. — *Time*

4. In jail and out, in Hollywood and during a self-imposed exile in Mexico, Dalton Trumbo wrote some 30 movies under assorted *pseudonyms*. —*Time*

5. A specialist in *gynecology* . . .

6. . . . Copernicus' universe carried shattering implications because it was *heliocentric*. —*Time*

7. It is felt that possible damage to the child's emotional and social adjustment will be avoided by keeping him with children of his own *chronological* age . . . —*Atlantic Monthly*

8. Only fourteen miles to the west of Athens, Greek *archaeologists* found the great sanctuary of Demeter at Eleusis . . . — *Atlantic Monthly*

9. This particular plant is *heliotropic*.

10. The doctors were so confident that . . . the diseased area showed no sign of malignancy that they did not bother to take a *biopsy* specimen . . . —*Time*

11. Publication of this novel was held up for two years in the Soviet Union because of its "*ideological* deviations." —*Time*

12. . . . and the islands, which so harmoniously unite earth and sea, farmer and fisherman, soldier and sailor . . . are, each individually, a *microcosm* of Greece, reflecting the whole course of its history. — *Atlantic Monthly*

13. To regard a prairie dog as belonging to the same species as a

cocker spaniel shows a complete ignorance of the rules of *taxonomy.*

14. A third guest was a hypochondriac, whose imagination wrought *necromancy* in his outward and inward world, and caused him to see monstrous faces in the household fires. — Hawthorne

15. Adequate *psychiatric* treatment is available in some hospitals.

16. The contentment of the Pygmies puzzled the *anthropologist,* and he searched for a reason for it. — *Time*

17. . . . *paleolithic* man, crouching in his cave a hundred thousand years ago . . . —*Atlantic Monthly*

18. Subject since 1954 to state control of jobs, salaries and classifications, the university protested that it was unable to compete for top teachers unless it had *autonomy* in hiring and firing. — *Time*

19. *Ethnologists,* classifying White men in accordance with their physical types, long heads and round heads, fair skins and dark skins, have sorted out three main White "races" . . . — Arnold Toynbee

20. . . . and the menace to that peace and freedom lies in the existence of *autocratic* governments backed by organized force which is controlled wholly by their will, not by the will of their people. — Woodrow Wilson

III. Given names generally have a meaning in the language in which they have originated. Thus, in French, *Lionel* means "young lion"; in Hebrew *Michael* means "Who is like God?" and in Anglo-Saxon *Edward* means "guardian of wealth." With the aid of your dictionary give the literal meanings of the following given names which are derived from Greek. (In WNCD and ACD see the special section at the back of the work; in WNWD names are listed alphabetically in the body of the work.)

1. Alexander	6. George
2. Anastasia	7. Peter
3. Christopher	8. Philip
4. Dorothea	9. Sophia
5. Eugene	10. Theodore

LESSON XIII   Sea Terms

The sea has always played a large part in the lives of the English-speaking peoples, and this fact is reflected by the many words and expressions in our language which have become so much a part of our general everyday speech that we have forgotten their source. But a realization of their original application should serve to remind us of the romantic days before the invention of steam power when the oceans were sailed by iron men in wooden ships. Thus *aloof,* from Dutch *loef,* "side toward the wind," was once used to describe a ship which kept well clear of the lee shore, toward which the wind might drive her, and it gradually passed into generalized use in the sense of remaining at a distance. "To be taken aback" referred to a vessel which had become unmanageable because its sails were pressed "backward" against the mast by a sudden shift of wind which struck their forward surface.

Rummage was originally the arrangement of cargo in a ship's hold, from Germanic *rum,* "room." The word acquired its present meaning of miscellaneous articles perhaps from the custom of holding "rummage sales," that is, sales of unclaimed articles at the docks; or perhaps the current meaning of the word was suggested by the confusion and clutter which seem to be present when goods are stowed in the hold. In the same way *junk* originally referred to pieces of old rope kept around a ship, from which were made mats and fenders and such.

Filibuster was a term at first applied to a privateer (by a series of changes in form ultimately from Dutch *vrijbuiter,* "freebooter"), in the seventeenth century little more than a pirate. Later it came to refer to one who made an unauthorized attack for personal gain against a country with which his own nation was at peace. Eventually, reflecting both the idea of irregular warfare and of piracy, the term was tranferred to a member of a legislative body who obstructs the passage of a bill by means of a long speech, and now it is used to designate the speech itself.

As a ship goes through the water, the wind striking against its side often causes a certain amount of lateral movement, and so in figuring a course some allowance must be made for this sideward motion, which is known as *leeway* (*lee,* the sheltered side, opposite to *windward*). This word has come into the language of landlubbers to mean margin for error.

Before the days of dry docks, it was the practice to tilt a vessel over on its side in order to make repairs on sections normally below the water line, and this was known as *careening* (Latin *carina,* "keel"). The term was also applied to a ship which a heavy sea caused to heel over, and eventually it came to refer to any moving object which lurches from side to side, as in the sentence, "The overloaded truck careened down the hill."

When we ask someone to lend us money to "tide us over" until payday, we are likewise using a nautical phrase, which originally meant to rely on a high tide to carry a ship over an obstruction. Some other common terms which were originally the exclusive property of sailors are *mainstay* (a line supporting the mainmast), *make headway,* and *arrive* (literally, "to reach shore," from Latin *ad,* "to," and *ripa,* "bank," "shore").

NOUN-FORMING SUFFIXES (COMBINING FORMS)

Learn the following combining forms and their meanings:

I. *-archy,* "rule by"

MON-	one	+	*-archy*	monarchy
MATRI-	mother	+	*-archy*	matriarchy

II. *-arch,* "one who rules"

MON-	one	+	*-arch*	monarch
MATRI-	mother	+	*-arch*	matriarch

A. Sometimes *arch(i)-* is placed in front of a base to mean "chief," "leading"

arch-	+	ANGEL	messenger	archangel
arch-	+	BISHOP		archbishop
archi-	+	TECT-	workman	architect

III. *-mania,* "madness about," "passion for"

KLEPT(o)-	thief	+	*-mania*	kleptomania
DIPS(o)-	thirst	+	*-mania*	dipsomania

IV. *-maniac,* "one having a madness or passion for"

KLEPT(o)-	thief	+	*-maniac*	kleptomaniac
DIPS(o)-	thirst	+	*-maniac*	dipsomaniac

V. *-phobia,* "abnormal fear of"

| CLAUSTR(o)- | lock, bar | + | *-phobia* | claustrophobia |
| AGORA | place of assembly, market place | + | *-phobia* | agoraphobia |

VI. *-phobe,* "one who fears or hates"

| ANGL(o)- | English | + | *-phobe* | Anglophobe |
| FRANC(o)- | French | + | *-phobe* | Francophobe |

ASSIGNMENT

I. Learn the following bases and their meanings:

ACR-	highest, the extremities	acrobat, acrostic
EGO- (Latin)	I	egotism, egoism
HIER-	sacred	hieroglyphic, hieratic
HYDR-	water	hydroelectric, hydraulic
MEGA-, MEGAL-	large, a million	megaphone, megacycle megalomania
OLIG-	few	oligarchy
PATR- (PATRI-, family, clan)	father	patriot, patristic patriarch
SOPH-	wise	philosophy, sophomore
TELE-	afar, operating at a distance	telephone, telegraph
XEN-	stranger, foreigner	xenogamy
ZO-	animal	zoology

II. Analyze the following italicized words and define them as they are used in the sentence or phrase.

1. (a) Johnson's profound reverence for the *Hierarchy* made him except from Bishops the highest degree of decorum. — James Boswell

(b) Professional baseball is now organized into a *hierarchy* as rigid as Virginia Society. At the top, of course, are the two major leagues . . . Below them stand the minor leagues, marshaled in carefully ordered ranks . . . —*Harper's Magazine*

2. I had always felt aversion to my uncourtly *patronymic* [Wilson]. —Edgar Allan Poe

3. Greek scholars reserved for themselves the area of Athens and excavated the *Acropolis.* —*Atlantic Monthly*

4. . . . lauding each other in terms that would make an *egomaniac* blush. —*Time*

5. He was introduced to *patristic* literature by finding at the bookseller's some volumes of the Fathers. — Thomas Hardy

6. Since several gasoline cans were found nearby, the fire seemed obviously the work of a *pyromaniac.*

7. . . . that *telepathy* with which as children they seemed at times to anticipate one another's actions as two birds leave a limb at the same instant. — William Faulkner

8. . . . climbed a 100-ft. tree, despite *acrophobia,* and with only one arm free . . . —*Time*

9. The ideal of many utopias is a philosophic *anarchism.*

10. . . . blending the incoherence of delirium with fragments of *theosophy* which might have been imported from old Alexandrian sources or from dim regions of the East. — John Addington Symonds

11. We Americans have felt, this time, at least some of the same war-weariness, the same *xenophobia,* that caused our revulsion from foreign responsibilities last time. — *Harper's Magazine*

12. To explain the solar system, Alfven says, other scientists have used plain old *hydrodynamics* (the behavior of fluids, including gases) . . . —*Time*

13. The high-risk driver's obvious faults are ill-concealed hostility lurking just below the surface, and an *egocentric* disregard for others' rights and feelings. —*Time*

14. The wings of bats are *homologous* to the front legs of mice.

15. The government of kings . . . gave place at long last, during a considerable lapse of time, to *oligarchies* of a few families. — John Stuart Mill

16. . . . the *Herald Tribune* and *World Telegram* printed new versions of their earlier prescient obits and brought their *necrology* up to date. —*Time*

17. He was a heavy man, with a *patriarchal* white beard, and of imposing stature. —Joseph Conrad

18. His particular egocentricity and *megalomania* made it seem that a composer who had not written for his ballet company was a composer whom he did not want . . . —*Atlantic Monthly*

19. In the adult it can cause *acromegaly* (a localized form of gigantism, with enlargement of the jaw and extremities). — *Time*

20. The development of reptiles began in the *Paleozoic* Era.

III. By combining Greek elements which have been previously studied, form English words with the following meanings. Then look up these words in a dictionary to make sure that they are listed there.

Example: abnormal fear of death — *thanatophobia.*

1. hatred of marriage
2. rule by women
3. madness for books
4. having a love for animals
5. palmistry, i.e., art of divination by means of the hand
6. a scientist who studies water
7. condition of hating new things
8. having many forms
9. the study of the teeth
10. abnormal fear of pain

LESSON XIV   Words from Sports and Games

The fact that many nautical terms have become a part of our general vocabulary indicates the large extent to which seafaring entered into the lives of our ancestors. But, if this is the case, what must we say about the emphasis which our forebears placed on sports and games? An even greater number of words and phrases from these activities have become generalized in meaning and have passed into our everyday language.

The word which perhaps best illustrates the pervasiveness of the influence of recreation upon our vocabulary is *check,* from the game of chess, the warning which one gives to an opponent that his king is in danger. (This word comes ultimately from the Persian *shāh,* "king," which is still the title for the ruler of Iran; *checkmate,* Persian *shāh māt,* means literally, "The king is dead or unable to escape.") So all of the various senses of *check* in modern English are metaphorical extensions of the original term, including *bank check* (the stubs act as a "check" or verification) and *checked,* "consisting of a pattern of small squares" (resembling a chessboard). *Exchequer,* a treasury, especially that of Great Britain, is likewise derived from the game of chess. In Norman England the accounts of public revenue were kept by placing counters on a table marked into squares like a chessboard.

Some words and expressions take us back to the sports of the Romans, "thumbs down," for instance, the supposed sign of the spectators at gladiatorial combats that the life of a beaten contestant should not be spared. Also *desultory,* "jumping from subject to subject, random," comes from the Latin *desultor,* an athlete who leaped from one horse to another while at full gallop.

In the Middle Ages the sport of falconry was popular, and though few people are interested in this today, it has left its mark on our vocabulary. *Haggard* originally referred to a hawk which had been captured at maturity and hence did not readily become used to captivity, keeping for a long time a wild, half-starved appearance. In the technical language of falconry a *lure* was a bunch of feathers used to recall a hawk which had been let fly, so the original meaning of *allure* was "to call back one's bird." *Reclaim* (Latin *re-,* "back," and *clamare,* "to cry out") also began as a technical term with the same meaning. Another popular medieval recreation is recalled by the expression "full tilt," which comes from tilting or jousting, the sport in which two horsemen galloped at one another, each trying to unseat his opponent with his lance.

Hunting, especially hunting with the hounds, has given our language many expressive terms and phrases. In the phrase "get wind of" *wind* refers of course to the air carrying the scent of the quarry. "At fault" originally meant having lost the trail, *fault* in hunting parlance referring to a dog's loss of scent. The expression became generalized to mean "perplexed and puzzled." Most people, however, are unaware of its origin, and it is normally used as the equivalent of "in fault," "guilty of error." The expression "at a loss" likewise first meant having lost the trail. "In full cry" referred to a pack of hunting dogs in pursuit of an animal; *cry* here describes the baying of the hounds.

Some methods of hunting unfamiliar to most of us, such as the use of beaters and nets, are recalled in the phrases "to beat around the bush" and "the toils of the law" (Old French *toile,* "net"). *Pitfall* originally denoted a concealed pit used as a trap for game.

In the case of various other sports, bowling has given us *bias* in its sense of "inclination," originally the oblique course which a ball follows, and *rub,* as in the expression "There's the rub," an obstacle which impedes a ball or turns it from its course. *Fluke* comes from billiards, where it meant a successful shot made by accident, while *bandy* is an old term from tennis and referred to a way of hitting the ball back and forth.

Less active and somewhat less respectable forms of recreation have also provided their share of additions to our general vocabulary. Even before the days of Julius Caesar and his traditional remark when crossing the Rubicon, "The die is cast," dicing had its devotees. *Hazard* meant originally a game of dice, the forerunner of craps (from Arabic *al-zahr,* "the die"). *Deuce,* though it is often used as a euphemism for devil, probably owes its origin to the exclamation of dismay from a gambler who has made the lowest possible throw, two. "Within an ace of" is also an expression derived from dicing, *ace* being originally a term for the single spot on a die, so the phrase means literally "within one point of."

Card games have of course provided many such terms. One of the most picturesque of these is the slang word *fourflusher,* "a person who makes a pretense." In poker a flush consists of five cards of the same suit, a relatively good hand, but a player with only four such cards may try to bluff his opponents into thinking he has a flush. "Pass the buck" also once was an expression used in poker; the *buck* was apparently a token which a player kept in front of him to remind him that it was his turn to deal next. If he did not care to deal, he "passed the buck" to the next player. The term *bunco,* "confidence game," reflects what happens all too often in gambling. It apparently comes from the Spanish *banco,* "bank," the name of an early card game. *Aboveboard* also suggests that cards are not always played fairly; the idea behind the term is that the players should keep their hands "above" the table so that they cannot substitute cards.

Finally, from cockfighting have come *crestfallen* and the slang *well-heeled* (referring originally to the custom of equipping the heels of the birds with sharp steel spurs); while "dark horse" has obviously been taken from racing and means specifically a horse whose background is little known, one about which we are "in the dark," in other words.

NOUN-FORMING SUFFIXES (COMBINING FORMS)

Learn the following combining forms and their meanings:

I. *-meter,* "measure," "instrument for measuring," "number of feet in poetry"

peri-		+	*-meter*	perimeter
dia-		+	*-meter*	diameter
PENTA-	five	+	*-meter*	pentameter

II. *-metry,* "art or science of measuring"

GE(o)-	earth			+	*-metry*	geometry
TRI-	three	+ GON(o)-	angle	+	*-metry*	trigonometry

III. *-graph,* "writing," "instrument for writing"

TELE-	far	+	*-graph*	telegraph
PHOT(o)-	light	+	*-graph*	photograph

IV. *-graphy,* "writing," "art or science of writing"

AUT(o)-	self	+ BI(o)-	life	+	*-graphy*	autobiography
TELE-	far			+	*-graphy*	telegraphy
PHOT(o)-	light			+	*-graphy*	photography

V. *-gram,* "thing written"

TELE-	far	+	*-gram*	telegram
dia-		+	*-gram*	diagram

VI. *-scope,* "instrument for viewing," "to view"

peri-		+	*-scope*	periscope
MICR(o)-	far	+	*-scope*	telescope
TELE-	small	+	*-scope*	microscope

A. When this is followed by an additional suffix, the *e* disappears.

TELE-	far	+	*-scope*	+	*-ic*	telescopic
MICR(o)-	small	+	*-scope*	+	*-y*	microscopy

ASSIGNMENT

I. Learn the following bases and their meanings:

BAR-	weight, pressure	barometer, barograph
CAL(L)-, KAL(L)-	beauty	calisthenics kaleidoscope
IS-	equal	isomerous, isosceles
MACR-	large, long	macron, macrocosm
ORA-	to see	panorama
PETR-	rock	petrify, petroleum
PHOT-	light	photograph, photosynthesis
TOP-	place	topic, utopia

II. Analyze the following italicized words and define them as they are used in the sentence or phrase.

1. But in her *topographical* ignorance as a late-comer to the place, she misreckoned the distance of her journey as not much more than half what it really was. —Thomas Hardy

2. . . . turning from the lonely *panorama* closed in by the distant Alps. —Dickens

3. The therapeutic application of radioactive *isotopes* is a broad field for future research. —*Atlantic Monthly*

4. The compass, the *chronometer,* the sextant gradually changed navigation from an art to a science . . . —*Time*

5. . . . —not *symmetrically* arranged like houses in a town, but helter-skelter here and there, as if the builders of them had no plan about it. —*Harper's Magazine*

6. The chief difficulty in learning to read Chinese is the great number of *ideographs* which must be studied.

7. In a nearby museum the battle is very realistically depicted in a *cyclorama*.

8. His eyes were examined for glasses by an *optometrist*.

9. After taking his degree in *petrography* he was employed by an oil company to explore new fields.

10. A *macroscopic* examination of this lesion fails to reveal its true nature.

11. How emancipated it sounds to dismiss in a moment's *epigram* an institution of nineteen hundred years! *—Harper's Magazine*

12. Within five months after his return from Nice, the deacon Athanasius was seated on the *archiepiscopal* throne of Egypt. —Edward Gibbon

13. It is believed that some of the Russian satellites have contained *telemetering* devices.

14. If she might speak of things worldly . . . she would hint to Mr. Warrington that his epistolary *orthography* was anything but correct. —Thackeray

15. We were warned by the sudden coldness of the weather, and the sinking of the mercury in the *barometer*. —Dickens

16. With the stilted gestures of *mimetic* tradition, he tells of his hopeless love for the leading lady of the troupe . . . *—Time*

17. The will was a *holograph,* for Mr. Utterson, though he took charge of it now that it was made, had refused to lend the least assistance in the making of it. —Robert Louis Stevenson

18. The difference in intensity of the two lights could only be determined by a very sensitive *photometer*.

19. For the Chinese art lover, the pleasure of viewing a painting includes enjoying the *calligraphy* of the written words as an art in itself . . . *—Time*

20. The daily weather maps published in many newspapers generally have the *isobars* marked on them.

III. According to many psychologists we live in an age of anxiety. At any rate, one exhaustive medical dictionary includes a special list of over a hundred phobias, the names of most of which have been formed from Greek elements. In this list are to be found such neological absurdities as *siderodromophobia,* "morbid fear of railroad trains" (*sideros,* "iron," and *dromos,* "course," as in *airdrome* and *hippodrome*), and *triskaidekaphobia,* "morbid fear of the number thirteen" (see Lesson XVI). The following are the names of some obscure phobias which you are not likely to encounter again but which will give you practice in the recognition of Greek word elements. Match Column B with Column A.

A	B
1. scopophobia	(a) fear of children
2. dysmorphophobia	(b) fear of people
3. pedophobia	(c) fear of rabies
4. ballistophobia	(d) fear of insects
5. ergophobia	(e) fear of animals' teeth
6. hydrophobophobia	(f) fear of being seen
7. odontophobia	(g) fear of certain places
8. topophobia	(h) fear of missiles
9. anthropophobia	(i) fear of deformity
10. entomophobia	(j) fear of work

LESSON XV   Military Terms

In the previous lesson we studied words contributed to our general vocabulary by various types of recreation. In this lesson we shall consider a grimmer set of words, those which have been drawn from war. Thus, for instance, several terms in English which begin with the syllable *har-* (connected with an early Germanic word for "army" *heri*) originally had to do with military life. *Harbor* once meant "a shelter for the army." *Harbinger,* now by metaphorical extension "a forerunner," as in the stereotyped phrase "harbinger of spring," formerly designated an officer who went ahead of the army to arrange lodging for it, or an advance party sent to prepare a campground. *Harry* first meant "to overrun with an army."

Some of our words recall the might of the Roman legions and the military organization which subjugated the Mediterranean World. *Salary* is one such word. The ancients were well aware that salt is necessary for bodily health as well as for seasoning food. Roman soldiers were consequently given an allowance for the purchase of salt, and this money was known as *salarium* (Latin *sal*, "salt," as in *saline, sal soda,* etc.), which has come into English as *salary*.

Pagan owes its modern meaning to its use as a bit of military slang by the soldiers of Rome. Originally the word meant "peasant" (from Latin *pagus*, "village"), but the legionaries applied it in a somewhat contemptuous fashion to anyone who was not a soldier, and so it became the equivalent of "civilian." Later, the Christians, who felt a strong similarity between the sacrament of baptism and a Roman soldier's solemn oath of allegiance to his commander, and who thus regarded themselves as "soldiers of Christ," adopted the word *pagan* to refer to non-Christians.

The words *interval* (*inter-*, "between," + *vallum*, "palisade," "wall") and *subsidy* (*subsidium*, "reserve troops," from SED-, SID-, "to sit;" i.e., "those sitting and waiting") are likewise metaphors drawn from the technical language of Roman warfare. *Trophy* goes back to ancient Greece, where it was originally a monument consisting of pieces of armor taken from the defeated enemy which the victors set up on the field of battle as a token of their victory. The word is derived from the base TROP-, "to turn" (see Lesson XII) and signified a "turning back" or defeat of the enemy.

Warfare in the age when knighthood was in flower has added *pioneer* to our general vocabulary. The term originally meant "foot-soldier" (Latin *pedo, pedonis,* from *pes, pedis,* "foot"). At a time when cavalry formed the most important part of the army, *pioneers* were not considered of any great consequence. (*Peon* and *pawn* are derived from the same word as *pioneer*.) But they were useful since they went ahead and cleared obstacles from the way of the knight in armor mounted on his cumbersome charger. Gradually, therefore, *pioneer* lost its original lowly significance and came to have the more elevated meaning of one who goes in advance and blazes a trail. From the same period have come *squire* and *esquire* (ultimately from Latin *scutum*, "shield"), originally a young man who attended a knight and carried his shield.

The less romantic aspect of war in those days is reflected by the word *havoc*, which was formerly the signal given to an army to pillage a conquered town, as in the line from Shakespeare, "And Caesar's spirit . . . shall . . . cry 'Havoc,' and let slip the dogs of war." Also, not all warriors were knights fighting for the right; *free-lance* was used originally to refer to a mercenary soldier, one whose weapon and services were free to be sold to the highest bidder or who took part in battle for the sake of plunder.

To conclude with a few miscellaneous examples, *boulevard* is a French corruption of the Dutch *bolwerc,* "bulwark," in this instance, the fortification surrounding a city. As cities expanded, the original walls became useless and were torn down. On the site of the demolished ramparts were laid broad, tree-lined streets known from their location as *boulevards. Belfry* etymologically has nothing to do with bells but was originally a wooden tower used in assailing a walled position. *Slogan* is from Gaelic, where it designated the distinctive battle cry of each of the Irish or Scottish clans and was usually the name of the chief.

VERB-FORMING SUFFIX

I. *-ize,* "to make," "to do something with," "to subject to," etc.
(This suffix has so many different senses that it is better in writing out the analysis of words to list it simply as "verbal suffix.")

ant- + AGON-	struggle			+	*-ize*	antagonize
CRI-	to judge	+	*-tic*	+	*-ize*	criticize
AMERICAN-				+	*-ize*	Americanize
ANGL-	English	+	*-ic*	+	*-ize*	anglicize

ASSIGNMENT

I. Learn the following bases and their meanings:

GON-	angle, angled figure	pentagon, trigonometry
LAB-, LEP- (LEM-)	to take, to seize	syllable, catalepsy dilemma
MES-	middle	Mesopotamia mesoderm
PHRA-	to speak	phrase, phraseology
STROPH-	to turn	strophe, catastrophe

II. Analyze the following italicized words and define them as they are used in the sentence or phrase.

1. The populace think that your rejection of popular standards is a rejection of all standard, and mere *antinomianism.* —Emerson

2. The instinctive act of human kind was to stand and listen, and learn how the trees on the right and the trees on the left wailed or chaunted to each other in the regular *antiphonies* of a cathedral choir. —Thomas Hardy.

3. Nevertheless, the *cosmologists* are now giving us a logical, consistent pattern of the development of the universe. —*Atlantic Monthly*

4. In this *paraphrase,* I have, for the sake of brevity, modernised the language . . . while seeking to preserve the meaning. —John Addington Symonds

5. . . . like an actor in a melodrama who *apostrophizes* the audience on the other side of the footlights. —Thomas Hardy

6. This specimen presents an *atypical* appearance.

7. By some process of *metathesis* he always pronounced "elevate" as "evelate."

8. The words came in a rush, broken by frequent *parenthetical* asides. —*Time*

9. It seems impossible for him to put pen to paper without inventing monstrous and ridiculous *periphrases.* —Symonds

10. . . . turning his head, glanced at the coloured *lithograph* of Garibaldi in a black frame on the white wall. —Joseph Conrad

11. . . . had *metastases* throughout his liver and bile ducts from a primary malignancy of the pancreas. —*Time*

12. Stephen looked at the black form of the adjacent house, where it cut a dark *polygonal* notch out of the sky. —Hardy

13. The co-operation in nature is most plainly visible in true *symbiosis.* The crocodile bird picks the teeth of the crocodile and is spared the fatigue of foraging. The crocodile is possibly saved from caries and trench mouth. —*Harper's Magazine*

14. He appeared to have the convulsive strength of a man in an *epileptic* fit. —A. Conan Doyle

15. New Englanders . . . are skeptical about visions of the future involving drastic changes, either millennial or *catastrophic.* —*Harper's Magazine*

16. In old Colonel Pyncheon's funeral discourse, the clergyman absolutely *canonized* his deceased parishioner, and . . . showed him seated, harp in hand, among the crowded choristers of the spiritual world. —Hawthorne

17. At the *autopsy,* the pathologists found no medical surprises.

18. The particles were *energized* by a high voltage current.

19. The *Mesozoic* life, animal and vegetable alike, was adapted to warm conditions and capable of little resistance to cold. —H. G. Wells

20. The dancers seemed unable to *synchronize* their leaps.

LESSON XVI The Arts

Since at any given time the fine arts appeal to a relatively small number of people, not many words from the language of painting, sculpture, and architecture appear in English. Yet those that are to be found reflect very interesting and unusual backgrounds. *Miniature,* for instance, looks as if it were related to *minus* and *minimum* since it expresses the idea of smallness, and no doubt these words have influenced its current meaning. Historically, however, the word is derived from *minium,* a red pigment used in the Middle Ages especially to decorate the large initial letters in manuscripts, and to designate this type of illumination the verb *miniare* was formed. Often in the space around such letters a scene was painted, and, although various colors were used, *miniare* came to refer to such painting as well. Then, because manuscript illuminations are of necessity small, the word, or rather its derivative *miniature,* lost its connection with a type of pigment and acquired its modern significance of "little."

The discovery in the Renaissance of some long-buried chambers among Roman ruins contributed two words to our language, *grotesque* and *antic.* The walls of these chambers were adorned with various fantastic pictures and, apparently from their location in a "grotto" or vault, these paintings were called "grotesque." Eventually anything fantastic or extravagant came to be called by this term, and it lost its original significance of "characteristic of a grotto." Since these pictures had been made in an earlier age, they were also referred to in Italian as *antico*, from Latin *antiquus*, "old," (which of course gives us *antique*). The Italian word, however, came into English as *antic*, with the meaning of posture or behavior as fantastic as that pictured in the "antique" style.

The origin of the word *maudlin*, "overly sentimental," might also be mentioned here. As we have seen, this comes from the name of St. Mary Magdalene, a woman of the Bible whom Christ redeemed from a sinful life. In early painting it became so customary to depict Mary Magdalene as deeply sorrowing in repentance for her past wickedness that her name has become proverbial for effusive sentimentality.

The language of sculpture has given us *colossal*. Originally *colossus* referred to a large statue like that at Rhodes where the gigantic bronze figure of a man stood across the entrance to the harbor. The Colosseum at Rome was so called from the fact that near it was a "colossal" statue of Nero. Eventually the word broadened in significance to include anything of tremendous size.

The fact that *story*, "narrative," "tale," and *story*, "level of a building," apparently have the same origin is again due to the influence of the fine arts. The latter word seems to have arisen from the friezes or painted windows representing scenes from history and legend which adorned some levels of buildings and which told a "story."

Flamboyant, "florid," "showy," was originally a term from architecture, where it meant in French "resembling a flame" and referred to the wavy, flamelike patterns of the later Gothic style, an extravagant, overly ornamented type of architecture.

The small room at the top of a house, the *attic*, likewise owes its name to a style of architecture. The word when capitalized means literally "pertaining to Attica," the old name for the section of Greece in which Athens is located, and it referred to a special type of Greek architectural decoration. Several centuries ago it was customary in building to include just under the roof a low story which was decorated with columns and other elements in the "Attic" style and which was consequently known as the Attic story. Later, although all connection with Greece disappeared, the word was kept for any room just under the roof.

Finally the word *character*, which has two apparently widely dissimilar meanings in English, "sign or token" and "distinctive trait or traits," referred in Greek times to an instrument for engraving or to a coin stamp. Thus the first meaning of this word in English comes from the idea of cutting a symbol in stone or metal, while the sense of the second meaning is that our characters are metaphorically speaking "stamped" upon us.

NUMERALS

Learn the following numeral bases and their meanings:

HEMI-	half	hemisphere
MON-	one, single	monotone, monorail
PROT-	first, original, primitive	protoplasm, protein
DI-	twice, double	dioxide
DICH-	in two	dichogamy
DEUTER-	second	deuterogamy, deuteragonist
TRI-	three	tripod, tricycle
TETR(A)-	four	tetraethyl
PENT(A)-	five	pentathlon, pentagon Pentecost
HEX(A)-	six	hexagonal
HEPT(A)-	seven	heptamerous
OCT(A)-	eight	octopus, octane, octagonal
DEC(A)-	ten	decathlon, decaliter
HECT-	a hundred	hectograph
KILO-	one thousand	kilocycle

Two other numeral bases in the series from one to ten which occur rather infrequently are HEN-, "one" (as in *henotheism*, which refers to the worship of one god without excluding belief in the existence of other gods) and ENNEA-, "nine."

ASSIGNMENT

I. Analyze the following italicized words and define them as they are used in the sentence or phrase.

1. By dint of long thinking about it, it had become a *monomania* with him, and had acquired a fascination which he found it impossible to resist. —Dickens

2. All this was part of the Pharaoh's larger plan to destroy the nation's pantheon of man-beast gods and substitute the world's first *monotheistic* faith, sun worship. —*Time*

3. The room lay in a high turret of the castellated abbey, was *pentagonal* in shape, and of capacious size. —Edgar Allan Poe

4. Playing on the pigeons' *monogamous* habits, they separate competitors from their mates for a week before the race . . . —*Time*

5. When he pontificated *polysyllabically* over the loudspeaker system, Olivier cracked: "He uses such big words I can't understand him." —*Time*

6. Hear the tolling of the bells,—
   Iron bells!
   What a world of solemn thought their *monody* compels! —Poe

7. Neither Statius nor Ausonius produced more musical *hexameters*. —John Addington Symmonds

8. It was appropriate to the situation of the actors, and intended to enhance the pathos of the *protagonist's* suffering. —Symonds

9. (a) The place took its name from a stone pillar which stood there, a strange rude *monolith*. —Thomas Hardy

   (b) Whether the Soviet Union can be anything but a *monolithic* state in which all opponents must, of necessity and for public instruction, be physically annihilated . . . —*Time*

10. British aircraft companies seldom produce enough *prototypes* of a new plane, thus face delays if a prototype is cracked up. —*Time*

11. . . . the unfathomable gloom amid the high trees on each hand, indistinct, shadowless, and spectre-like in their *monochrome* of grey. —Hardy

12. You could see the strengths and weaknesses of each with *stereoscopic* clarity. —Joseph and Stewart Alsop

13. Household silver became an index of financial status, and decorated with *monograms* and coats of arms, it became a highly personal way for a Dutch burgher to advertise his worth. —*Time*

14. . . . subjected to the *dilemma* of suffering their friends to be slain and themselves to be plundered, or openly appealing to arms. —Francis Parkman

15. It is clear that the three plays of this *trilogy* are closely bound together. —Symonds

16. They recognize no *dichotomy* between mind and body; so all their medicine is, in a sense, psychosomatic. —*Time*

17. The whole establishment had an air of *monastic* quiet and seclusion. —Washington Irving

18. Termites eat wood, but they can't digest it; that is done for them by several species of flagellate *protozoans* in their intestines. —*Harper's Magazine*

19. I have made a special study of cigar ashes — in fact, I have written a *monograph* upon the subject. —A. Conan Doyle

20. In this masterpiece of Shakespeare's art, as in . . . Browning's dramatic *monologues,* a single actor virtually monopolizes the stage. —Arnold Toynbee

III. The following rather technical terms are all connected with religion. Match the words in Column A with the definitions in Column B.

A	B
1. Decalogue	(a) belief in two antagonistic gods, one good and one evil
2. Deuteronomy	(b) the first six books of the Old Testament
3. ditheism	(c) the ruler of a fourth part of a province
4. Heptateuch	(d) the first five books of the Old Testament

5. Hexateuch   (e) the Ten Commandments

6. Monophysite   (f) the first one to suffer death for a cause

7. Pentateuch   (g) the doctrine that the Father, Son, and Holy Spirit are three distinct gods

8. protomartyr   (h) a book of the Bible which contains the second appearance of the Law of Moses

9. tetrarch   (i) one who believes that the nature of Christ is single

10. tritheism   (j) the first seven books of the Old Testament

LESSON XVII The Law

In this lesson we shall consider some of the words in English which were once legal terms but which have since made their way from the law courts to become part of our common language. Ancient Greek legal procedure is reflected by the word *martyr,* which in classical times meant "witness" and was a perfectly ordinary word for a person who testified at a trial. The early Christians, however, used it in reference to those who bore "witness" for Christ and, because so many of them died for their faith, the word has come to mean "one who suffers in behalf of a cause." Also from Greek has come *paraphernalia* (*para,* "beside," and *pherne,* "dowry"), which in a legal sense referred to the property, exclusive of her dowry, belonging to a wife.

One of Rome's greatest contributions to European Civilization has been a systematized body of law and, in addition, respect for the body of precedent established by law. *Prejudice* (*pre-,* "before," and *judicium,* "judgment") in Roman legal procedure referred to a previous judgment or decision which affected the case at hand. *Privilege* (*privus,* "private," and *lex, legis,* "law") signified originally a law made in favor of or against an individual. *Peculiar* likewise reflects the pervasive influence of Roman Law; it comes from *peculium,* which was the private property given to a slave, a wife, or a child as his own, and was eventually generalized to mean "pertaining to any individual characteristic." The fact that the word is in turn derived from *pecus,* "cattle," shows its antiquity, for it must go back to the early period when property consisted mainly of sheep and cows (cf. *pecuniary*).

The somewhat primitive legal standards of the Middle Ages are indicated by the word *ordeal,* which in Anglo-Saxon meant "judgment." The term has acquired its modern meaning of "difficult or painful experience" from the fact that in those times it designated a type of trial in which the accused was subjected to physical dangers, such as the plunging of his hand into a caldron of boiling water or being forced to carry red-hot irons, on the theory that if innocent he would be preserved from harm by the will of Heaven.

Another reminder that at one time the penal code was considerably harsher than it is today is *roué,* "a dissipated person, a grossly immoral individual." The word comes from a verb which in French means "to break on the wheel," a most excruciatingly painful form of execution, and signified that, in the opinion of some, such debauchees should be subjected to this torture. It was first used in regard to the dissolute companions of the Duc d'Orleans in the eighteenth century.

The word *pain* likewise reflects the punitive aspect of the law. It is derived from the Latin *poena* (ultimately from Greek), "penalty," "punishment," (cf. "on *pain* of death"), which became more general in meaning to refer not just to the "pain" inflicted by a court of law, but to pain from any source. *Poena* is familiar in the term *subpoena* (*sub,* "under threat of"), the first words of such a writ when it appeared in Latin, which in effect had the meaning, *"Under threat of punishment* you are hereby ordered to be present in court."

Culprit would seem to indicate that in some ages the prosecution has carried greater weight than the defense. The term is taken from the courtroom procedure of Norman England, where trials were conducted in the French language, and is an abbreviation of the words of the prosecutor at the opening of the case. When the prisoner pleaded "not guilty," the representative of the Crown recited the formula *culpable, prit,* "guilty, ready (to prove our case)," and this became shortened to *cul-* and *prit.*

Size, reflecting jurisdiction over commerce, is a shortened form of *assize* (ultimately from Latin *ad* and *sedere,* "to sit"; cf. *assess*), referring to a "sitting" or session of a legislative body and its ordinances, especially those regulating weights and measures.

Bailiwick (*bailiff* and *-wick,* "village") was once a district under the supervision of a bailiff, formerly a representative of a lord or the king, in charge of collecting taxes and administering justice. Another type of tax collector in England at one time was an *escheator.* In the language of lawyers *escheat* refers to the reversion of property without legal heirs to the government, and these officers, whose duty it was to look after such property, acquired a reputation, deserved or not, of being generally dishonest. From their designation, consequently, has come the word *cheater*.

Matter of fact, despite having undergone a process of weakening in popular usage, as in the merely introductory phrase, "Well, as a matter of fact . . ." is still in use in strictly legal terminology to mean the part of an inquiry concerned with the truth or falsity of the alleged facts, as distinct from *matter of law,* having to do with the legal interpretation of the case.

Ignoramus, literally "we do not know" in Latin, was formerly an indorsement applied to an indictment when a grand jury found the evidence insufficient to bring the defendant to trial. It acquired its modern meaning of "dunce" from a 17th-century play by George Ruggle about an ignorant lawyer who was given the legal-sounding as well as suggestive name of *Ignoramus*.

ASSIGNMENT

I. Learn the following bases and their meanings:

CHORE-	dance	chorus
ER-, EROT-	love	erotic
GLYPH-	to carve	hieroglyphic, triglyph
NAUT-	sailor	nautical, Argonaut
NES-	island	Indonesia, Melanesia

II. Analyze the following italicized words and define them as they are used in the sentence or phrase.

   1. . . . an appearance of benevolence, kindness, pity, and the championship of the helpless is a gloss that covers a *pathological* misanthropy . . . —*Harper's Magazine*

   2. At intervals sections of the highway were carefully measured and marked as a means of *odometer* testing.

   3. Before the war Guam was the only United States possession in *Micronesia*.

4. Water, backed up by the great new dam at The Dalles, will soon cover the strange rock carvings in *Petroglyph* Canyon. — *Time*

5. ... weeds whose red and yellow and purple hues formed a *polychrome* as dazzling as that of cultivated flowers —Thomas Hardy

6. ... *Polynesian* navigators in flimsy open canoes, without chart or compass. — Arnold Toynbee

7. *Demographers* are much concerned about the population explosion.

8. But the antiquity of the scrolls was soon proved conclusively by *paleographical* and archaeological evidence ... —*Time*

9. An immediate interest kindled within me for the unknown Catherine, and I began forthwith to decipher her faded *hieroglyphics*. —Emily Brontë

10. ... beyond this "mild *aphasia*" ... Eisenhower's doctors could find no other symptoms. — *Time*

11. *Psychometrists* strongly defend the use of tests to determine college entrance.

12. Agnostics challenged the *theistic* basis of his philosophy.

13. The one had a *kinetic* and the other a static temperament. — Allan Nevins

14. Just to describe the new rash of alphabetese, linguists were forced to invent a new word: *acronym* ... which first appeared in dictionaries in 1947. — *Time*

15. No Russian *cosmonaut* had been sent into space in the year and five days since Gherman Titov's 17-orbit flight ... — *Time*

16. He devised the *choreography*, commissioned the music, directed the dancers and the camera, and he dances a leading part ... —*Time*

17. The flowers of the orchids present a multitude of curious structures which a few years ago would have been considered as mere *morphological* differences without any special function. — Darwin

18. His poetry is rather too *erotic* and passionate, you know, for some tastes. —Hardy

19. . . . U. S. space officials now plan to send *astronauts* on at least three more three-orbit flights . . . —*Time*

20. *Pathogenic* bacteria . . .

LESSON XVIII Literary Terms

In this lesson we shall consider some of the words which our language has drawn from literature. The literary form which has made the greatest contribution of such terms is drama, and the fact that a number of these words have come down into modern English reflects the great influence of the classical theater on later culture. Thus *hypocrite* was originally a term for an actor. *Episode,* which means literally "a coming in besides" (*epi-,* "upon," "in addition to," *eis,* "into," and OD-, "way," "road," Lesson V) in the technical language of Greek tragedy designated a part of the play between two songs of the chorus, roughly the equivalent of an act; in early times dialogue scenes between actors were regarded as interpolations or interruptions in the choral songs, which were originally the sole element of Greek tragedy.

Because of the historical development of Greek drama the meaning of *chorus* has changed considerably. In its earliest form, Greek tragedy was performed by a group of fifty dancers, and the original meaning of *chorus* is "dance in a ring" (cf. English *choreography*). The performers, however, sang songs while they danced, and, as the drama of the Greeks developed a polished literary style, the role of the chorus became primarily that of a singing group. *Orchestra* has undergone a somewhat similar evolution. In the early theater it designated the area where the chorus danced (*orcheisthai,* "to dance"). As it is used today, however, it generally refers to the group of musicians who now sit in this place.

Scene likewise reflects the primitive period of Greek tragedy, when the word referred to the tent or booth located behind the playing area, where the actors changed into their costumes. Eventually, when elaborate theaters of stone were built, the word came to be used for the back of the stage, and later for the stage itself.

From the Roman theater has come the word *person* (also its doublet *parson*), which in Latin meant "actor's mask." In Roman comedy there was an appropriate mask for each of the stock characters, the slave, the old man, etc., and so the word *persona* came to mean "a character in a drama, "as in the phrase *dramatis personae.* In the course of its passage into modern English *person* later acquired the meaning of "one who plays a part" and by metaphorical extension "one who plays a part in life." Finally the idea of sustaining a role was lost, so that *person* now means simply "individual." The Roman Theater has likewise given us *explode* (*ex-,* "from," and *plaudere, plodere,* "to clap," as in *applaud*), literally "to drive off the stage by loud clapping," referring to a practice of showing displeasure which, although the reverse of our own, was common in the past.

The word *pants* has come from Italian comedy, in which there was a stock character named *Pantalone,* a lean, foolish old man who usually appeared costumed in a kind of tight-fitting pair of trousers called after him *pantaloons* and eventually shortened to *pants.*

In the theater of the previous century, before the days of electricity, when an especially brilliant, concentrated light was needed to mark out some star performer, a dazzling white beam was produced by directing a flame of oxygen and hydrogen on a cylinder of lime, and it was consequently known as a *limelight.*

Robot is of relatively recent origin (1923). The term comes from the name given to mechanical men in a play by Karel Capek entitled *R.U.R.* (*Rossum's Universal Robots*) and was originally a Czech word *robota,* "cumpulsory service."

Words such as these have of course come from forms of literature other than drama. Most college students have wondered at one time or another what the connection is between the *Romance* languages (French, Spanish, etc.) and *romance,* having to do with adventure, excitement, and especially love. In the Middle Ages most literature was in Latin; but some lighter works were written in the native dialects which were beginning to emerge from the language of the Romans, and, since such works were in the Romance dialects, they were called by this name. The best known of them dealt with the exploits of knights who slew dragons and rescued fair damsels in distress, and so *romance* has become a term for the characteristics of such fiction.

Finally, literary criticism figures in the origin of *namby-pamby,* a contemptuous nickname for the eighteenth-century English poet, Ambrose Philips (fancifully based on his name), whose insipid, weakly sentimental style has been immortalized by this epithet.

ADDITIONAL MATERIAL

I. For additional practice, with the help of the list of bases at the end of Part II, analyze the following italicized words and define them as they are used in the sentence or phrase.

1. The features expressed nothing of monastic austerity or of *ascetic* privations; on the contrary, it was a bold bluff countenance. — Sir Walter Scott

2. In the thick of traffic shepherds pass along with *bucolic* slowness and serenity, clad in clothes like those worn by their ancestors. —*Atlantic Monthly*

3. Central belief of the cargo cults is that the world is about to come to a *cataclysmic* end . . . —*Time*

4. Here was a young man who, from a very humble place, was mounting rapidly; from the *cynosure* of a parish, he had become the talk of a county. — Robert Louis Stevenson

5. My poem was evidently too *didactic*. The public was wise enough. It no longer read for instruction. — Washington Irving

6. It was perhaps true that *hedonism* is an impotent gospel, for now it could be seen that pleasure means nothing to many men. — *Harper's Magazine*

7. . . . part of their centuries-old struggle for *hegemony* in modern Europe. — *Time*

8. The face was well shaped, even excellently. But the mind within was beginning to use it as a mere waste tablet whereon to trace its *idiosyncrasies* as they developed themselves. — Thomas Hardy

9. For a number of years he had been a *peripatetic* scissors grinder.

10. The worst offence of this kind which can be committed by a *polemic* is to stigmatise those who hold the contrary opinion as bad and immoral men. — John Stuart Mill

II. The following italicized words are also derived from Greek; define them as they are used in the sentence or phrase.

1. Though four Ankara professors resigned in protest and students walked out on a one-day strike, the government remained *adamant.* —*Time*

2. His simple patriotism that puts country above home and family is expressed in one of his *aphorisms.* —*Time*

3. Is it not almost a self-evident *axiom* that the State should require and compel the education . . . of every human being who is born its citizen? —John Stuart Mill

4. Positively ionized air was discovered to have *deleterious* effects upon human well-being . . . —*Harper's Magazine*

5. . . . have scarcely been able to refrain from breaking out into fierce *diatribes* against that complicated, enormous, outrageous swindle. —Thackeray

6. This was a disbelief in the evidence of the senses, a despair of *empirical* knowledge. —John Addington Symonds

7. Everywhere, some fragment of ruin suggesting the magnificence of a former *epoch* . . . —Hawthorne

8. I have experienced this pleasure when I have drunk the liquor of the *esoteric* doctrines. —Thoreau

9. Its steeples and towers, and its one great dome, grow more *ethereal;* its smoky housetops lose their grossness in the pale effulgence. — Dickens

10. When the Vandals disembarked at the mouth of the Tiber, the emperor was suddenly roused from his *lethargy* by the clamours of a trembling and exasperated multitude. — Edward Gibbon

11. The London *Gazette* announced his appointment, not with official dryness, but in the fervid language of *panegyric.* — Macaulay

12. Marstan had sprung out of his chair in a *paroxysm* of anger. — A. Conan Doyle

13. The progressivists treat the schools as laboratories of experience in which students learn chiefly by *pragmatic* problem solving. — *Time*

14. . . . at his gentlest tells nothing less than the bitter truth and at his worst dismisses humanity with a *sardonic* jeer. *—Time*

15. If the game was chess, the officers had to stand throughout, and Napoleon almost invariably lost unless the other player *sycophantically* threw the game. *—Time*

III. Give the source and meaning of each of the following words which arose in connection with literature.

1. bowdlerize
2. Gargantuan
3. Lilliputian
4. Mrs. Grundy
5. pamphlet

6. Pollyanna
7. Rabelaisian
8. sadism
9. simon-pure
10. yahoo

LESSON XIX   Terms from Various Occupations

In Part I (page 62) we saw some of the words which originally belonged to the language of farming and which came to be used figuratively, so that their meanings broadened or changed, words such as *delirium* (literally "out of the furrow") and *rehearse* (literally "to harrow over again"). In this lesson are some terms drawn from various other ways of earning a livelihood.

The work of making cloth is represented by the word *tease,* literally "to separate or pull apart" (the fibers of wool, flax, etc.), and by *heckle,* "to comb out" (flax or hemp in preparation for spinning). *Subtle* (Latin *sub-* "under," and *tela,* "woven material") originally referred to a fabric which was finely woven, while "to be on tenterhooks" was a figure of speech taken from a finishing process in the manufacture of cloth, where the material is stretched by means of hooks on a wooden frame known as a *tenter,* so that it will dry evenly without shrinking.

Dicker apparently has a very interesting origin; it is thought by some authorities to come from the fur trading carried on between the early Germans and the Romans, which must have involved much the same sort of bargaining that took place in more recent times between frontiersmen and Indians. Furs were customarily handled in groups of ten known as *decuriae* (from Latin DECIM-, "ten," "tenth"; see Part I, Lesson VI), and so *dicker,* a much later form of this word, once meant "to argue over a lot of ten furs."

Shambles, "a scene of bloodshed or general destruction," is a term formerly used to refer to a butcher shop; it once meant the bench or table (Latin *scamellum,* "little bench") on which the meat was cut and sold.

Ton and *broker* both recall the early wine trade. *Ton* represents the Anglo-Saxon *tunne,* "a large cask" (which is still the meaning of its doublet *tun*). It was first used for "wine cask," then for "weight of a wine cask," and finally acquired its current meaning of unit of weight in general. A *broker* was originally one who "broached" a cask of wine, that is, a retailer who sold wine from the barrel in small amounts. From this beginning the word became generalized in its use to mean any middleman.

Chap has been contributed by merchandising; it is a shortened form of *chapman,* "trader," "merchant" (Anglo-Saxon *ceap,* "trade," "a bargain," which also gives us *cheap*) and came to mean "person" in the same way as the word *customer* in the colloquial expression "a tough customer" (meaning "a tough person to deal with"). *Untrammeled* is a figure of speech drawn from fishing. A *trammel* is a kind of net (Latin *tri-,* "three," and *macula,* "mesh"), so *untrammeled* originally meant "free from the confines of a net." Blacksmithing has contributed *brand-new,* which once meant "fresh from the fire," *brand* here being "flame." Shakespeare in fact speaks of articles "fire-new from the mint."

To turn once again to the language of farming, *pester* (from Latin *pastorium,* "tether," "hobble," related to *pasture*) formerly referred to the practice of shackling the feet of horses so as to prevent them from wandering out of the pasture. *Ruminate,* "to ponder," was once a very picturesque figure of speech. It originally meant "to chew the cud," and so whoever first applied the term to mental activity intended to convey the idea of going over and over a problem in one's mind. As a matter of fact, the zoological term *ruminant* is still used to designate animals that chew the cud.

Season was originally "sowing time" (ultimately from Latin *satio,* "sowing"). *Greenhorn* apparently once referred to a young animal with horns which were new and hence called "green"; so today *greenhorn* is applied to a person who is inexperienced, usually because of youth.

According to one explanation, the expression "gone haywire" has arisen from the nature of the wire used around bales of hay. Such wire is stretched very tight and when cut it coils up into a jumbled mass that is quite suggestive of a machine which has broken down. Another possibility, however, is that the expression originally referred to logging camps with rundown equipment patched together by means of miscellaneous pieces of wire such as those salvaged from bales of hay. In these "hay-wire camps," as they were called, the machinery was generally out of order.

ADDITIONAL MATERIAL

I. The following italicized words have entered English from Greek without having become completely anglicized; thus they still retain their Greek, or in some cases their Latin, endings (since, as we have seen, such words have often come into English by way of Latin; see Introduction to Part II, (pp. 135-136). Define them as they are used in the sentence or phrase.

1. The brilliancy of the foliage has passed its *acme*. —Hawthorne

2. We had soup today, in which twenty kinds of vegetables were represented, and manifested each its own *aroma*. —Hawthorne

3. You weaken the *aura* of all good laws every time you break a bad one . . . *Harper's Magazine*

4. I like you more than I can say; but I'll not sink into a *bathos* of sentiment . . . —Charlotte Brontë

5. In this casual and sinisterly impermanent manner the Soviet *colossus* had marked the boundary with its tiny neighbor. — *Harper's Magazine*

6. . . . the ultimate and all-embracing movement of a stellar *cosmos* in which our local solar system has now dwindled to the diminutiveness of a speck of dust. —Arnold Toynbee

7. . . . there seems to be no intelligible *criterion* by which the merits of the quarrel can be judged. — *Harper's Magazine*

8. . . . a Rag and Bottle shop, and general *emporium* of much disregarded merchandise. — Dickens

9. Yet their discipline was such as to draw forth the *encomiums* of the Spanish conquerors. — William Hickling Prescott

10. I cannot forecast to you the action of Russia. It is a riddle wrapped in a mystery inside an *enigma;* but perhaps there is a key. — Sir Winston Churchill

11. ... the standards of conduct which civilization has over *eons* gradually imposed upon human nature. — *Harper's Magazine*

12. What we are headed for is a sort of social structure in which the highbrows are the elite, the middlebrows are the bourgeoisie, and the lowbrows are *hoi polloi*. —*Harper's Magazine*

13. There is not an *iota* of truth in this accusation.

14. ... ("image" in Madison Avenue's *lexicon* means what the public thinks about a person or corporation when it is not thinking very hard). — *Time*

15. These appearances, which bewilder you, are merely electrical phenomena not uncommon — or it may be that they have their ghastly origin in the rank *miasma* of the tarn. —Edgar Allan Poe

16. ... and today he writes of the New Deal with the *nostalgia* usually found in men who have narrowly missed a famous war. — *Time*

17. But conscription — that much favored *panacea* for national security — will not meet the problem. — *Harper's Magazine*

18. Her anxiety . . . had given a strange tremor to her voice and made her eyes more eloquent in their silent *pathos*. —W. H. Hudson

19. Actuated by these sentiments our ancestors arrayed themselves against the government in one huge and compact mass. All ranks, all parties, all Protestant sects, made up that vast *phalanx*. —Macaulay

20. ... amused them by explaining some of the strange *phenomena* exhibited by the ocean in the tempest, which had filled their superstitious minds with mysterious dread. —Prescott

21. The tragedy has been so uncommon, so complete, and of such personal importance to so many people that we are suffering from a *plethora* of surmise, conjecture, and hypothesis. — A. Conan Doyle

22. In a lengthy *prolegomenon* he stated the underlying philosophical ideas on which his work was based.

23. What most men feared was not the moral verdict of society, pronouncing them degraded by vicious or violent acts, but the intellectual estimate of incapacity and the *stigma* of dullness. — John Addington Symonds

24. There were no short cuts to learning, no comprehensive lexicons, no dictionaries of antiquities, no carefully prepared *thesauri* of mythology and history. —Symonds

25. It took him months to recover from the emotional *trauma* produced by the false accusations brought against him.

II. Give all of the plurals listed in your dictionary for each of the following words:

1. colossus	9. miasma
2. cosmos	10. octopus
3. criterion	11. phalanx
4. diagnosis	12. prolegomenon
5. emporium	13. stigma
6. encomium	14. synthesis
7. enigma	15. thesaurus
8. lexicon	16. trauma

LESSON XX   Scientific Language

In the previous lessons we have encountered a number of scientific terms. The remainder of the book, however, will be devoted exclusively to the study of technical terminology, which to so great an extent has been derived from Greek. Science figures so largely in present-day life that even the general student should have some acquaintance with its language and should acquire the ability to analyze its complex terms.

Many of the words which you will encounter in the following lessons are extremely technical and, you may feel, unnecessarily so. There has always been a tendency to regard the specialized language of scientists as merely the mark of pompousness. In some cases, it is true, technical terms have been manufactured needlessly, but there are several reasons why a specialized vocabulary is desirable.

In the first place, the fact that such words are confined to a specialized sphere is of value in insuring precision of language. Technical words as a rule have but one application, and this makes them more useful tools for the expression of scientific ideas. Words in general use often have many applications and shades of meaning, and, although their richness of meaning may enhance their value for literary purposes, it is not desirable in scientific writing. *Speechlessness* and *aphasia* (PHA-, "to speak") at first glance seem to refer to the same thing, yet *speechlessness* actually has several meanings; the word may designate stage fright, it may refer to a momentary loss of the power to express oneself because of surprise or anger, it may apply to a condition present from birth where a child has never learned to talk. *Aphasia,* on the other hand, refers to a specific abnormal state involving loss of speech, usually the result of brain damage. Similarly, to say that a man has acromegaly is quite different from saying that he has large hands and feet. *Acromegaly* is a specific diseased condition characterized by the enlargement of the bones of the extremities and caused by excessive activity of the pituitary gland.

The fact that such words are generally unfamiliar and are employed almost exclusively by specialists who know their application tends to keep their meaning precise. Technical terms which come into general use sometimes lose their exactness. The word *allergy* is a good example of this. In medicine it refers to an abnormal sensitivity to certain substances which are harmless to most people; but it is often used by nonphysicians loosely to mean indigestion or simply dislike. Many of the terms from psychology which have passed into popular circulation show this same looseness of application. *Complex,* for instance, has come to mean popularly unusual fear or dislike, and you have no doubt often heard *phobia* and *mania* used in an exaggerated sense.

Finally, technical terms allow for economy of language while still maintaining precision of meaning. It is much shorter to write or say "thrombosis" than "formation of a clot in the heart or a blood vessel which obstructs the circulation," just as "H_2O" is a shorter means of expression than "two atoms of hydrogen and one of oxygen."

SUFFIXES USED IN MEDICAL TERMS

The following suffixes are used almost exclusively in connection with medicine.

I. *-itis,* "inflammation of," "inflammatory disease of"

APPENDIC-	appendix	+	*-itis*	appendicitis
ARTHR-	joint	+	*-itis*	arthritis
TONSILL-	tonsil	+	*-itis*	tonsillitis

II. *-oma*, usually, "tumor arising in or composed of"; occasionally, "swelling containing"; rarely, "diseased condition," "result of" (related to *-ma*, "result of"; see Lesson XI)

Usually this suffix is attached to a base which designates a type of body tissue, such as bone, muscle, etc., but the commonest term which ends in *-oma, carcinoma*, a type of cancer, does not follow this pattern. The base CARCIN-, means "crab," and the word originated in ancient times when the nature of malignant growths was little understood. One explanation for the term is that the swollen veins surrounding the diseased area resembled the claws of a crab (cf. the term *cancer*, which in Latin means "crab," as in the sign of the zodiac and in the phrase *Tropic of Cancer*).

MELAN-   black, dark   +   *-oma*   melanoma
(a highly malignant tumor, i.e., cancer, composed of dark pigment-bearing cells)

OSTE-   bone   +   *-oma*   osteoma
(a benign tumor composed of bone tissue)

HEMAT-   blood   +   *-oma*   hematoma
(a swelling containing blood)

TRACH(Y)-   rough   +   *-oma*   trachoma
(an infectious disease of the eyes in which granulations form on the inside of the eyelid)

A. If *-oma* is followed by an additional suffix, it becomes *-omat-*.

CARCIN-   crab   +   *-omat-*   +   *-ous*   carcinomatous
TRACH(Y)-   rough   +   *-omat-*   +   *-ous*   trachomatous

III. *-osis*, "diseased condition of"; sometimes, "act of," "process of," like *-sis*, of which this is a form (see Lesson XI)

PSYCH-   mind   +   *-osis*   psychosis
TUBERCUL-   nodule   +   *-osis*   tuberculosis
HYPN-   sleep   +   *-osis*   hypnosis

A. The adjectival form of this suffix is usually *-otic*.

PSYCH-   mind   +   *-otic*   psychotic
HYPN-   sleep   +   *-otic*   hypnotic

ASSIGNMENT

I. Learn the following bases and their meanings:

ARTHR- "joint," "speech sound or articulation"
>*arthritis* — inflammation of a joint
>*arthropod* — a member of a large group of animals with jointed legs, including insects and spiders
>*anarthria* — the lack of ability to articulate words because of brain damage

CARDI- "heart"
>*electrocardiogram* — a record of the heart's action
>*cardiologist* — a heart specialist
>*pericardium* — the membranous sac which encloses the heart

CHONDR- "cartilage"
>*hypochondriac* — one who has a morbid anxiety about his health (The term originally referred to one suffering from melancholy in general and reflects the discarded notion that melancholy arose in the particular part of the body "under the cartilage" of the breastbone.)
>*chondrocyte* — a cartilage cell
>*synchondrosis* — a joint where connection is made by a plate of cartilage

CYAN- "dark blue"
>*cyanophil* — having an affinity for blue dye
>*anthocyanin* — a pigment found in flowers and plants
>*cyanide* — a derivative of cyanogen, which is involved in the process of making the dye Prussian blue

CYT- "cell"
>*cytology* — the branch of biology dealing with the nature of cells
>*hemocytozoon* — a parasite living within blood corpuscles
>*anisocytosis* — inequality in the size of red blood cells

ENTER- "intestine"
>*dysentery* — an infectious disease of the intestines
>*archenteron* — the primitive digestive tract of an embryo
>*exenterate* — to eviscerate

HEPAT- "liver"

> *hepatomegaly* — enlargement of the liver
>
> *hepatization* — the change of tissue into a liverlike substance
>
> *hepatica* — a small plant with leaves which resemble the lobes of the liver

MELAN- "black," "dark"

> *melanin* — the dark pigment found in skin, hair, etc.
>
> *melanosis* — the abnormal presence of dark pigment in the body tissue
>
> *melangeophilous* — dwelling in loam
>
> *Melanesia* (NES-, "island") — a group of islands in the South Pacific, so called from the blackness of the inhabitants' skin
>
> *melancholy* — literally, "the presence of black bile," a term going back to the humoral theory of physiology (see pp. 87-88), according to which a predominance of black bile was thought to cause sadness.

MYC-, MYCET- "fungus," "mold"

> *mycology* — the branch of botany concerned with the study of fungi
>
> *mycotrophic* — referring to plants which live in a symbiotic relationship with fungi
>
> *Aureomycin, Chloromycetin, neomycin* — various antibiotic drugs, the names of which contain this base because they were originally prepared from mold substances

NEPHR- "kidney"

> *nephritis* — inflammation of the kidneys
>
> *pronephros* — the foremost of the three pairs of embryonic kidney structures
>
> *nephrolith* — a kidney stone

OST(E)- "bone"

> *osteopath* — originally, a practitioner whose method of treatment was based on the theory that most diseases are caused by disarrangements of the bone structure and consequent interference with nerves and blood vessels
>
> *osteotome* — a surgical instrument for cutting bone
>
> *acrostealgia* — pain in the bones of an extremity

SCLER- "hard"

> multiple *sclerosis* — a disease in which there is a gradual hardening of tissue in brain and spinal cord
>
> *arteriosclerosis* — hardening of the walls of the arteries
>
> *sclerometer* — an instrument for determining the hardness of materials

II. Analyze the following words and define them:

1. endocarditis	11. scleroid
2. periostitis	12. macrocyte
3. osteoclast	13. enteritis
4. sclerodermatous	14. cyanosis
5. cytolysis	15. cardiograph
6. parenteral	16. enarthrosis
7. exostosis	17. necrosis
8. melanism	18. diathermy
9. mycosis	19. hemophilia
10. hepatitis	20. embolism

III. The following words contain elements which have been studied in this or previous lessons. Match Column B with Column A.

A	B
1. hematocytolysis	(a) inability to see the color blue
2. anenterous	(b) inflammation of the kidney associated with a kidney stone
3. acyanopsia	(c) impairment of speech articulation
4. megalocardia	(d) pertaining to a condition of the skin characterized by increase in dark pigment
5. hepatoma	(e) having no intestine
6. lithonephritis	(f) the dissolution of blood cells
7. dysostosis	(g) the enlargement of the heart
8. dysarthria	(h) a tumor of the liver
9. acromycosis	(i) defective formation of bone
10. melanodermic	(j) the growth of fungus on the hands and feet

LESSON XXI Combining Forms Used in Medical Terms

Learn the following combining forms and their meanings:

I. *-ectomy,* "surgical removal of" (from the base TOM-, "to cut";
see Lesson III)

APPEND- appendix + *-ectomy* appendectomy
TONSILL- tonsil + *-ectomy* tonsillectomy

II. *-tomy,* "surgical operation on," "surgical cutting of"

GLOSS(o)- tongue + *-tomy* glossotomy
GASTR(o)- stomach + *-tomy* gastrotomy
LOB(o)- lobe (of the brain) + *-tomy* lobotomy

III. *-rrhea (-rrhoea),* "abnormal discharge"

dia- + *-rrhea* diarrhea
PY(o)- pus + *-rrhea* pyorrea
LOG(o)- word + *-rrhea* logorrhea

(a term from abnormal psychology which refers to excessive and
usually incoherent loquacity)

ASSIGNMENT

I. Learn the following bases and their meanings:

ADEN- "gland"

adenoid — (1) like a gland (2) a growth of lymphoid tissue
in the throat

lymphadenitis — inflammation of a lymph gland
ectadenia — ectodermal reproductive glands in insects

ANGI- "vessel"

cholangiotomy — incision into the bile ducts

sporangium — a spore case

angiitis — inflammation of a blood or lymph vessel

CEPHAL- "head"

mesocephalic — referring to a head with a medium ratio of length to breadth

cephalopod — one of a class of molluscs to which belong squid, octopuses, etc., having tentacles (i.e., "limbs") around the front of the head

en- + CEPHAL- "brain"; *electroencephalograph* — an instrument for measuring brain waves

archencephalon — the primitive forebrain

CHOL(E)- "bile," "gall"

cholangiitis — inflammation of the bile ducts

cholelith — a gallstone

cholagogue — an agent which induces the flow of bile

choleric — prone to anger, since, according to the humoral theory of physiology (see pp. 87-88), a predominance of yellow bile, usually simply termed bile, made a person wrathful (cf. *melancholy,* in the preceding lesson)

HYSTER- "uterus," "hysteria" (The two meanings arise from the belief of the ancients that, since hysteria was observed mostly in women, it must somehow be associated with the organ peculiar to women.)

hysterotomy — a surgical incision into the uterus

hysteroepilepsy — hysteria associated with symptoms of epilepsy

LIP- "fat"

lipase — an enzyme which breaks down fats during the digestive process

lipophil — having an affinity for fatty tissue

lipuria — the presence of fat in the urine

MAST-, MAZ- "breast"

> *mastectomy* — the surgical removal of a breast
>
> *mastoid* — a nipple-shaped projection of the temporal bone behind the ear
>
> *mastodon* — a prehistoric mammal named from the nipple-like projections on its teeth (ODONT-).

OO- "egg"

> *ootheca* — an egg case
>
> *oosphere* — an egg before fertilization
>
> OO- + PHOR- ("to bear"), "ovary;" *oophoritis* — inflammation of an ovary

OT- "ear"

> *otoscope* — an instrument for examining the ear
>
> *otorrhea* — a discharge from the ear
>
> *dichotic* — affecting the two ears differently, so that, for instance, a single sound will be heard simultaneously in one way by one ear and in another way by the other ear

PHLEB- "vein"

> *phlebectomy* — surgical removal of a vein
>
> *phlebosclerosis* — hardening of the walls of a vein

PY- "pus"

> *arthroempyesis* — the formation of pus in a joint
>
> *pyogenesis* — the formation of pus
>
> *pyonephritis* — inflammation of a kidney accompanied by the presence of pus

UR- "urine"

> *melanuria* — the presence of black pigment in the urine
>
> *dysuria* — difficulty in urination

II. Analyze the following words and define them:

1. diuretic	11. enuresis
2. angioma	12. adenoma
3. lipolysis	13. phlebitis
4. acephalous	14. pyuria
5. empyema	15. oogenesis
6. oolite	16. hysterectomy
7. hydrocephalous	17. angiologist
8. parotitis	18. encephalitis
9. phlebotomy	19. pyorrhea
10. mastoidectomy	20. polyuria

III. Match Column B with Column A:

A	B
1. otomycosis	(a) having a well-developed head (applied to certain insect larvae)
2. cholangiography	(b) a tumor composed of blood vessels
3. barotalgia	(c) the presence of blood and fatty substance in a joint
4. adenectopia	(d) inflammation of the inner coat of a vein
5. antipyogenic	(e) the presence of blood in the urine
6. lipohemarthrosis	(f) the growth of a fungus inside the ear
7. eucephalous	(g) the presence of a gland in an abnormal place
8. hematuria	(h) preventing the formation of pus
9. endophlebitis	(i) pain in the ear caused by (air) pressure
10. hemangioma	(j) X-ray of the bile ducts

LESSON XXII   Combining Forms Used in Medical Terms

Learn the following combining forms and their meanings:

I. -*path*, "one who suffers from a disease of," "one who treats a disease" (from the base PATH- "to feel," "to suffer;" see Lesson X)

PSYCH(o)-	mind	+	-*path*	psychopath
OSTE(o)-	bone	+	-*path*	osteopath

II. *-pathy*, "disease of," "treatment of disease of or by"

NEUR(o)-   nerve   +   *-pathy*   neuropathy
(a disease or disorder of the nervous system)

HYDR(o)-   water   +   *-pathy*   hydropathy
(the treatment of disease by means of water)

OSTE(o)-   bone   +   *-pathy*   osteopathy

III. *-iasis*, "diseased condition" (often referring to an infestation by parasites)

PSOR-   itch   +   *-iasis*   psoriasis
(a chronic itching disease of the skin)

ELEPHANT-   elephant   +   *-iasis*   elephantiasis
(a disease resulting from an infestation of worms which causes the skin of the affected part to resemble an elephant's hide)

AMEB-   amoeba   +   *-iasis*   amebiasis
(an infestation by amoebas)

IV. *-therapy*, "treatment of or by"

CHEM(o)-   chemical   +   *-therapy*   chemotherapy
HELI(o)-   sun   +   *-therapy*   heliotherapy
PSYCH(o)-   mind   +   *-therapy*   psychotherapy

ASSIGNMENT

I. Learn the following bases and their meanings:

BRACHY- "short"

     brachyglossal — having a short tongue

     brachypodous — having a short foot or stalk

     brachylogy — shortness of expression

BRADY- "slow"

     bradycardia — abnormal slowness of the heart action

     bradylogia — abnormal slowness of speech

     bradykinesia — abnormal slowness of movement

CHLOR- "green," "yellowish-green;" also, "chlorine" (a yellowish-green gas)

chlorophyll — the green coloring matter in plants

achlorhydria — the absence of hydrochloric acid in the stomach

DOLICH- "long"

dolichofacial — having an abnormally long face

dolichomorphic — having a long form

ERYTHR- "red"

erythrocyte — a red blood corpuscle

erythrophilous — having an affinity for red dye

hemoerythrin — a red pigment found in the blood of certain animals

EURY(S)- "wide," "broad"

eurybaric — able to withstand wide variations in pressure

eurycephalic — having an unusually broad head

LEUC-, LEUK- "white"

leukemia — a disease characterized by an abnormal increase in the number of white blood cells

leukoderma — absence of skin pigmentation occurring in patches or bands

leucoma — a white opacity in the cornea of the eye as a result of an ulcer or injury

MER- "part"

hexamerous — having six parts

dysmerogenesis — the production of unlike parts

merogony — development of normal young from part of an egg

PLATY-, "flat," "broad"

platyhelminth — a flatworm

platysma — a broad sheet of muscle

amphiplatyan — flat at both ends

STEN- "narrow"

stenography — shorthand writing

stenothermic — capable of existing only within a narrow range of temperature

stenopetalous — having narrow petals

TACHY- "swift;" TACH- "speed"

tachylogia — extreme rapidity of speech

tachistoscope — an instrument for providing very brief exposure of visual material

XANTH- "yellow"

xanthoderma — yellowness of the skin

xanthodont — referring to certain rodents with yellow-colored teeth

xanthin — a yellow pigment found in flowers

II. Analyze the following words and define them:

1. brachycephalic	11. homeopathy
2. leucocytosis	12. arthromere
3. hemostat	13. aneurysm
4. tachylyte	14. tachometer
5. erythrocytometer	15. physiotherapist
6. stenosis	16. osteophyte
7. hydrotherapy	17. chlorosis
8. erythrism	18. isomerous
9. dolichocephalic	19. idiopathic
10. pentamerous	20. urolith

III. Match Column B with Column A

A	B
1. eurythermic	(a) division into parts
2. erythrophobia	(b) a yellow pigment-bearing cell
3. orthodolichocephalous	(c) slowness of speech articulation
4. angiostenosis	(d) capable of withstanding wide variations of temperature
5. bradyarthria	(e) defect of vision in which all objects appear green
6. xanthophore	(f) excessively fast beating of the heart
7. merotomy	(g) fear of the color red
8. platycephalic	(h) the narrowing of a blood vessel
9. chloropsia	(i) having a long straight head
10. tachycardia	(j) characterized by a flat head

IV. While most people are not likely to be called upon to coin new words, one useful method of becoming familiar with scientific terminology is to try to form words on the basis of a knowledge of bases and affixes. For each of the following definitions, therefore, give a single word with this meaning. Since the words are all in current use, they have been listed as they appear in dictionaries on p. 264.

Example: inflammation of a gland — *adenitis*

1. a tumor composed of fatty tissue
2. pain in a joint
3. narrowing of the heart
4. blueness of the extremities
5. a fungus infection of the skin
6. surgical incision into the liver
7. inflammation of the ear
8. smallness of the heart
9. condition of having a black tongue
10. the study of bones

LESSON XXIII Combining Forms

Learn the following combining forms and their meanings:

I. *-emia,* "condition of the blood;" occasionally, "congestion of blood in" (from HEM-, HEMAT- "blood"; see Lesson V)

LEUK- white + *-emia* leukemia
(a disease marked by the presence of large numbers of white corpuscles in the blood)

an- + OX- oxygen + *-emia* anoxemia
(a condition in which there is a deficiency of oxygen in the blood)

hypo- + GLYC- sugar + *-emia* hypoglycemia
(a condition in which there is a deficiency of glucose in the blood)

TULAR- + *-emia* tularemia
(an infectious disease commonly found among animals but transmissible to man, named from Tulare County, California, where it was discovered)

II. *-hedron,* "solid figure with a (specified) number of faces"

POLY- many + *-hedron* polyhedron
OCTA- eight + *-hedron* octathedron
ICOSA- twenty + *-hedron* icosahedron

ASSIGNMENT

I. Learn the following bases and their meanings:

ACOU-, ACU- "to hear"

> *acoustics* — the study of sound

> *paracusia* — any defect in the hearing

> *acoumetry* — the measurement of hearing ability

MENING- "membrane;" specifically, the membranes around the brain and spinal cord, the meninges

> *meningoencephalitis* — inflammation of the brain and its surrounding membranes

> *meningomyelitis* — inflammation of the spinal cord and its surrounding membranes

MY-, MYS-, MYOS- "muscle"

    myograph — an instrument for recording muscular action

    myomere — a muscle segment

    amyotaxia — lack of muscular coordination

    myositis — inflammation of a muscle

MYEL- "bone marrow," "the spinal cord" (The two meanings arise from the failure of early anatomists to differentiate between the two substances, since the spinal cord as well as marrow is found within bone.)

    poliomyelitis (POLI- "gray") — inflammation of the gray matter of the spinal cord

    myelocyte — a cell of bone marrow

    myelencephalon — the posterior portion of the brain

NEUR- "nerve," "the nervous system"

    neuralgia — pain along the course of a nerve

    neurosis — a type of mental disorder

    neuropsychiatry — a branch of medicine concerned with both the mind and the nervous system

    neurosurgery — surgery of the nervous system

OPHTHALM- "eye"

    ophthalmia — inflammation of the eyeball or surrounding tissue

    ophthalmologist — a physician who specializes in the treatment of diseases of the eye

    photophthalmia — inflammation of the eyes caused by excessively bright light

PHREN- "mind," "diaphragm" (The two meanings arise from the fact that the ancients generally regarded the region of the diaphragm as the seat of the emotions and intellect.)

    phrenogastric — pertaining to the stomach and diaphragm

    hebephrenia (HEBE- "youth") — a form of mental illness occurring at puberty *bradyphrenia* — slowness of mental activity

phrenology — an outmoded system of diagnosing personality by analyzing the surface irregularities of the skull; popular in the 18th and 19th centuries

(*Frenzy* and *frantic* are also derived from the Greek word *phren.*)

PLEG- "paralysis;" PLEX- "(paralytic) stroke"

paraplegia — paralysis of the lower half of the body

diplegia — paralysis of the same part on both sides of the body

apoplexy — a stroke; a sudden paralysis and loss of consciousness caused by the rupture or blocking of a blood vessel in the brain

RHIN- (-RRHIN-) "nose"

rhinitis — inflammation of the nose

otorhinolaryngologist — a specialist in diseases of the ear, nose, and throat

rhinoceros (CER- "horn") — so called from the horn on its nose

rhinencephalon — the portion of the brain concerned with the sense of smell

SOM-, SOMAT- "body"

chromosome — any of several deeply staining bodies in a cell which determine hereditary characteristics

somatology — in anthropology, the study of the physical characteristics of the human body

merosome — a body segment

STHEN- "strength"

> *asthenopia* — weakness of the eyes
>
> *anisosthenic* — referring to pairs of muscles of unequal power
>
> *adenohypersthenia* — greater than normal activity of a gland

THYM- "mind," "strong feeling"

> *dysthymia* — melancholy, despondency
>
> *hyperepithymia* — exaggerated desire
>
> *prothymia* — alertness

TON-, (-TONUS) — "a stretching," "tension"

> *tonic* — a medicine which invigorates and braces
>
> *ophthalmotonometer* — an instrument for measuring tension within the eyeball
>
> *angiohypertonia* — abnormal constriction of blood vessels
>
> *peritonitis* — inflammation of the peritoneum, the membrane that encloses, i.e., is "stretched around," the internal organs

II. Analyze the following words and define them:

1. meningitis	11. calisthenics
2. exophthalmic	12. myocarditis
3. platyrrhinian	13. schizophrenia
4. uremia	14. psychosomatic
5. neurasthenia	15. decahedron
6. atony	16. neurologist
7. ophthalmoscope	17. osteomyelitis
8. hemiplegia	18. isotonic
9. cyclothymia	19. pyemia
10. rhinoscope	20. catatonic

III. Match Column B with Column A:

A	B
1. myasthenia	(a) perception of bodily sensations
2. ophthalmoplegia	(b) an excess of fat in the blood
3. oligophrenia	(c) paralysis of a single limb or part of the body
4. hyperacusia	(d) paralysis of the eye
5. somatotopagnosia	(e) lack of muscle tone
6. rhinophonia	(f) muscular weakness
7. hyperlipemia	(g) feeble-mindedness
8. monoplegia	(h) inability to identify one's body or its parts
9. somesthesia	(i) exceptionally acute hearing
10. amyotonia	(j) a nasal tone in speaking

LESSON XXIV   Suffixes

Learn the following suffixes and their meanings:

I. *-in, -ine,* "chemical substance" (of Latin derivation)

anti- + TOX- poison + *-in* antitoxin
MELAN- black, dark + *-in* melanin
(a dark pigment found in skin, hair, etc.)

HEM(o)- blood + CYAN- blue + *-in* hemocyanin
(a pigment found in the blood of some invertebrates)

epi- + NEPHR- kidney + *-ine* epinephrine
(another name for adrenalin; Latin REN- "kidney")

II. *-ium,* "part," "lining or enveloping tissue," "region"

endo- + CARDI- heart + *-ium* endocardium
(the membrane lining the cavities of the heart)

peri- + NEPHR- kidney + *-ium* perinephrium
(a tissue surrounding a kidney)

epi- + NEUR- nerve + -ium epineurium
(a sheath of tissue surrounding a peripheral nerve)

ASSIGNMENT

I. Learn the following bases and their meanings:

BLAST- "bud," "formative substance," "embryonic cell"

blastomere — any of the cells formed during the first few divisions of a fertilized ovum

blastula — an embryo in an early stage of development, consisting of one or several layers of cells around a central cavity

myoblast — an embryonic cell which develops into muscle tissue

COCC(US)- "berry," "seed," "spherical bacterium"

pentacoccous — having five seeds or carpels

streptococcus (STREPT- "twisted," here meaning "twisted chain") — any of a particular genus of bacteria some species of which cause serious disease and which are named from their arrangement in chains

meningococcemia — the presence in the blood of the bacteria which cause meningitis

CYST- "bladder," "sac," "sac containing morbid matter"

cholecystitis — inflammation of the gallbladder

cystolithiasis — condition caused by a stone in the urinary bladder

cystectomy — surgical removal of a cyst

statocyst — a fluid-filled sac found in many invertebrates which serves as an organ of balance

DACTYL- "digit," "finger or toe"

dactylosymphysis — adhesion of fingers or toes

hexadactylism — the condition of having six fingers or toes

brachydactyly — the condition of having abnormally short digits

DROM- "a running," "a course"

> *hippodrome* (HIPP- "horse") — originally, a track for horse races
>
> *dromomania* — a morbid desire to wander
>
> *homodromy* — a condition of having spirals which turn in the same direction

HIST-, HISTI- "tissue"

> *histamine* — a substance occurring in all animal and vegetable tissue
>
> *histometaplastic* — changing tissue into that of another type
>
> *histozoic* — living within tissue, as a parasite

ICHTHY- "fish"

> *ichthyosaur* — a prehistoric marine reptile with a fish-like body
>
> *Chondroichthyes* — a class of vertebrates, mainly fish, with cartilaginous skeletons

ORNIS-, ORNITH- "bird"

> *ornithophilous* — pollinated through the agency of birds
>
> *archaeornis* — a type of prehistoric bird
>
> *ichthyornis* — a type of prehistoric bird

PHAG- "to eat"

> *sarcophagus* (SARC- "flesh") — a stone coffin, so called because early sarcophagi were made of limestone, which caused the body to disintegrate rapidly
>
> *geophagy* — the eating of earth
>
> *glossophagine* — securing food with the tongue

PLAS(T)- "to form"

> *plasma* — the fluid part of the blood (literally, "something formed")
>
> *encephalodysplasia* — defective development of the brain
>
> *-plasty*, surgical operation to form, plastic surgery, as in *arthroplasty* — formation of an artificial joint
>
> *hyperplasia* — excessive development of tissue

PTER-; PTERYX, PTERYG- "wing," "fin"

helicopter — literally, "spiral (HELIC-) wing"

arthropterous — referring to fishes with jointed fin-rays

Lepidoptera (LEPID- "scale") — an order of insects to which belong butterflies and moths

coleopterous (COLE- "sheath") — belonging to an order of insects having hard anterior wings which cover the membranous posterior ones

ichthyopterygia — paired fish fins

STOM-, STOMAT- "mouth," "opening"

amphistomous — applied to certain worms which have suckers at both ends of the body

stomatoplasty — plastic surgery on the mouth

exostome — an opening in the outer wall of an ovule

-stomy — an operation to make an artificial opening in an organ, as enterostomy — the making of an opening through the abdominal wall into the intestine for the purpose of drainage

II. Analyze the following words and define them:

1. pericardium
2. syndrome
3. anthropophagous
4. protoplasm
5. anastomosis
6. erythroblast
7. syndactyl
8. ichthyosis
9. phytophagous
10. neuropterous
11. micrococcus
12. anadromous
13. ornithology
14. osteoplasty
15. orthopterous
16. polydactylism
17. histology
18. phagocyte
19. chiropter
20. epigastrium
21. pterodactyl
22. osteoblast
23. ichthyology
24. neoplasm
25. hemolysin

III. Match Column B with Column A:

	A		B
1.	rhinoplasty	(a)	the dissolution of tissue
2.	ornithosis	(b)	stone-eating (as certain birds)
3.	lithophagous	(c)	fish-eating
4.	endomysium	(d)	having two wings
5.	cholecystokinin	(e)	the condition of having abnormally long fingers or toes
6.	pteropod	(f)	the making of an opening into the gallbladder
7.	ichthyophagous	(g)	the connective tissue between fibers and muscle
8.	dipterous	(h)	a hormone which causes the gallbladder to contract
9.	macrodactylism	(i)	plastic surgery on the nose
10.	histolysis	(j)	a disease found in birds
11.	cholecystostomy	(k)	a fossil fish
12.	ichthyolite	(l)	small molluscs having feet with wing-like lobes

LESSON XXV Diminutive Suffixes

Learn the following suffixes and their meanings:

I. *-ium, -ion,* "little" (often difficult to distinguish from *-ium* in the preceding lesson)

BACTER-	staff, rod	+	*-ium*	bacterium
POD-	foot	+	*-ium*	podium

(in zoology, a part which serves as a foot)

| THEC- | case | + | *-ium* | thecium |

(a part of a fungus which contains sporules)

| ASTER- | star | + | *-ion* | asterion |

(the meeting point of various sutures or seams in the skull, forming a star-shaped pattern)

| STOM- | mouth | + | *-ion* | stomion |

(a skin pore of a sponge)

II. *-idium,* "little"

BAS-   base   + *-idium* basidium
(a fungus cell which bears spores on a stalk)

OO- egg + PHOR- to bear + *-idium* oophoridium
(a spore case in certain plants)

STOM-   mouth   + *-idium* stomidium
(the terminal pore of a tentacle)

III. *-arium, -arion,* "little"

CON-   cone   + *-arium* conarium
(an old term for the pineal gland)

HIPP-   horse   + *-arion* Hipparion
(a genus of extinct mammals related to the horse)

IV. *-isk, -iscus,* "little"

ASTER-   star   + *-isk* asterisk

MEN-   moon, month   + *-iscus* meniscus
(a crescent-shaped object, in particular, a type of lens; also, the curved upper surface of a column of liquid)

ASSIGNMENT

I. Learn the following bases and their meanings:

ACTIN- "ray," "radiating structure"

    actinobiology — the branch of biology which studies the effects of radiation upon living organisms

    actinodromous — referring to a leaf with veins radiating from a common center

    actinodermatitis — inflammation of the skin caused by the actinic rays in sunlight

ANTH- "flower"

    chrysanthemum — literally, "golden (CHRYS-) blossom"

    anthology — originally, a collection of choice passages, , the "flowers," of literary works *anthema* — a skin eruption, literally, a "blossoming"

anthophilous — attracted by flowers, as certain insects

CARP- "fruit"

amphicarpous — producing two kinds of fruit

carpolith — a fossil fruit

angiocarp — a fruit with an external covering

DENDR- "tree," "tree-like structure"

dendrolatry — the worship of trees

dendron — the branching process of a nerve cell

philodendron — an ornamental climbing plant (one which "clings to trees")

GON- "generative" "reproductive," "sexual" (related to GEN-, "to be produced;" see Lesson VII)

archegonium — the female reproductive organ in certain plants

gonorrhea — a venereal disease

gonoblast — a type of reproductive cell in animals

GYMN- "naked"

gymnasium — (in ancient Greece clothes were not worn during athletic exercises)

gymnorhinal — referring to birds with nostril region not covered with feathers

gymnanthous — having uncovered flowers, with no floral envelope

HIPP- "horse"

hippopotamus (POTAM- "river"; cf. *Mesopotamia*) — literally "river horse"

hippodrome — originally, a course for race horses

HYGR- "wet," "moist"

hygroscope — an instrument which indicates humidity, hence *hygroscopic* — absorbing moisture from the air *hygrophyte* — a plant which lives in a moist environment

euryhygric — able to withstand wide variations in humidity

PHYLL- "leaf"

chlorophyll — the green coloring matter found in leaves

phyllophagous — eating leaves

oligophyllous — having few leaves

THEC(A) "case" (related to THE- "to place," "to put;" see Lesson X; originally, "a case in which to put something")

bibliotheca — a library

amphithecium — the external layer of cells in the spore case of certain plants

pterotheca — the wing case of a chrysalis

neurothecitis — inflammation of the sheath of a nerve

THROMB- "a clot"

thrombin — a substance in the blood which causes clotting

thromboangiitis — clot formation accompanied by inflammation of a blood vessel

thrombocyte — a blood platelet, a type of cell important in clotting

TOX- "poison"

intoxicate — originally, to poison

toxin — a poisonous substance produced by microorganisms or by plants and animals

antitoxin — a substance which counteracts a toxin

zootoxin — a toxin derived from an animal

XYL- "wood"

xylophone — a percussion instrument played by striking wooden bars

xylocarp — a hard woody fruit

xylophyte — a woody plant

II. Analyze the following words and define them:

1. perianth
2. schizocarpous
3. phyllopod
4. gonidium
5. xylotomous
6. actinomorphic
7. carpophagous
8. prothrombin
9. heterophyllous
10. xylophagous
11. toxemia
12. oogonium
13. xanthophyll
14. monocarpic
15. ootheca
16. thrombosis
17. anthocyanin
18. acrocarpous
19. pseudopodium
20. exanthema
21. dendrite
22. toxicology
23. phyllotaxy
24. nephridium

III. Match Column B with Column A:

A	B
1. gonidangium	(a) referring to a moisture-loving plant
2. geocarpy	(b) having bare wings
3. melanophyllous	(c) the reversion of flower petals to ordinary green leaves
4. podotheca	(d) the determination of dates by the study of tree rings
5. actinotherapy	(e) the practice of eating horse meat
6. epixylous	(f) having hard leaves
7. hygrophilous	(g) the ripening of fruits underground
8. hippophagy	(h) a structure containing minute reproductive bodies
9. chloranthy	(i) growing upon wood
10. gymnopterous	(j) treatment by means of rays
11. dendrochronology	(k) a foot covering (of birds or reptiles)
12. sclerophyllous	(l) having dark-colored leaves

IV. For each of the following definitions give a single word with this meaning. Since these words are all in current use, they have been listed as they appear in dictionaries on p. 264.

1. paralysis of the tongue
2. having hidden flowers
3. eating only one thing

4. pertaining to the formation of bone
5. having small wings
6. fear of flowers
7. with winged fruit
8. bearing leaves
9. deficient hearing
10. inflammation of the nerve of the eye

ANSWERS TO EXERCISE IV OF LESSON XXII

1. lipoma
2. arthralgia
3. cardiostenosis
4. acrocyanosis
5. dermatomycosis
6. hepatotomy
7. otitis
8. microcardia
9. melanoglossia
10. osteology

ANSWERS TO EXERCISE IV OF LESSON XXV

1. glossoplegia
2. cryptanthous
3. monophagous
4. osteoplastic, osteogenic
5. micropterous
6. anthophobia
7. pterocarpous
8. phyllophorous
9. hypacusia
10. ophthalmoneuritis

LIST OF SUFFIXES AND COMBINING FORMS (GREEK)

The Roman numerals in parentheses indicate the lesson in which each suffix is to be found.

-ac, see *-ic*

-al, pertaining to, like, belonging to, having the character of (VIII)

-an (-ian) pertaining to, like, one concerned with (VIII)

-arch, one who rules (XIII)

-archy, rule by (XIII)

-arion, see *-arium*

-arium, -arion, little (XXV)

-ast, -st, one who does (X)

-cracy, rule by, etc. (XII)

-crat, one who advocates or practices rule by (XII)

-ectomy, surgical removal of (XXI)

-emia, condition of the blood (XXIII)

-gram, thing written (XIV)

-graph, writing, etc. (XIV)

-graphy, writing, etc. (XIV)

-hedron, solid figure (XXIII)

-ia, see *-y*

-iasis, diseased condition (XXII)

-ic (-ac), -tic pertaining to, etc. (VII)

-ician, specialist in, etc. (IX)

-ics, -tics, art, science, or study of (VII)

-idium, little (XXV)

-in, -ine, chemical substance (XXIV)

-ine, see *-in*

-ion, see *-ium,* little

-iscus, see *-isk*

-isk, -iscus, little (XXV)

-ism, belief in, etc. (IX)

-ist, one who believes in, etc. (IX)

-ite, one connected with, etc. (IX)

-itis, inflammation of, etc. (XX)

-ium, -ion, little (XXV)

-ium, part, etc. (XXIV)

-ize, verbal suffix (XV)

-logy, science of, etc. (XII)

-m, see *-ma*

-ma, -m, -me, result of (XI)

-mania, madness about, etc. (XIII)

-maniac, one having a madness for (XIII)

-me, see *-ma*

-meter, measure (XIV)

-metry, art or science of measuring (XIV)

-nomy, science of, etc. (XII)

-oid, like (VII)

-oma, tumor, etc. (XX)

-osis, diseased condition of, etc (XX)

-ous, (-ious), full of, pertaining to, like (VIII)

-path, one who suffers from a disease of, etc. (XXII)

-pathy, disease of, etc. (XXII)

-phobe, one who fears or hates (XIII)

-*phobia*, abnormal fear of (XIII)

-*rrhea* (-*rrhoea*), abnormal discharge (XXI)

-*scope*, instrument for viewing, etc. (XIV)

-*se*, see -*sis*

-*sia*, see -*sis*

-*sis*, -*se*, -*sy*, -*sia*, act of, etc. (XI)

-*st*, see -*ast*

-*sy*, see -*sis*

-*t*, -*te*, he who, etc. (X)

-*te*, see -*t*

-*therapy*, treatment of or by (XXII)

-*tic*, see -*ic*

-*tics*, see -*ics*

-*tomy*, surgical operation on, etc. (XXI)

-*y*, -*ia*, quality of, etc. (X)

LIST OF BASES (GREEK)

The Roman numerals in parentheses following the meanings indicate the lesson in which each base is to be found.

A

ACU-, see ACOU-

ACOU-, ACU-, to hear (XXIII)

ACR-, highest, the extremities (XIII)

ACTIN-, ray, radiating structure (XXV)

ADEN-, gland (XXI)

AESTHE-, ESTHE-, to feel, to perceive (VII)

AGOG-, -AGOGUE, to lead (IX)

AGON-, struggle, contest (V)

ALG-, pain (IV)

ALL-, other (X)

ANDR-, man, male (XI)

ANGEL-, messenger, message (V)

ANGI-, vessel (XXI)

ANTH-, flower (XXV)

ANTHROP-, human being, man (VII)

ARCHA(E)- (ARCHE-), ancient, primitive, beginning (VII)

ARCHE-, see ARCHA(E)-

ARTHR-, joint, speech sound or articulation (XX)

ASCE-, to exercise (XVIII)

AST(E)R-, star (VII)

AUT-, self (XII)

B

BALL-, BOL-, BLE-, to throw, to put (VI)

BAR-, weight, pressure (XIV)

BI-, life (IV)

BIBLI-, book (III)

BLAST-, bud, formative substance, embryonic cell (XXIV)

BLE-, see BALL-
BOL-, see BALL-
BRACHY-, short (XXII)
BRADY-, slow (XXII)
BUCOL-, cowherd (XVIII)

C

CAC-, bad (X)
CAL(L)-, KAL(L)-, beauty (XIV)
CANON-, a rule (III)
CARDI-, heart (XX)
CARP-, fruit (XXV)
CAU-, CAUS-, to burn (X)
CENTR-, center (V)
CEPHAL-, head (XXI)
CHEIR-, see CHIR-
CHIR- (CHEIR-), hand (IX)
CHLOR-, green, yellowish-green, also chlorine (XXII)
CHOL(E)-, bile, gall (XXI)
CHONDR-, cartilage (XX)
CHORE-, dance (XVII)
CHROM-, CHROMAT-, color (VIII)
CHROMAT-, see CHROM-
CHRON-, time (IV)
CINE-, see KINE-
CLA-, to break (X)
CLYS-, to wash (XVIII)
COCC(US), berry, seed, spherical bacterium (XXIV)
COSM-, universe, order (IX)
CRA-, to mix (XVIII)
CRI-, to judge, to decide, to separate (VIII)
CRYPH-, see CRYPT-
CRYPT-, CRYPH-, hidden, secret (III)

CYAN-, dark blue (XX)
CYCL-, circle, wheel (III)
CYN(OS)-, dog (XVIII)
CYST-, bladder, sac, sac containing morbid matter (XVIV)
CYT-, cell (XX)

D

DACTYL-, digit, finger or toe (XXIV)
DAEMON-, see DEMON-
DEC(A)-, ten (XVI)
DEM-, people (V)
DEMON- (DAEMON-), spirit, evil spirit (IV)
DENDR-, tree, tree-like structure (XXV)
DERM-, DERMAT-, skin (VI)
DERMAT-, see DERM-
DEUTER-, second (XVI)
DI-, twice, double (XVI)
DICH-, in two (XVI)
DIDAC-, to teach (XVIII)
DO-, to give (X)
DOG-, see DOX-
DOLICH-, long (XXII)
DOX-, DOG-, opinion, teaching (VI)
DROM-, a running, a course (XXIV)
DYN-, DYNAM-, force, power (X)
DYNAM-, see DYN-

E

EGO-, I (Latin) (XIII)
ENTER-, intestine (XX)
ER-, EROT-, love (XVII)

ERG-, URG-, work (X)
EROT-, see ER-
ERYTHR-, red (XXII)
ESTHE-, see AESTHE-
ETHN-, race, cultural group
  (VIII)
EURY(S)-, wide, broad (XXII)

G

GAM-, marriage (V)
GASTR-, stomach (XII)
GE-, earth (IV)
GEN(E)-, GON-, to be
  produced, to originate, to
  produce (VII)
GEN(E)-, kind, race (XI)
GERONT-, see GER-
GER-, GERONT-, old age, old
  people (VII)
GLOSS-, GLOT(T)-, tongue,
  language (III)
GLOT(T)-, see GLOSS-
GLYPH-, to carve (XVII)
GNO-, to know (VI)
GON-, generative, reproductive,
  sexual (XXV)
GON-, angle, angled figure (XV)
GON-, see GEN(E)-, to be
  produced
GYMN-, naked (XXV)
GYNEC-, see GYN(E)-
GYN(E)-, GYNEC-
  (GYNAEC-), woman, female
  (XI)

H

HAEM-, see HEM-
HAEMAT-, see HEM-
HECT-, a hundred (XVI)

HEDON-, pleasure (XVIII)
HEGEMON-, leader (XVIII)
HELI-, sun (XII)
HEMAT-, see HEM-
HEM- (HAEM-), HEMAT-
  (HAEMAT-), blood (V)
HEMER-, day (V)
HEMI-, half (XVI)
HEPAT-, liver (XX)
HEPT(A)-, seven (XVI)
HETER-, other, different (IX)
HEX(A)-, six (XVI)
HIER-, sacred (XIII)
HIPP-, horse (XXV)
HIST-, HISTI-, tissue (XXIV)
HOD-, see OD-, way, road
HOL-, whole (VII)
HOM-, HOME-, same
  (HOMAL-, regular) (VI)
HOMAL-, see HOM-
HYDR-, water (XIII)
HYGR-, wet, moist (XXV)
HYSTER-, uterus, hysteria
  (XXI)

I

IATR-, physician, medicine
  (VII)
ICHTHY-, fish (XXIV)
ICON- image (III)
IDE-, thought, idea (XII)
IDI-, one's own, peculiar (XI)
IS-, equal (XIV)

K

KAL(L)-, see CAL(L)-
KILO-, one thousand (XVI)
KINE-, CINE-, to move (XI)

L

LAB-, LEP- (LEM-), to take, to seize (XV)

LAT(E)R-, to worship excessively, to be fanatically devoted to (X)

LECT-, see LOG(UE)

LEM-, see LAB-

LEP-, see LAB-

LEUC-, LEUK-, white (XXII)

LEUK-, see LEUC-

LIP-, fat (XXI)

LITE, see LITH-

LITH-, LITE, stone (XI)

LOG-, -LOGUE, speech, word, proportion, reasoning (IV)

LOG(UE), LECT-, to speak, to choose (VIII)

LY-, to loosen (IV)

M

MACR-, large, long (XIV)

MANC-, MANT-, to divine by means of (XII)

MANT-, see MANC-

MAST-, MAZ-, breast (XXI)

MAZ-, see MAST-

MEGA-, MEGAL-, large, a million (XIII)

MEGAL-, see MEGA-

MELAN-, black, dark (XX)

MENING-, membrane (XXIII)

MER-, part (XXII)

MES-, middle (XV)

MICR-, small, one millionth part of (XII)

MIM-, to imitate (III)

MIS-, hatred (XI)

MNE-, to remember (IV)

MON-, one, single (XVI)

MORPH-, form, shape (VI)

MY-, MYS-, MYOS-, muscle (XXIII)

MYC-, MYCET-, fungus, mold (XX)

MCET-, see MYC-

MYEL-, bone marrow, the spinal cord (XXIII)

MYOS-, see MY-

MYS-, see MY-

N

NAUT-, sailor (XVII)

NE-, new, new and different form of (IX)

NECR-, the dead, corpse, dead tissue (XII)

NEPHR-, kidney (XX)

NES-, island (XVII)

NEUR-, nerve (XXIII)

O

OCT(A)-, eight (XVI)

OD-, song, poem (III)

OD-, HOD-, way, road (V)

ODONT-, tooth (IX)

OLIG-, few (XIII)

ONYM-, name, word (VI)

OO-, egg (XXI)

OP-, OPT-, eye, to see (IX)

OPHTHALM-, eye (XXIII)

ORA-, to see (XIV)

ORNIS, ORNITH-, bird (XXIV)

ORNITH-, see ORNIS

ORTH-, straight, correct (IX)

OST(E)-, bone (XX)

OT-, ear (XXI)

P

PAED-, see PED-

PALAE-, see PALE-

PALE- (PALAE-), old (XII)

PAN-, PANT-, all, every (IV)

PANT-, see PAN-

PATE-, to walk (XVIII)

PATH-, to feel, to suffer, disease (X)

PATR-, father; PATRI-, family, clan (XIII)

PATRI-, see PATR-

PED- (PAED-), child; -PEDIA, education (IX)

PENT(A)-, five (XVI)

PEP(T)-, to digest (VII)

PETR-, rock (XIV)

PHA(N)-, to show, to appear (VIII)

PHA-, see PHE-

PHAG-, to eat (XXIV)

PHE-, PHA-, to speak; PHEM-, voice (XI)

PHEM-, see PHE-

PHER-, PHOR-, to bear, to go (VI)

PHIL-, to love (VIII)

PHLEB-, vein (XXI)

PHON-, sound, voice (VIII)

PHOR-, see PHER-

PHOT-, light (XIV)

PHRA-, to speak (XV)

PHREN-, mind, diaphragm (XXIII)

PHY-, to grow; PHYSI-, nature (X)

PHYLL-, leaf (XXV)

PHYSI-, see PHY-

PLAS(T)-, to form (XXIV)

PLATY-, flat, broad (XXII)

PLEG-, paralysis; PLEX-, (paralytic) stroke (XXIII)

PLEX-, see PLEG-

POD-, foot (IV)

POL-, POLIS, city, state (IX)

POLIS, see POL-

POLEM-, war (XVIII)

POLY-, many, much (VIII)

PROT-, first, original, primitive (XVI)

PSEUD-, false (XII)

PSYCH-, mind (XII)

PTER-, wing; PTERYX, PTERYG-, wing, fin (XXIV)

PTERYG-, see PTER-

PTERYX, see PTER-

PY-, pus (XXI)

PYR-, fire (III)

R

RHIN- (-RRHIN-) nose (XXIII)

-RRHIN-, see RHIN

S

SCHIS-, see SCHIZ-

SCHIZ-, SCHIS-, to split (XI)

SCLER-, hard (XX)

SOM-, SOMAT-, body (XXIII)

SOMAT-, see SOM-

SOPH-, wise (XIII)

STA-, to stand, to stop (X)

STAL-, see STOL-

STEN-, narrow (XXII)

STERE-, solid, three dimensional (XI)

STHEN-, strength (XXIII)

STLE-, see STOL-

STOL-, STAL-, STLE-, to send,
to draw (V)
STOM-, STOMAT-, mouth
(XXIV)
STOMAT-, see STOM-
STROPH-, to turn (XV)

T

TACH-, see TACHY-
TACHY-, swift· TACH-, speed
(XXII)
TACT-, TAX-, to arrange, to put
in order (VI)
TAPH-, tomb (V)
TAUT-, the same (VIII)
TAX-, see TACT-
TECHN-, art, skill, craft (VII)
TELE-, afar, operating at a
distance (XIII)
TETR(A)-, four (XVI)
THANAS-, see THANAT-
THANAT- (THANAS-), death
(V)
THE-, to place, to put (X)
THE-, god (IV)
THEC(A), case (XXV)

THERM-, heat (VIII)
THROMB-, clot (XXV)
THYM-, mind, strong feeling
(XXIII)
TOM-, to cut (III)
TON- (-TONUS), a stretching,
tension (XXIII)
TOP-, place (XIV)
TOX-, poison (XXV)
TRI-, three (XVI)
TROP-, to turn (XII)
TROPH-, to nourish, to grow
(IV)
TYP-, stamp, model (XI)

U

UR-, urine (XXI)
UR-, tail (XVIII)
URG-, see ERG-

X

XANTH-, yellow (XXII)
XEN-, stranger, foreigner (XIII)
XYL-, wood (XXV)

Z

ZO-, animal (XIII)